SOUTHERN ITALY
TRAVEL BIBLE

Enjoy the Dolce Vita with a Complete Guide to Discover the Hidden Gems of
Puglia, Campania, Calabria, Sicily & Basilicata, Savoring the Best Food
& Traveling Like a Local

CONTENTS

WHY SOUTHERN ITALY?

As dawn spills over the horizon, staining the Mediterranean Sea with blush hues, Southern Italy comes alive. Waves softly kiss the shoreline, the olive trees sway gently in the morning breeze, and the cobblestones of age-old towns glow in the tender light. The day breaks, the symphony of life crescendos, and the regions of Campania, Puglia, Basilicata, Calabria, and Sicily welcome you into their embrace.

Southern Italy is an epic poem, its verses written by nature, history, and the vibrant tapestry of cultures and traditions. Here, you won't just visit places; you'll embark on a soulful journey, immerse in sensory experiences, and become a part of an ongoing story that has unfolded for centuries.

In Campania, the land is a palette of colours and textures, where azure coastlines meet emerald-hued vineyards and fields ablaze with poppies. At the heart of this visual spectacle, Naples stands proud, a pulsating hub of life and culture. Narrow streets wind around baroque churches and medieval castles, leading you to hidden treasures – street art masterpieces, inviting trattorias, vibrant piazzas, and the sweet aroma of fresh sfogliatella pastries filling the air. No journey to Campania is complete without a visit to Pompeii, where the silent ruins echo tales of a thriving Roman city, and the Royal Palace of Caserta, a testament to the architectural grandeur of a bygone era.

As you continue south to Puglia, the landscape morphs into a patchwork of sun-drenched olive groves and vineyards that stretch as far as the eye can see. The region's charm is steeped in its distinctive architectural jewels, like the cone-roofed Trulli houses of Alberobello and the ornate baroque buildings of Lecce, aptly dubbed 'the Florence of the South.' Puglia's coastline is a siren's call to beach lovers, with white sand beaches, dramatic cliffs, and crystal-clear waters creating postcard-perfect vistas that captivate and enchant.

Journeying further, Basilicata is a treasure trove of historical and natural splendors. Matera, known for its labyrinthine 'Sassi' cave dwellings, takes you back to ancient times, while the untouched wilderness of the Pollino National Park offers breathtaking vistas and a sanctuary for a myriad of wildlife. It's a region where nature and history intertwine, creating a harmonious blend that intrigues and fascinates.

At the tip of the Italian boot, Calabria awaits, where the rugged landscapes offer a stark contrast to the serene beauty of the Tyrrhenian and Ionian coastlines. The mighty Pollino mountains, the dense forests, and the vast plateaus speak of a raw, unspoiled beauty, while the coastal town of Tropea, with its pastel-colored buildings perched on a cliff overlooking the turquoise sea, evokes an air of timeless charm.

Beyond the Strait of Messina, Sicily beckons, an island steeped in history, culture, and an unyielding spirit that is tangible in every corner. Here, the sandy beaches and azure waters are backdropped by the snow-capped peak of Mount Etna, while the ancient Greek temples of Agrigento and the stunning mosaics of Villa Romana del Casale provide a journey into the island's rich past. Whether you're wandering through the bustling markets of Palermo or exploring the baroque streets of Catania, every experience is a sensorial delight.

Southern Italy's gastronomic landscape is as diverse and vibrant as its physical one. The region serves a culinary symphony that showcases local produce and centuries-old recipes. From the creamy buffalo mozzarella of Campania to Puglia's crumbly burrata, from Calabria's fiery 'nduja spread to Sicily's delectable cannoli, every dish is a love letter to the region's bountiful produce and culinary heritage.

As you journey through this southern paradise, the locals' warmth and hospitality will move you. They carry a pride and joy that comes from their rich heritage and love for their homeland. The lively festivals, passionate music, vibrant dances, and gastronomic feasts are shared with open hearts, inviting you to become a part of their world and experience Southern Italy in its most authentic form.

This journey through Southern Italy is more than a travel itinerary; it's an immersion into a rich cultural tapestry, a treasure trove of sensory experiences, a testament to the timeless allure of this enchanting land.

So, come, let the magic of Southern Italy unfold before your eyes. Let it touch your heart with its warmth, charm you with its beauty, inspire you with its history, and leave an indelible mark on your spirit. Remember, Southern Italy is not just a destination; it's an experience, a state of being, a chapter in your life's journey. As the Italians say, 'la vita è un viaggio' (life is a journey), let this journey through Southern Italy be the one that enchants, captivates, and stays with you forever.

I am Francesco Giampetruzzi, an Apulian in love with southern Italy, and I am ready to take you friends on an unparalleled journey. Welcome, and let your adventure commence!

ABOUT FRANCESCO

Hello to you who have this book in your hands and are probably planning to come and visit my beloved Puglia!

Before I leave you to read, I wanted to introduce myself: my name is Francesco Giampetruzzi, known to my friends as "Petrù", I live in Puglia, and I am 26 years old.

I am a farmer with over 7000 trees, including olive, almond, and many other types of fruits, but I also have a passion for traveling and welcoming tourists from all over the world. In particular, Finland kidnapped my heart and continues to kidnap it whenever I return.

But as much as I adore Finland, my love for the land where I was born remains indescribable. I live in the center of many of Puglia's beauties, such as Polignano a Mare, Alberobello, Castellana Grotte, Matera, Monopoli, Bari, Ostuni, Locorotondo, and many other towns full of history, culture, and traditions that, besides me, tourists love!

In addition, the food we produce here has something extraordinary: genuine, high-quality, farm-to-table flavors and ingredients with exceptional properties conferred by the land, sea, and wind of this region, which I would very much like you to taste.

Therefore, after sending dozens of boxes to Finland for my friends to discover Apulian products, I decided to create a box full of delicious foods from my land!

Why did I do all this?

I aim to become your Apulian friend from Italy and show you all the wonders of Puglia through its unique cuisine and places.

But let's go back to the book you are about to read.

Now that you are planning to visit Puglia, I must warn you that you are getting into a lot of trouble: it will not be easy at all to choose what to visit among the hundreds of wonderful places Puglia has to offer.

That's why I created this guide, which will help you decide which stops to include in your Puglia tour and how to organize your itinerary!

As mentioned above, I love welcoming tourists from all over the world, so if you ever need help visiting Puglia, I suggest you check out my site.

You may decide to let an authentic Apulian guide you to discover the most beautiful places in my country!

Now it is time for us to immerse ourselves in a journey among the beauties of my Puglia, so I wish you a fantastic read, with the hope of seeing you here soon!

A hug, Francesco

PUGLIA

TRAVEL GUIDE

Are You Ready to Visit Southern Italy?

Discover the Best Places of This Wonderful Region Following the Advice
of an Apulian Native, and Don't Miss Its Incredible Typical Flavors

EXPLORE
Puglia

Get ready for some amazing adventures in Apulia that I've personally collected just for you!

From mouthwatering local delicacies to exploring charming towns and soaking up the sun on stunning beaches, we've got it all covered.

Let's dive into the fun and excitement that awaits you in this fantastic region of Italy. Get set for a blast in Apulia!

Don't miss out! Scan the QR code and let the adventure begin!

Let's make unforgettable memories in Apulia!

SCAN ME

INTRODUCTION TO PUGLIA

How beautiful is Puglia?

Answering this question is not difficult at all: Puglia is truly beautiful.

Indeed, according to national and international news outlets, Puglia is so beautiful that it is considered one of the most beautiful regions in the world.

But before we delve into the sumptuous magnificence of this region, let us say right away where it is located.

Puglia is a region of Italy located in its easternmost part in the south. It is a peninsula, washed by the Adriat- in the East and the Ionian Sea western part. It is bordered by Molise, and Campania re- tion is about 4 million.

presence in the region has been at- tested since the Stone Age, as evi- denced by the numerous artifacts and findings throughout its territory. In some areas, there are even footprints and fossils ing to the presence of dinosaurs.

Apulia has always played an important role, not only in the history of Italy but also in Europe, as a real bridge to the East. To go eastward, it was necessary to start from the ports of Apulia; to return from the East, the nearest and oblig- atory landing place was only one, Apulia.

The comings and goings of people, goods, information, and ideas has dramat- ically influenced the Apulian territory in every aspect. The succession of Greeks, Romans, Byzantines, Normans, French, Arabs and many other peoples helped create, century after century, an extremely rich, layered, vibrant, and, above all, living culture and tradition. As a result, even today the region main- tains its role as a bridge to the East.

In this book, the intent is to capture the essence of Puglia encapsulated in its inhabitants, in their customs, in an area that manifests its beauty in different forms, in its food, in its traditions, and in its history.

In fact, it would be necessary to describe every single aspect of this fantastic region.

I could also just talk about its coast, which stretches for hundreds of kilometers hiding wonderful natural spectacles within every bay and inlet; or about its hinterland, with its woods, forests, natural areas, such as the Murgia and its particular conformation, within which rock civilizations have thrived. Or again, of Apulian gastronomy, which has taken the traditional elements of its cuisine and further enhanced them: bread, oil, cultivated products, and those that grow wild, making Apulia a veritable treasure trove of tastes and flavors.

Take as an example Apulian viticulture, which has been attested to since ancient times.

It was overshadowed by the rest of Italy for a long time, using wines produced in Puglia to "cut" Italian wines, meaning they were used to give body and color to wines from other areas of Italy and Europe.

For the past few decades, however, Apulian winemakers have put all their strengths into bringing Apulian wines to the forefront. They are now known for their quality and are exported worldwide. Red wines, white wines, rosé wines... Puglia is now among the leading areas of quality wine production.

We could also talk about the great religious devotion of this region, manifested in its churches and its rituals related to Christmas, Holy Week and many other religious holidays.

Even more surprising is how the landscape within it, whether historical, natural or gastronomic, is extremely varied, complex, and rich even though the region nevertheless has its common identity character, which makes it immediately distinguishable to those from outside.

In order not to dwell too long and start this journey among Apulian wonders, let us say that Apulia has as many as four sites considered UNESCO World Heritage Sites, with two more "intangible" sites that are candidates to be so in the coming years.

To add more would be useless. So let us end this introduction with a phrase from Emperor Frederick II of Swabia, who loved and gave so much to this region:

"It is evident that the God OF the Jews did not know Apulia and Capitanata. Otherwise, He would not have given His people Palestine as the Promised Land."

❝*It is evident that the God OF the Jews did not know Apulia and Capitanata. Otherwise He would not have given His people Palestine as the Promised Land.*❞

CHAPTER 1

THE PUGLIA REGION

To reveal Puglia to you reading this book, I will start with the natural areas that will leave you spellbound.

Let's start by specifying that Apulia can be divided into 6 main natural areas:

1. The Gargano area: located in the north of the region, with its beautiful beaches, Umbra Forest, and the islands of Lesina and Varano;
2. The central Adriatic coast, with the regional capital and beautiful coastal towns full of life and history;
3. The Murgia area: a vast area that includes incredible villages with centuries-old history, culture, and culinary traditions and beautiful landscapes;
4. Itria Valley area, the Trulli area: in this incredible area next to the Trulli (typical world-famous local stone dwellings), you will come across fairy-tale landscapes, as well as taste truly unique traditional products;
5. The Salento area: the Salento peninsula is famous everywhere for its clear waters, coastline, local produce, and festive atmosphere 365 days a year.
6. The Doric-derived city of Taranto and its hinterland that seems like an enchanted world.

Although not part of the region, we can consider the city of Matera and its surroundings as part of the Murgia itinerary.

Matera is a unique city in the world, thanks to the so-called "sassi", rock dwellings directly dug into the rock thousands of years ago. It is enough to think that this is where lived the third oldest civilization ever existed, dating back more than ten thousand years.

It has entered the UNESCO list of World Heritage Sites and today is a destination for tourists worldwide. Here the presence of the peasant civilization is still very strong, and you can still feel it in the narrow alleys that characterize the old part of the city.

DISCLAIMER: As mentioned earlier, this guide does not claim to be exhaustive and complete about all the beauties of Puglia. However, I will try to indicate what is from my experience that I was born and have lived in Puglia all my life, the best itinerary among the many possible of this magnificent region and the different areas that make it up.

GARGANO AREA

The Gargano area encompasses the entire northern part of Apulia: towards the east, there are many beautiful and characteristic coastal villages, set among rocks and headlands, inlets and sea caves, while continuing inland, the terrain becomes more mountainous, and villages settle on hilltops or in the woods. We move from the Adriatic Sea to an area where

we can already smell the scent of mountains because the chain of the Apennines is not far away. The great Umbra Forest is a magnificent and impervious place between the two parts.

MARGHERITA DI SAVOIA AND THE SALT PANS

Among the most interesting areas in the entire northern part of Puglia is the town of Margherita di Savoia, with its salt pans (the largest in Europe) and the whole area attached to them, whose ecosystem has been placed under protection (the so-called wetland). In fact, the site has quite unique characteristics compared to the surrounding area, and over time it has been colonized by pink flamingos. These magnificent birds contribute to the spectacular nature of this place.

But it is not only flamingos that inhabit this area. Indeed, the whole park is a reference point for several species of birds, both migratory and resident.

SOME HISTORICAL BACKGROUND

Margherita di Savoia and its salt pans have recorded human presence since ancient times.

Abandoned at a specific time as a malarial area, from the 17th century, it underwent a gradual process of re-foundation and continuous expansion until its 20th-century industrialization, extending to the point of being the first salt marsh in Europe both in terms of extension and salt production.

Precisely to understand this development, there is a museum dedicated to the salt marshes and their history; meetings, special projects, and guided tours are often organized to learn about the relevance and secrets of this entire so important area.

Read more:

http://www.museosalina.it/il-museo.html

HOW TO VISIT THE SALT PANS AND NATURE PARK

Both the salt pans and the wetland can be visited, with prior reservation at info@salinamargheritadisavoia.it, or at the telephone number 0883 657519.

The salt pans can be visited year-round. However, different types of tours are arranged depending on the season (trekking or bicycle tours are also provided in summer). Whichever type of tour you choose, the presence of a guide is mandatory. It will take you between the salt mining areas and the nature area, explaining how the process takes place, up to the large and impressive salt mountain, the collection point.

You can also do birdwatching activities: in addition to pink flamingos, the area is considered a protected area that hosts more than 200 species of birds, some of whom are endangered. However, even for this type of activity, it is necessary to make reservations and be directed by a guide.

Also linked to salt mining are other types of activities, such as the world-famous thermal baths of Margherita di Savoia.

THE THERMAL BATHS OF MARGARET OF SAVOY

The Thermal Baths of Margherita di Savoia is a spa complex located in the town of Margherita di Savoia. The thermal complex makes use of sulfur waters from the area, which have proven useful in treating a variety of health problems, including skin diseases, respiratory and rheumatic problems. The thermal waters are rich in sulfates, chlorides, bicarbonates and calcium, which are useful in alleviating a variety of ailments.

The spa complex includes swimming pools, saunas, steam baths, and beauty and beauty treatments. In addition, the Margherita di Savoia Thermal Baths also offer rehabilitation and physical therapy programs for patients with injuries or chronic diseases.

The thermal complex also has several facilities to accommodate visitors, including single and double rooms, apartments, and vacation homes. Restaurants, bars, stores and entertainment services are available for visitors. They are open year-round and offer customized treatment packages to meet the needs of anyone who intends to stay here It goes without saying that these spas do not only have a "curative" function; people also come here to relax and enjoy a few hours of pure tranquility, useful for regenerating themselves from the toils of everyday life.

VIESTE AND ITS WONDERFUL BEACHES

Vieste is a coastal town located at the easternmost part of the Gargano promontory. It is known for its natural beauty, particularly its 30 km of unspoiled beach, sea caves (which can be visited by boat), reefs and varied wildlife. The town sits on a peninsula and overlooks the Adriatic Sea, surrounded by a series of bays and inlets, with a crystal-clear sea and sandy and rocky beaches.

But Vieste is not just about nature; the town's historic center attracts tourists with numerous churches and historic buildings, including the Swabian Castle and the Cathedral of Santa Maria di Merino. In a special way, the old part of town

is distinguished by its narrow, winding streets with white houses and red roofs, interspersed with beautiful small squares and courtyards.

To this we add the excellent local food, including vegetables and fresh fish, the very lively nightlife and a series of shows and events that make Vieste a must-visit tourist hub.

We have already mentioned how renowned and famous the beaches of Vieste are, sandwiched between coves and beautiful landscapes, some hidden, others a destination for mass tourism. Let's try to list the best-known ones.

THE CASTLE BEACH

It is Vieste's most famous beach, thanks to its golden-white sand and a seabed that gently slopes into the sea. It lies south of the town and is greeted by the first Gargano sun. There are numerous access points on the Enrico Mattei promenade, making it easy for anyone to enter. It has modern bathing establishments and areas of free beach. The area is

equipped with accommodations, restaurants, bars and discos. "Guarding" the beach are the Swabian Castle and the "Pizzomunno" monolith (which we discuss in the paragraph below), a symbol of the town, linked to a legend of sailors in love and jealous mermaids. The Punta San Francesco peninsula shelters the northern part of the beach from the mistral winds.

THE BAY OF PIZZOMUNNO

What gives this bay its name is a large 25-meter-high monolith called Pizzomunno, about which a sad legend hovers:

> **❝***In fact, the legend tells of a young boy named Pizzomunno, who was in love with the young Cristalda. Every night, when he was out at sea fishing, Pizzomunno was tempted by the sirens' calls, calls to which the young fisherman yielded. Then the sirens, jealous of Cristalda, decided to kidnap her and take her to the depths of the sea. The boy, from his pain, turned into the huge white rock that can be seen today. Thus it was that the sirens, moved to compassion, allowed the two lovers to be able to meet again once every 100 years.*❞

The beach is considered one of the most beautiful of all the Gargano: as mentioned earlier, it has lovely golden sand and crystal-clear waters and is lapped by a cliff.

It features numerous services and is also within walking distance, given its proximity to the town.

Fun fact: tradition says that whoever makes a complete circle around the Pizzomunno monolith will be able to fulfill one's wish.

SCIALMARINO BEACH

Scialmarino Beach is located in Vieste, within the Gargano National Park, in a natural area that also includes a forest, lakes, and picturesque villages. The beach is 3 km long, and its crystal-clear waters are warmer than most of Vieste's coastline. The seabed is exceptionally shallow, which makes bathing safe for children. Because it is exposed to winds from the north and northeast, the beach is popular with surfers, kite-surfers and windsurfers. The beach is free, but nearby bathing establishments still offer facilities for an enjoyable day at the beach. From the beach, you can also see the Porticello trebuchet. The Trabucco is a wooden structure used in the past for fishing, is included in the cultural heritage of the Gargano. Several can be found along the coast, many of which have been restored

CHIANCA BEACH

Chianca beach is located 8 km north of Vieste and is named after the rock in the bay's center. The beach is about 200 meters wide and has a shallow sandy seabed, suitable for both those with children and those who like to dive. A striking feature of the area is a sea cave partially open at the top, which was once a refuge for some monk seals.

CROVATICO BEACH

Crovatico Beach is a little-known beach located in a hidden bay along the north coast of Vieste, about 10 km from the town center. It is protected by thick vegetation and the cliff that surrounds it. There is no road to reach it since it is surrounded by a holiday village that occupies the entire inland side. Access is possible only through the town, or the cliff, in case you want to climb it. The beach is very quiet and relaxing because of this not-so-easy access. The sandy beach has crystal clear waters and shallow, gently sloping seabed. Located north of the Gargano, it is exposed to the Mistral and Tramontana winds and sheltered from winds coming from the south, such as the sirocco and libeccio. The presence of the reef, however, makes the area not particularly windswept.

PESCHICI AND THE BAY OF MANACCORA

Vieste is surrounded by beautiful beaches known for their natural beauty. But it is not the only one: proceeding north, particularly following the road to the town of Peschici, it is possible to reach the wonderful Manaccora Bay: Manaccora Beach is famous for the extraordinary beauty of its nature and its crystal-clear waters. During the summer season, it exerts a strong tourist attraction, thanks also to a wide range of water activities such as snorkeling or being able to dive,

while equally high is the offer of the various accommodations and restaurants in the surroundings.

Manaccora is also known for the "trabucchi," these ancient fishing structures typical of the Gargano region. Trabucchi are built on stilts, allowing them to extend to sea and make it easier for fishermen to use their nets in deep water.

Manaccora's Trabucchi is particularly famous for their beauty and panoramic location, allowing spectacular coastline and beach views. Today the trabucchi are used as restaurants or for tourist activities, which allows for unique and crazy views of the Gargano coastline while sampling the local cuisine.

TREMITI ISLANDS ARCHIPELAGO

The Tremiti Islands are an Italian archipelago located in the Adriatic Sea, 12 miles off the coast of Gargano. Their power of attraction is due to the clarity of the waters and the pristine, clean seabed. The climate is pleasant for much of the year, while the air proves unpolluted, the vegetation lush, with unspoiled wilderness. The coastline features bays, headlands, low and sandy shores, and high and rocky cliffs with sheer cliffs.

The archipelago comprises five islands: San Domino, San Nicola, Capraia, Cretaccio, and Pianosa. San Domino is the largest island covered with an Aleppo pine forest, while San Nicola is rich in historical and artistic monuments. Capraia, on the other hand, is covered with grasses and flowers. Cretaccio is the smallest of the islands, the largest rock in the entire archipelago, while Pianosa is part of the Marine Park reserve. All the islands have small inlets and coves, some well-known, such as Cala delle Arene, Cala Matano, and Cala degli Inglesi.

The Tremiti Islands were once known as "Insulae Diomedeae," named after the Greek hero Diomedes, whose burial place was believed to be in the archipelago.

Legend has it that Diomedes, after the Trojan War, discovering the conspiracy hatched against him by his wife and her lover, fled and took refuge on the coast of Gargano, where he married the daughter of King Dauno, here he threw three boulders into the sea that gave rise to the islands of San Domino, San Nicola, and Capraia.

Legend also says that Diomedes died during a duel and that his fellow adventurers, transformed into birds by the goddess Venus, wept and watched over his grave. ✑

The documented history of the Tremiti begins with the construction of the Santa Maria a Mare abbey on the island of San Nicola, which was expanded by the Benedictines and fortified by Charles II of Anjou. Then, in the 19th century, King Ferdinand II of the Two Sicilies settled several destitute people from the Neapolitan slums to repopulate the islands, who were thus able to take advantage of the sea's abundance of fish, giving rise to a second colonization of the Tremiti.

THE SEA PARK

The Tremiti Islands Marine Park, established in 1989 and included in the Garga-no National Park, is one of the most beautiful natural habitats in the Mediterra-nean, a nature reserve encompassing the coastal area surrounding the five is-lands with a unique fish stock of fish and crustaceans that live protected in the depths of the sea. The underwater panorama of the Tremiti is of rare beauty. Scuba diving allows visitors to appreciate the natural treasure and the many relics and shipwrecks. The economy of the Tremiti Islands is based mainly on fishing and summer tourism. However, the wild nature and rugged coastline have encouraged slow tourism, making it an ideal destination for those seeking a vacation in total freedom in contact with nature. Nowhere else offers the same warm, genuine, and relaxing atmosphere as the Tremiti Islands.

LAKES OF LESINA AND VARANO

Another Gargano area of unspoiled natural beauty is the two lakes of Lesina and Varano, located in the northernmost part of the Gargano area. Their proximity to the Adriatic Sea means that the water in both lakes is salty.

As with the Tremiti Islands, tourism in this area is designed for those who want to get in touch with nature, perhaps observing the countless species of birds that make this area a place to nest or winter. The fish fauna also features fascinating species.

This is why there are several laws and restrictions in place to protect the area, and anyone visiting both lakes is required to observe and respect them.

Several portions of both lakes are considered protected areas. Mass tourism would be detrimental to the ecosystem of these delicate environments, which they are trying to preserve.

There are several activities that can be carried out at the lakes of Lesina and Varano: near the natural area of Lake Lesina is the visitor center "Laguna di Lesina," from which it is possible to organize guided excursions both on foot on land and by the sea with boats such as sandals and catamarans. Night fishing and sport fishing are also possible, as well as birdwatching.

LAKE LESINA

Lake Lesina covers about 50 square kilometers. It is the shallowest, whose bottom fluctuates between 70 centimeters and 2 meters deep. A strip of land separates the lake from the Adriatic Sea, with which it communicates through the two channels Acquarotta and Schiaparo.

The eastern part of the lake is considered a protected area. Here, fish and migratory birds have found an ideal habitat to thrive and nest. In addition, Lake Lesina is navigable, and several companies offer this service.

Sailing the lake at sunset can be a unique experience, as can walking along the shores of the lake. Here the setting of the sun creates an incredible spectacle.

In Lesina, there is a 400-meter-long footbridge that allows you to walk along the lake until you reach the remains of an islet dedicated to St. Clement, now used by birds for nesting, on which a monastery once stood.

Near Lesina, it is possible to see fishermen whose techniques are still those used by their ancestors. Here, in fact, eel fishing is a significant tradition.

LAKE OF VARANO

Lake Varano, the largest lake in Italy, is separated from the sea by a strip of beach (considered a protected area) and has an area of 60 square kilometers, and within it, there is also an island, considered a protected area, home to many species of birds and plants.

Boat trips and fishing can also be organized here.

A tip for those who love to ride a bike: there is a dedicated bike path called "Pista Ciclabile del Lago di Varano. It is a path that winds along the coast of Lake Varano, about 20km long, offering incredible panoramic views of the body of water and the surrounding hills. The route is suitable for everyone, as it is flat and has no particular technical difficulties.

The bike route runs between the town of Vieste and the Varano Nature Reserve. It passes through many towns and villages, such as Mattinata, Peschici, and Vico del Gargano. It is an excellent opportunity to admire the extraordinary beauty of

this stretch of Gargano coastline while also stopping in the various villages and enjoying what they offer.

Lake Varano is navigable. In fact, several companies offer this service, providing different types of boats.

A unique experience for those who love nature and adventure could be to visit the lake by kayak. The lake is ideal for kayaking, from which, while paddling, you can admire the lush vegetation and rich wildlife, including waterfowl and fish. By kayak, you can navigate between the lake's islands, where you can reach caves and different inlets. While sailing, it is also possible to spot dolphins and sea turtles. To visit the lake by kayak, it is advisable to do so with an experienced guide or in an organized group. Several on-site companies provide kayak rental services and logistical support for organized excursions.

The undoubtedly most evocative area of Lake Varano is its eastern part: in fact, here it is possible to see a wooden statue from the 1300s depicting Jesus Christ, placed in the middle of the lake, about which various legends hover.

One such legend states that the one depicted is the true face of Christ and that the statue itself is a reminder of the cross that was on top of the church of a nearby village, obliterated by the wrath of God because of the impiety of its inhabitants.

The lake area is full of caves. The most famous of these caves is that of St. Michael the Archangel (in this area, religious tourism is very strong, later, we will talk about two other important shrines also in the same area, one of which is related to the same archangel).

Legend says that St. Michael the Archangel had escaped from the nearby town of St. Mark and hid in one of the many cavities in the area and, to leave a sign of his passage, imprinted the shape of his wings on the rock.

The cave's interior contains all the natural elements typical of the environment: stalactites and stalagmites, rocks, and a basin containing water with miraculous powers. The bay is named "Pila di Santa Lucia," a saint traditionally considered the patron saint of sight, so much so that tourists stop to wet their fingers to rub them over their eyes. At the entrance to the cave, it is possible to see what legend says are the imprint of the saint's wings and his horse's hoof.

Unfortunately, dampness has almost completely obliterated the frescoes, while graffiti and inscriptions left by visitors over the centuries can be seen on the floor.

This mixture of religion, history, and legend is found almost everywhere in Italy, but it is particularly pronounced in this area.

Two other religious places annually attract thousands, if not millions, of faithful and non-faithful people from all over the world: we are talking about San Giovanni Rotondo, the place where Padre Pio lived, and the sanctuary of St. Michael the Archangel.

A RELIGIOUS TOURISM: SAN GIOVANNI ROTONDO AND MONTE SANT'ANGELO

The town of San Giovanni Rotondo is famous for housing the remains of Padre Pio, a monk of the Capuchin order who, according to Christian tradition, bore the marks of Christ's passion on his body for many years. Millions of pilgrims come each year to pay homage to the saint's remains.

The presence of this figure for long years has made the small Gargano town a true center of religious tourism, where it is possible to visit:

1. The church of Santa Maria delle Grazie, where are the saint's remains, the golden altar, and the moonstone with the trace of the stigmata;
2. The new church of St. Pio, built in 2003;
3. The monastery caves where the friar prayed;
4. The civic museum dedicated to Padre Pio.

Much of San Giovanni Rotondo's tourism revolves around this figure, considered sacred. However, remember that we are in the heart of the Gargano, and its national park with the Umbra Forest, which we will discuss later.

If the cult of Padre Pio is pretty recent, since his life took place in the last century, the cult that grew up for the Archangel Michael in Monte Sant'Angelo is much older.

The same saint we have already encountered at Lake Varano appears to have also appeared here.

Legend has it that a local man had lost a bull and found it inside a cave. Seized with fury, he kills the bull by shooting an arrow at it. However, the arrow changes its path, thunders back, and wounds the man.

After the news of the prodigious event spread and ecclesiastical representatives were called to verify what had happened, the Archangel appeared, explaining that he had diverted the course of the arrow.

The second apparition was on the occasion of a siege by the Goths on the city of Siponto; here, St. Michael appeared to the bishop to say that everything would soon end with a victory for the local population and the retreat of the Goths. ❧

The cave of the first apparition was elevated to a shrine that became a destination for pilgrims, but especially for crusaders, who, before leaving for the Holy Land, passed by Mount St. Michael as a sign of devotion and to ask to be protected from the dangers of the journey to the Holy Land.

Ideally, this very ancient shrine, known since the 6th century, is linked to other important shrines scattered throughout Europe:

- St Michael's Mount (Cornwall); Mont Saint Michel (France);
- Sacra di San Michele in the Susa Valley;
- The Hermitage of San Michele di Coli near Bobbio.

Monte Sant'Angelo is considered a UNESCO heritage site precisely because of the shrine and the traces left here by the Lombard population.

The town's historic center is also considered heritage to be protected: walking through the narrow medieval streets, you get the impression that time has stood still centuries ago. It should be considered that the town stands on a point that towers over the entire Gargano, which contributes to a truly unique and evocative atmosphere.

Among these narrow streets, it is possible to catch a glimpse of the skill of the local artisans, who, thanks to their ability to work with wood,

stone, and wrought iron, create objects dedicated to religious worship as well as utensils for daily life.

In the upper part of the town also stands the castle, which dominates the area below, dating from the Middle Ages and built by the Normans. The castle today houses a museum with historical artifacts dating back to the Middle Ages and the Renaissance.

A legend associated with the castle has it that the ghost of Bianca Lancia, fourth wife of Emperor Frederick of Swabia, roams its rooms; out of jealousy, he kept her segregated in the castle. Finally, the woman, tired of this confinement, decided to throw herself off the castle's highest tower. From that moment on, her ghost wanders the rooms of the structure with cries and cries, dressed in a light white dress.

This wonderful village, precisely because of its history and culture, can be considered an actual open-air museum: among the various monuments to visit, we also have the monumental complex of San Pietro, which encloses the baptistery of San Giovanni and the church of Santa Maria Maggiore.

The territory of Monte Sant'Angelo also includes another element that has been named a UNESCO heritage site, this time of natural origin: the beech forests of Monte Sant'Angelo.

This forested area is of great ecological importance, home to a beech forest over 500 years old. The beech forests are an ideal habitat for several species of birds and insects and an important wildlife refuge. Various hikes and nature walks can be taken in the area, admiring the beauty of the local vegetation and wildlife. The beech forests of Monte Sant'Angelo are also a place of great historical and cultural value, as they have been used as hunting grounds since ancient times.

These beech forests are located within the magnificent Umbra Forest, which we will discuss below.

THE UMBRIAN FOREST AND ITS MAGNIFICENCE

The Umbra Forest is an important part of Gargano Park, covering 10,000 hectares and having areas that reach up to 800 meters above sea level and almost touching the sea.

The Umbra Forest is so called because of the dense vegetation whereby the sun's rays can hardly get through the barrier created by the plants.

It is an area considered most important for several reasons:

There is 40% of the Italian flora; 70% of the birds nesting in Italy;

It is possible to study the phenomenon of macrosomatism: plants are larger than the norm;

There are more than 2000 plant species: beeches, oaks, holm, downy oaks, maples, Aleppo pines, and many others as one descends towards the sea, where the vegetation takes on more of the typical characteristics of the Mediterranean maquis; The fauna is very rich and varied: roe deer, badgers, dormice, eagle owls, barn owls, to name just a few.

There are several areas designed for children, such as an artificial lake where they can observe and feed carp, catfish, toads, and other aquatic animals.

There is also an area where there are deer, with whom you can interact, thanks to the presence of a net.

Still, near this area, a magnificent playground is designed for the youngest children.

For the older ones, several and numerous trails can be followed, both on foot and by bike.

The Umbrian Forest is a truly enchanting place where you can touch the purest and wildest nature and breathe uncontaminated air.

My only advice: always bring something warm to wear, even in the middle of summer. As mentioned, the sun's rays hardly reach the ground, making the forest have a totally different climate than outside it.

FOODS TO ABSOLUTELY ENJOY IN THE GARGANO AREA

There are several gastronomic specialties in the Gargano. Here the sea's flavors meet the hinterland's flavors, resulting in dishes characterized by strong flavors using simple ingredients.

These dishes, in addition to enhancing the products of the area, bear witness to a thousand-year-old culinary tradition.

Here is what you absolutely must taste:

The fish soup, called "ciambott" by the locals, made with very fresh and delicious fish;

The caciocavallo, a typical Apulian cheese, here produced in its podolica variant: the milk used comes from podolica cows raised in the semi-wild state. After aging, caciocavallo is a feast for the palate.

Paposcia, a sandwich stuffed with cheese and grilled vegetables, all produced locally;

At Lake Lesina, I recommend tasting eel, prepared in various ways, and a prized wild herb, salicornia, also known as sea asparagus.

The Gargano is also famous for citrus production, especially fragrant oranges, and lemons.

As for the wines, these are those typical of the Gargano area.

Nero di Troia: highly prized black wine, the production of which has also enabled some economic growth in the area. It has a very dark color and a characteristically spicy flavor. While in the past it tended to be mixed with other "gentler" wines given its qualities, for the past few years it has begun to be produced to keep it pure, with excellent characteristics

Cacc'e Mitt: wine suitable for accompanying first courses, especially ragú sauce, with an intense aroma and a full, harmonious flavor. Its name derives from the fact that those who possessed the tools for crushing grapes made them available to different vintners who, by the end of the day, had to complete all the operations to allow another vintner to crush them.

San Severo: wine with three variants, red, rosé and white. It is particularly suitable for enjoying with typical Gargano products such as fish and seafood.

CHAPTER 2

APULIA AND THE SEA: BARI AND THE ADRIATIC CITIES

Moving down south, we come to the heart of Puglia: focusing on the side that faces the Adriatic, there are lovely towns full of history, traditions, great food, and more.

A series of sandy and rocky beaches, dunes, cliffs, sea caves, and a wide range of wildlife and flora characterize the coast. The Apulian Adriatic coast is highly popular for summer tourism, thanks to a beautiful sea, unparalleled scenic beauty, delicious cuisine like few in the world, and cities that can welcome tourists but not only, also full of historical treasures to discover and visit. In short, the Apulian Adriatic coast is one of the most popular tourist destinations in the region, with a long tradition of tourism, great cultural and recreational offerings, warm hospitality, and many services to suit every need.

BARI

Let's start immediately with what is the largest city in Puglia, as well as the region's capital, the magnificent city of Bari.

I am particularly attached to this city because it is only half an hour from the small town where I was born, raised, and currently live, so I have had several opportunities to experience the beauty that Bari has to offer fully.

Bari will overwhelm you with its enthusiasm, traditions, food, and beauty.

A saying goes like this: "If Paris had the sea, it would be a little Bari."

The cheerfulness of the people of Bari is irrepressible; they will welcome you like family members, ready to guide you through the city's beauty and make you feel at home. They will immediately offer you what are typical foods, among the best in the world:

- Panzerotti
- Orecchiette con le cime di rape
- Crudo di mare
- Fresh homemade pasta with meat sauce

CATHEDRAL OF SAINT NICOLAS

Among the first places you should visit is the basilica of St. Nicholas: the protector of the city.

The church is an example of Apulian Romanesque, where Norman and Byzantine elements are blended. It was erected in the 11th century on the ruins of an earlier Byzantine church, which arose on the ruins of a pagan temple. The church consists of three large naves with a chancel and a semicircular apse. The crypt below contains part of the relics of St. Nicholas, whose body was stolen from Myra, Turkey, by some Italian merchants in 1087. it is also possible to observe magnificent frescoes dating from the 12th century.

The church is the site of a pilgrimage from all parts of the world, the figure of St. Nicholas being the object of worship and devotion by different religious denominations.

During the patronal feast days in May, the Bari waterfront fills with people, lights, sounds, and music. The festive air is everywhere, so great is the devotion of the entire city to the patron saint. Civil and religious events create a unique atmosphere to be experienced firsthand.

BASILICA OF SAN SABINO

Walking through the narrow streets of Bari's old town, not far from the cathedral, is another Apulian Romanesque-style church dating from the same period as the basilica: the Cathedral of St. Sabinus, inside whose crypt are the remains of the saint.

The cathedral's facade is of white stone decorated with geometric patterns, animals, and a rose window, while inside, there are Byzantine mosaics on the floor.

NORMAN-SWABIAN CASTLE

As well as the cathedral, the castle overlooks the sea and is located in the old part of the city.

Built in the 12th century by the Normans, the Swabians later expanded it. Today it houses a medieval museum that is well worth seeing. From the well-preserved central tower, it is possible to see an overview of the entire city and its beautiful sea.

For information, you can visit the official Facebook page or the website:

https://musei.puglia.beniculturali.it/musei/castello-svevo- di-bari/

Staying still in the old town, getting lost in the alleys and lanes can lead you to discover priceless treasures: unique views, breathtaking views, but also crafts and traditions that, despite efforts to protect, are disappearing.

One of the most famous streets in old Bari is the so-called "Strada delle orecchiette": here, you will find old women intent on making fresh pasta typical of the place, ready to welcome you with their enthusiasm and cheerfulness, and from whom you can also buy the pasta they make every day. Not only that, if you want you can book a lunch or dinner prepared by these women, of course, based on orecchiette!

ST NICHOLAS PIER

On the other hand, if you want to taste raw fish such as sea urchins or octopus, accompanied by a bottle of strictly "Peroni" beer, St. Nicholas Pier is the best place. Here you can see fishermen's spears loaded with freshly caught fish ready to be sold. In addition, if you are lucky, you will be able to witness a "ritual" handed down from fisherman to fisherman over the centuries: the curling of the octopus. A process that is divided into several stages and is designed to make the octopus more tender. Not suitable for the faint-hearted, it nevertheless remains a truly unique process.

From the San Nicola pier, you can see the Margherita Theater and walk along Bari's magnificent waterfront.

The historic center of Bari is wonderful, and I will never tire of saying that. Besides gorgeous places, here you can taste the best of the best that Bari cuisine offers.

The city is teeming with places where you can taste incredible delicacies, including focaccia, panzerotti, rice potatoes and mussels, orecchiette with sauce, and braciole.

We'll point you to a few places, but we assure you that there are more than a few places where you can taste great food. If you want to taste focaccia made according to tradition, then the right place is the "Panificio Fiore," located behind the cathedral in "Strada palazzo di Città, 38."

As for panzerotti, you can usually also find them where focaccia is sold. However, we recommend "Cibò" in Piazza Mercantile, where you can enjoy several variations of them, open, however, only from 8:30

p.m. onward. You can choose from a wide variety of fillings for panzerotti. Still, the one that most represents Bari is the panzerotto stuffed with minced meat and turnip tops, vegetables that grow flavorfully and luxuriantly in the Murgia area and that you won't be able to taste anywhere else.

If, on the other hand, you are undecided and don't really know your way around, several agencies offer different packages of historical- gastronomic tours through the streets of old Bari, where alongside the secrets of history that lurk in the alleyways, you can savor the best of the best in local cuisine.

Bari food tours:

https://www.civitatis.com/it/bari/tour-gastronomico-bari/?aid= 6811&cmp=vederebari

Walking tours and homemade pasta:

https://www.getyourguide.it/bari-l721/bari-tour-a-piedi-e-pasta- fatta-in-ca-sa-t181841/?partner_id=XE5R8WQ&utm_medium= platforms_and_communities&-placement=button-cta&cmp= vederebari&deeplink_id=38a147ae-c226-5bfa-9e1f-1258086650c8

Guided tour of Bari:

https://www.civitatis.com/it/bari/visita-guidata-bari/?aid= 6811&cmp=vederebari

Guided tours and street food:

https://www.getyourguide.it/bari-l721/bari-tour-a-piedi-con-cibo-di- stra-da-t181481/?partner_id=XE5R8WQ&utm_medium= platforms_and_communities&-placement=button-cta&cmp= vederebari&deeplink_id=83b09fcc-d40d-5664-a14d-c0d7092051db

TRANI, THE PEARL OF THE ADRIATIC

Another wonderful city overlooking the Adriatic, the city of Trani is located further north than Bari, and is a true wonder to discover and visit.

Precisely because of its beauty and the treasures it contains, Trani is considered a "city of art," so much so that it has earned the nickname "Pearl of the Adriatic."

TRANI CATHEDRAL

When one speaks of Trani, the thought immediately runs to its magnificent cathedral that rises above the sea and dominates the large square in front, combining its white color with the colors of the sea and sky, creating a fascinating contrast.

In fact, the structure, dedicated to St. Nicholas Pellegrino and erected in the 12th century, was built using a stone typical of these places, white tuff.

Inside we find mosaics and works of art of great value. In general, the church is considered a splendid example of the Gothic architecture of southern Italy.

The church can be visited free of charge, while a ticket is charged to climb the bell tower.

THE HARBOR OF TRANI

Another symbolic place of the city is its harbor, from which not only goods and people pass and have passed, but also centuries of history.

Built on an inlet, it is always bustling with life and movement, full of fine establishments ready to send your taste buds into a feast, but also ideal for an evening stroll amid the moon reflecting in the water and boats being rocked by the gentle movement of the waves.

The port is also one of the landing points for cruises passing through the Adriatic.

HISTORIC CENTER

The historic center of Trani looks like a maze of narrow streets and small squares, with houses and buildings made of white stone, in which the smells coming out of the many restaurants present permeate. I recommend stopping, even if only to enjoy a coffee or ice cream, while enjoying the quiet and serenity atmosphere of one of Puglia's most beautiful towns.

Within the historic center, it is worth visiting the church of All Saints and the Jewish quarter with the synagogue.

SWABIAN CASTLE

Another place rich in history and charm is the Swabian-Norman castle, a fine example of Apulian medieval architecture.

The castle stands on a rocky promontory above the sea and, like Bari's, is of Norman origin, with extensions in later centuries.

The castle is perfectly visitable in all its structures, it also houses a museum with various artifacts, and it is something not to be missed.

But how is it possible that we are talking about one of the most beautiful coastlines and we have not yet mentioned its beaches?

BEACHES IN TRANI

Trani's beaches are characterized by alternating stretches of fine, golden sand with others composed of pebbles. The water is always crystal clear.

The strong presence of services and accommodation facilities means that every tourist or visitor can satisfy their needs, whether they want to relax or go searching for adventure.

Facilities on the Cristoforo Colombo promenade, as well as those on the Mongelli promenade, provide a wide range of services to please both families with children and the grim of young people looking for fun.

BARLETTA AND MOLFETTA

Let's stay still north of Bari to meet two more splendid cities on the Adriatic coast, two charming towns full of life, in which ancient and modern merge, creating a scenario that cannot help but surprise those who visit them. We are talking about Barletta and Molfetta.

BARLETTA

Barletta is also considered a city of art, with a port that has always been a very important landing and departure point over the centuries.

The first thing that comes to mind when thinking of Barletta is the famous "disfida": in 1503, thirteen Italian knights (who sided with the Spanish), and 13 French knights, fought over a matter of honor as part of the struggle for control of the territory. Victory went to the Italians, led by Ettore Fieramosca, an Italian leader.

Such "disfida" is annually commemorated with a giant re-enactment of those events, involving the entire city with processions, performances, figures, and events related to the entire historical context of the city in the 1500s. Typically such a major event takes place between late August and October.

The re-enactment is engaging and exciting, as the whole city seems to return 500 years ago. The spectacle and atmosphere that is created is truly amazing and incredible.

WHAT TO SEE IN BARLETTA

Like other Adriatic cities, Barletta is not only sea, but also history, art, and culture.

For example, its Norman-era castle houses a library, the Barletta Civic Museum, which includes artifacts and artifacts related to the city's history, as well as paintings by great past artists and a lapidarium, a collection of stone inscriptions and funerary monuments in Greek and Latin. The history of a region inhabited since ancient times emerges through tombstones, epigraphs and other artifacts. The "De Nittis" picture gallery is also worth visiting, dedicated precisely to the impressionist painter from Barletta (also known by the much better-known French impressionist painters). The picture gallery was once housed in the castle; however, it was feared that the proximity to the sea might damage the canvases, and it was preferred to move it to the Marra palace.

For art lovers and non-art lovers alike, it is worth seeing, especially for the organized temporary exhibitions.

BASILICA OF THE HOLY SEPULCHRE

The Basilica of the Holy Sepulcher is one of those places you absolutely must visit.

Apparently, it was founded by the Knights of the Holy Sepulcher returning from the holy land, and today it houses several treasures, some of them directly from Palestine. Numerous frescoes can be seen.

The other wonder next to the basilica is the "Colossus of Barletta," considered one of the greatest examples of Byzantine sculpture. The bronze statue, 4.50 m high, would represent the Byzantine emperor Theodosius II.

If you want to enjoy Barletta's beaches and sea, there is a seafront promenade fully equipped with services and eateries. In contrast, the two beaches of Ponente and Levante are easily accessible and ideal as much for relaxing as for those looking for fun.

THE INNER PART

When we talked about Barletta as a city of history and culture, reference was also made to the hinterland: first of all, the magnificent Castel del Monte, which we will talk about later, and then the archaeological park of Canne della Battaglia, where the clash between Rome and Carthage led by the leader Hannibal took place. Visiting this area means retracing the region's entire history, from prehistory to the Middle Ages. In fact, there are numerous finds, fragments, and ruins that testify to the extent to which humans have always inhabited these places.

Visiting the hinterland of Barletta also means seeing what the extreme edges of the Murgia area, within which other inestimable natural and historical beauties are waiting to be discovered by travelers are.

MOLFETTA

The other Adriatic town north of Bari that we want to talk about is Molfetta, located between Bari and Barletta, a quiet and welcoming seaside town where you can enjoy the beach to relax, do activities, or even go in search of its extraordinary cultural, gastronomic, and natural treasures.

Let's start with the sea: the waters here are crystal clear and limpid, with a predominantly rocky coastline.

There are few free beaches, especially those near the city, where private lidos take care to meet any kind of special need or condition. The sea in Molfetta is also well-known because anyone can easily access it.

Notable among the free beaches is Cala San Giacomo, a very old city port that later fell into disuse. The view is wonderful, and here nature has decided to combine sand, pebbles, and rocks. Even sitting and watching the scenery in a quiet area can prove to be something fulfilling, from which to spiritually get in touch with the soul of this beautiful sea and its equally wonderful nature. In addition, you can bring your animal friends for much of the area of this ancient harbor. What could be better than enjoying a beautiful landscape with your four-legged friend?

The other free beach is Prima Cala, where a small pine forest surrounds a mixture of pebbles and sand. This, as well as Cala Sant'Andrea, has some facilities to allow disabled people to swim.

Molfettesi's free beaches are often considered by those who love tranquility and seek proper relaxation.

If, on the other hand, the intention is to try one's hand at doing activities, whatever they may be, or to always have comfort at hand, there are many private lidos available such as Lido Bahia or Villaggio Lido Nettuno, which both day and night are always active and with many proposals made available to vacationers.

HISTORIC CENTER

Like many other villages in the surrounding area, Molfetta has centuries of history and art behind it. And here, too, the historic center, which stands on a small promontory called " St. Andrew's Island" with its peculiar herringbone structure, awaits you with its scents and flavors to make you relive the atmosphere of the past, in its narrow, winding streets, among which we find ancient churches and palaces set.

On the edge of the historic center stands the cathedral of St. Conrad, located by the sea and artistically distinctive, considered a splendid example of unique Apulian Romanesque architecture.

In fact, the nave has a singular feature: three aligned domes of different sizes along the entire length of the center. The arrangement of the chianche roofing is very reminiscent of the trulli of Alberobello, while the exterior features twin bell towers 39 meters high. A place that certainly does not go unnoticed.

The historic center is charming: among a café, restaurants and many churches with a few secrets hidden inside, such as the Baroque church of San Pietro with its tower towering over the entire old town.

Staying in the historic center, we find the Passari tower: a circular structure on 3 floors built in the 1500s for defensive purposes. Today, however, it hosts exhibitions and cultural events, while from its top, you can enjoy a fabulous view of the city and the Adriatic Sea.

Next to the cathedral is the splendid port, a wonderful place that houses a large lighthouse and a series of shipyards, which can be visited with a guide: they are some of the last remaining in Apulia and have been active since the Middle Ages.

BEYOND THE CITY

Outside the town is a special church, the Church of Our Lady of the Martyrs, built in the Middle Ages next to a shelter where knights returning from the Crusades were treated. Together with St. Conrad, this saintly figure is the town's patron saint, and every year her statue is carried in procession by the sea.

THE PULO OF MOLFETTA

We remain outside the city, and this time we talk about a truly unique place: the Pulo of Molfetta.

The Pulo is nothing but a doline, a cavity due to the erosive action of water on limestone rock.

The one in Molfetta has a diameter of 170 m for a maximum depth of 30 m. Caves and natural cavities are present along the walls.

The Pulo has its importance both in terms of biodiversity and because important finds, some of which date back to the Neolithic period, have been found.

The Pulo can be visited free of charge, although reservations are required.

There is also a civic museum dedicated to the Pulo, which contains a variety of artifacts from the Neolithic to the 1800s, a period when it was exploited to extract mineral products.

If you still want to explore the coast north of Bari, the advice is to pass through the two towns of Giovinazzo and Bisceglie. In these places, too, culture and tradition go hand in hand with the search for fun and carefree living.

POLIGNANO AND MONOPOLI

This time we move further south than Bari to discover two other seaside towns that are more than wonderful, and amazing and have been experiencing incredible development in recent years: Monopoli and Polignano a Mare.

All of these towns on the Adriatic are experiencing a very strong development, with the number of tourists increasing yearly, and consequently, the supply is also adjusting to the demand.

Let's start with Monopoli: the first thing that stands out about Monopoli is the huge historic center, called the "old town" by the locals.

Initially, you may be overwhelmed by its size, but soon you become fascinated by the ancient squares, noble palaces, and whitewashed houses. In addition, this area has a high concentration of cultural heritage and churches.

Walking through the narrow-cobbled streets and arches, you can smell the sea air and scents of local food. At nightfall, the fishing fleet arrives at the harbor, and a veritable microcosm comes alive with sounds, scents, and colors representing the values of Mediterranean and Levantine traditions. Within the old town are numerous restaurants and trattorias where you can enjoy excellent fresh fish. There are also bars and clubs for young people, as well as artisans' stores and grocery stores. In this historic area, everything is at your fingertips.

16TH CENTURY CASTLE

An important element of the historic center is the 16th-century castle built by Charles V, part of the defensive system of fortifications desired by the emperor.

The castle's perimeter is characterized by five pentagonal bastions, while much of the ancient walls are still excellently preserved.

Inside the castle, there are very interesting spaces to visit:

- A 10th-century rock church dedicated to St. Nicholas;
- The weapons room, with four gunboats at "water's edge," two facing the sea, the other two facing the harbor;
- A large Roman gate with two guardhouses and two octagonal towers incorporated into the castle's structure: the latter was erected on ancient Messapian walls, based on a fortification that is traced back to prehistoric times.

THE SEA OF MONOPOLI

Monopoli is also famous for its crystal-clear water sea and splendid 15 km of beach. In fact, there are several awards from different bodies for the beauty and quality of the sea waters that bathe this magnificent seaside town.

In addition, the beaches of Monopoli are distinguished to the north and toward the center by the succession of low cliffs to inlets and coves, while to the south, there are long stretches of sand.

A landscape that, thanks to the many services and facilities present, allows for various activities, such as surfing, boat trips or exploration.

It is also possible to visit the cliffs, that is, caves created by the erosive action of the waters on the rock. If you are brave enough, there are some cold currents along the coast where you can dive.

I suggest some of the beaches in Monopoli that you absolutely must see:

CALA PORTA VECCHIA

This beach is one of the most famous in Monopoli. It has shallow waters and is easily accessible. If you are fond of photography, this beach hosts between September and November the "PhEst," an international festival of photography and more, which involves the whole town with exhibitions and events.

Porto Rosso

Porto Rosso beach is very popular due to its advantageous location and size. It consists of fine sand with a shallow seabed and crystal-clear water, making it ideal for families with young children and young people. During the summer, concerts are often organized here.

Porto Bianco

The conformation of this cove, with wide beach and shallow water, is among the favorites for those with children. Ramps and wooden stairs facilitate its access.

It is also considered the ideal starting point to reach nearby beaches by boat.

Cala Paradiso

This bay, entirely surrounded by cliffs, can be easily reached by public transportation.

The area is in private hands who organize different kinds of sports activities and events. There are also summer camps here organized by neighboring countries.

Porto Paradiso

Despite its centrality to the town, this small sandy beach is favored by those seeking tranquility and convenience, thanks to the services provided by private individuals. It is easily reached by public transportation.

Porto Marzano

This small beach is also sandy, and to reach it you have to walk along a path surrounded by greenery.

Because of the rock walls surrounding it, and the rocky outcrop near the shore, this beach is also known as "Devil's Peak."

Cala Sottile

Like the previous beach, this bay is hidden and can be reached by a dirt path that runs alongside a campsite.

Thanks to the pine forest surrounding the small bay, the waters remain calm and peaceful even on the windiest days.

RUPESTRIAN CIVILIZATION

Traces of an ancient past can be found in every corner of Apulia. Monopoli is no exception in this. You can treat yourself to a magnificent experience with a hike among Byzantine frescoes, rare rock churches and houses carved into the rock.

These places are lost or hidden in the historic center and make for an exciting hike, making you feel like you are the protagonist of an adventure movie. The rock churches are evidence of ancient worship that survived the barbarian hordes and Saracen assaults. They were carved into the rock and entirely frescoed. The greatest presence of these rock settlements is recorded south of the city. The territory lends itself very well to developing a rock civilization due to the presence of "lame," small canyons of karst origin that slope down toward the sea.

Visiting these settlements takes on a special charm, as it means moving in search of art treasures and early forms of Christianity in this area. These houses and churches were created as "negative architecture" by digging into the rock,

out of sight of possible enemies, during an age when assaults, especially from the sea, were frequent. First to inhabit these "shelters" were the Greek-Apulian monks who followed the rule of St. Basil. These churches were the meeting point between East and West, between Catholic liturgy and Greek Orthodox worship, which overlapped and merged into a single mindset and religious expression. Some of these churches existed as early as 1180, as confirmed by a bull of Pope Alexander III.

PHEST

Monopoli has been hosting The PhEst, an open-air exhibition of photography and art of international caliber for the past few years. It aims to investigate the relationship between the Mediterranean Sea and those who overlook its basin.

So not only Monopoli and Apulia but also the Balkan areas, North Africa, and the Middle East are involved in this splendid series of events in which the whole city participates, and the best photographers from around the world beyond leave their mark. The festival takes place between September and November through events, stages, and routes.

POLIGNANO A MARE

We now come to one of the most beautiful places in the region: Polignano a Mare.

Polignano is simply gorgeous, and this is evidenced by the fact that the number of registered tourists increases dramatically year by year.

Anyone who has been to Polignano a Mare can only speak of it in one way: positively.

The first thing that steals the spirit of those who arrive in town is a beautiful deep blue sea, whose waves go poetically crashing over cliffs and sea caves, many of which can be visited.

But Polignano's beauty does not end there: its historic center, built on a rocky outcrop, spreads out among white hovels and Baroque-era buildings that, starting from the marquis arch, wind through a maze of narrow streets and alleyways to astonishing balconies overlooking the sea from where the Adriatic and its coastline offer a spectacle unique in the world.

Within the historic center, there are several monuments to visit: the statue of the great Polignano-born singer Domenico Modugno, the church of Santa Maria Assunta in Cielo and the other churches scattered in the various narrow streets, the bridge over Lama Monachile, and the Pino Pascali Museum of Contemporary Art, with several exhibitions inside.

Polignano is worth visiting at any time of the year: events, concerts, festivals, and ceremonies of all kinds are always present. At Christmas, the historic center is decorated and decked out with lights and Christmas motifs.

Let's now consider the picturesque beaches of Polignano, its coastline, and the various caves that make it magnificent:

CALA PORTO or Lama Monachile

We can say that it is the symbolic beach of Polignano. Located just outside the historic center, you can enter it by crossing the ancient Via Traiana bridge.

The small beach, composed of pebbles, is an inlet surrounded by rocky walls overlooked by houses and buildings. A truly picturesque place. It is precisely here that an essential scene of the well-known soap-opera Beautiful was filmed;

Lido Cala Paura

This beach, just over 1 km from the city center, has always escaped mass tourism and is much sought after by those looking for quiet places to relax.

The beach is mainly free, although there is plenty of part of it where access is charged.

It is accessed by a flight of steps carved into the rock, and both the beach and the seabed are rocky.

By moonlight, this small piece of coastline offers an awe-inspiring spectacle, creating a romantic and unforgettable setting;

Cala San Vito

Cala San Vito's free beach in Polignano is a little more than 3.5 kilometers from the city center.

The name is due to the Abbey dedicated to the Saint located nearby, where there is also find an observation tower, a common element along the entire Adriatic coast.

The beach of Cala San Vito in Polignano a Mare is quite wide and mostly rocky, as is the seabed, which turns out to be shallow near the coast. Access is via a footbridge, which facilitates passage to the beach;

Porto Cavallo

Porto Cavallo is a charming free beach located about 3 km from the center of Polignano. It is small and has a sandy part and a more significant part of rocky coastline. The seabed is sandy and shallow. However, moving away from the shore, the water quickly becomes very high. Its location makes it a sheltered place from the winds. To reach it, it is necessary to travel along a narrow, bumpy road;

Cala Fetente

Cala Fetente is one of the enchanting beaches on the coast of Polignano a Mare. It has a free part and a private part. It is very suitable for children, and it is possible to rent beach chairs, umbrellas, and equipment for water sports. The beach has fine, light-colored sand, and the crystal-clear waters are ideal for snorkelers.

THE SEA CAVES

The Caves of Polignano a Mare are a must-see attraction for those visiting the Apulian city.

These underwater caves, famous for the beauty of their colors and shapes, are a popular destination for scuba diving enthusiasts. Visiting them, you cannot help but notice the imaginative shapes assumed by stalactites and stalagmites over the millennia or natural pools that create a unique and fascinating environment. In addition, these caves are important historical sites, as they have been used over the millennia by humans, for example, as places of worship.

As many as 21 caves have been recorded in Polignano, of which these are the most famous.

Grotta Della Rondinella

This cave is so named because tradition tells of a small swallow that nested and hatched its pups inside the cavity.

One year due to a sea storm, the cave was flooded entirely, so swallowed and the pups did not survive.

That is why it is said that if you hear the swallow's cry and swallows on stormy days, doom is impending.

Reaching this cave is easier by sea, while the route is quite difficult by land.

Grotta Ardito

This cave is named after its former owners. At one time, it was possible to access it by a ladder.

Inside the cave is a huge column called the "Column of Hercules," as it gives the impression that it is holding up the whole world from its position.

Grotta Palazzese

The best-known cave in Polignano, as well as being the most remarkable in size. It has been known for centuries, so much so that men like Diderot have spoken of it.

Here, too, there was once a ladder to access its interior.

In the twentieth century, it was transformed, first into a bathing establishment, then into a restaurant overlooking the sea, which is now very popular.

By sea, the cave has two natural entrances leading to a large room, connected to a smaller one with a small pebble beach.

Grotta di Sella

It is characterized by its natural suspension bridge, created after the gradual collapse of the inner part of the sea cave vault.

Grotta delle monache

It was so named because, in the past, the hospital nuns used the small beach nearby without being disturbed.

Grotta dei colombi

In addition to being a nesting place for birds, the cave is also home to significant archaeological findings.

These are just some of the caves in Polignano a mare. There are others, such as the cave of San Lorenzo, Grotta Azzurra, Grotta dei Ladroni, Grotta della foca, and many others.

Many of these can be visited in different ways.

By boat or amphibious vehicle: many of the smaller caves are accessible only by boat or amphibious vehicle, which will allow you to navigate inside the caves;

By organized tour: several agencies organize tours of the caves of Polignano a Mare. Usually, there are also local guides who will explain all the secrets and beauties of the various caves; Independently: here, adventure lovers can indulge themselves. By following prepared paths and signs, it is possible to visit some of the caves independently.

The advice is to check the availability and condition of caves before you go, as some may be closed for conservation or safety reasons.

RED BULL CLIFF DIVING

An event that has now found a home in Polignano is the spectacular Red Bull Clidd Diving.

It takes place a real extreme diving competition in which, some of the most daring to famous athletes in the world, dive from 25 meters high into the blue waters of the Adriatic Sea.

Polignano's stage of this type of competition has proved to be particularly popular with both athletes and spectators, where the spectacular nature of the sport combines with the beauty of the rocky cliffs and white houses directly overlooking the Adriatic, providing a spectacle unique in the world.

FOODS TO ABSOLUTELY ENJOY ON THE ADRIATIC COAST

As for food on the Adriatic coast, there is plenty to indulge in. The list would be very long. However, these are the foods that you cannot help but taste:

Fresh fish: octopus, anchovies, squid, sea urchins, mussels... you name it; served raw as an appetizer, roasted, or cooked in tomato sauce. We are on the coast, and here the catch, in addition to being of excellent quality, is always very fresh.

Focaccia barese: delicious and perfect for breakfast, lunch, dinner, or snacks. Crispy outside and soft inside. Tradition calls for it to be topped with fresh or peeled tomatoes. Enjoy while sitting on the Bari waterfront (but other cities are fine, too) accompanied by a cold beer.

Panzerotti fritti: another must-have. A golden, crispy wrapper contained a combination of mozzarella and tomato sauce. A food as good as few others in the world. Also excellent in its dozens of variations: with ground meat, turnip tops, and ham.

Rice, potatoes, and mussels (tiella): a first course you will never forget. A delicious combination of land and sea elements. Tradition calls for the three main ingredients to be prepared and cooked in the same pan.

Braciole al sugo: slices of veal or horse stuffed seasoned with cheese, salt, and parsley and simmered for hours in tomato sauce. The meat becomes tender and soft, and the flavor is indescribable.

Homemade pasta: Some foods, such as homemade pasta, are found throughout the region, but they take different forms and characteristics depending on the area of reference. In the area of the Adriatic coast and Bari we go for orecchiette and cavatelli (strascinati).

Sgagliozze: fried pieces of polenta, a typical street food to eat while walking through the streets of the old city.

As for wine to go with these dishes, there are several types from the central Adriatic coast.

Barletta red wine: its color is a ruby tending to garnet, with orange highlights emerging as it ages. Its flavor is very dry and full-bodied. Its alcohol content does not exceed 12%.

Moscato di Trani: The grapes for producing this wine are harvested when almost withered. It has a yellow color and a characteristic aroma when aged inside wooden barrels. At the same time, its flavor is sweet, so much so that it is indicated as ideal to accompany dry pastries or delicate desserts.

Aleatico: red wine, very sweet and aromatic. Its aroma is intense and fruity, with notes of cherry and plum. It needs an aging period of a few years to fully develop all its qualities.

CHAPTER 3

THE MURGIA AREA

If you love to discover the hidden secrets of small towns perched on the slopes of rolling hills with their flavors and traditions still intact, or if you want to explore nature with its incredible biodiversity, you must pass through the Murgia area.

The Murgia is an area of karst origin, which characterizes much of the region, whose distinctive elements are hills and plateaus within which caves, canyons, and almost magical places develop.

The Murgia territory spans the entire central Apulian area, from Barletta to the Itria Valley, and includes part of the bordering region of Basilicata, within whose borders are the very famous Sassi di Matera (more on this later).

In this area, the bond with nature is very strong, so much so that there is an effort to promote a form of "slow" tourism, where those who arrive are almost obliged to stop to savor the tranquility, the quietness of these territories, to take a moment to understand the richness of a territory that at first glance may appear unkind, almost arid, and in which it seems impossible that civilizations had managed to develop.

Instead, behind this appearance lies an absolute treasure trove of natural, historical, and cultural riches, with a tradition that in the face of modernity, has been able to renew itself without losing its identity. Therefore, proceeding slowly and stopping, if necessary, is the first step to capturing the essence and beauty of this wonderful corner of Puglia.

Much of the Murgia territory has been included in the "High Murgia National Park" as an area to be valued and protected precisely because of its biodiversity and how man interacted with it.

The first of the places that immediately comes to mind when thinking of the Murgia is Castel del Monte, on the UNESCO heritage list.

CASTEL DEL MONTE

The castle is near Andria, not far from Barletta (about 30 km). It was built by Emperor Frederick II of Swabia on a rocky bank elevated above the surrounding area, over which it dominates with its imposing figure.

Its octagonal plan is unique, with eight towers at its eight vertices, which are themselves octagonal in plan. From whichever angle you look at it, this presents itself as an incredible spectacle that leaves you speechless Just this particular design of its own has caused various legends to arise around the castle: some consider it to be a kind of place of initiation for those who wanted to initiate themselves into elitist knowledge, according to others the castle has the same shape as those that were the emperor's crown. Still, others claim that the Holy Grail was kept in the castle.

Whether these stories are true or not, they indicate how much wonder this beautiful structure, which had a function of defense, but also of recreation and study, has always caused. The emperor regarded it as a place where he could take refuge and devote himself to his passions, such as falconry.

Its importance is such that the effigy of the castle is imprinted on the Italian one-cent coin.

The castle can only be visited by reservation. No more than 30 people are allowed inside at a time.

Inside, it is possible to roam freely around the two floors that make up the castle, as well as the courtyard and the winding spiral staircase found inside the towers.

Car parking is a mile away, and a shuttle bus is available to take you to the foot of the castle if you want to avoid walking.

ALTAMURA

One of the most important centers in the Murgia area is Altamura, a city famous all over the world for its bread, but not only.

Altamura is nicknamed "The Lioness of Apulia" because of its history, importance, and beauty.

At the behest of Frederick II, a splendid cathedral was built here, dedicated to Santa Maria Assunta, with two of its imposing bell towers and the two 16th-century lions placed on either side of the entrance.

The church, as seen today, majestic on the town's main square, is the result of stratifications and interventions over time. Nevertheless, it retains all its splendor as a medieval cathedral, which is well worth a visit.

During the Middle Ages, thanks in particular to the thrust of Frederick II, Altamura became a very important center. We could say cosmopolitan today, where small neighborhoods related to different ethnic groups such as Arabs, Jews or Greeks were created. These neighborhoods correspond to today's historic center in a set of small streets and small, characteristic squares called claustrum.

These small squares are distributed throughout the historic center of Altamura and are evidence of community life. Some of them possessed a well from which the inhabitants could draw water. Their function was also defensive, as this was where enemies who were unlikely to escape could be attracted.

Within these enclosed spaces, it is possible to observe a whole series of loggias, staircases, balconies, and other architectural elements that highlight the coexistence and intermingling of different cultures and ornamental elements different natures carved in the tuff.

Throughout the city's historical center there are about 80 cloisters; it is worth "getting lost" to search these very characteristic places.

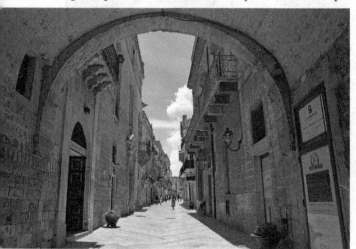

But Altamura and its territory also have a history that predates man: here, in fact, about twenty years ago, thousands of dinosaur footprints were discovered in a private area, which are still the result of studies and research.

For the time being, it is possible to visit them only during the period from May to October by reservation, as explained on the website:

https://www.comune.altamura.ba.it/index.php/it/novita/ notizie/item/1215-preno-tazioni-e-visite-guidate-alla-cava-dei- dinosauri-linee-guida-e-modulo

Staying still in ancient times, Altamura was the site of an incredible discovery: inside the cave of Lamalunga, a complete skeleton was found, dating back to a man who lived hundreds of thousands of years ago and according to recent estimates, classifiable as Neanderthal man.

The exceptionality of the find lies in the fact that the entire human structure has come down to us in an exceptional state of preservation, thanks to the gradual "incorporation" of the body by the surrounding rocks.

These remains are still there where they were found. Removing them is impossible, even though this possibility has been discussed for a long time.

It is precisely around this find that a museum circuit has sprung up, which also allows us to understand the nature and history of the Murgia area:

- The Lamalunga visitor center: about 3 km from the village, from which an exciting journey to discover the area and how Neanderthals came to be discovered. This is also the privileged point to set off in search of extraordinary places, such as "the bat room," where you can experience echolocation, that is, orienting yourself and understanding the presence of obstacles through ultrasound.

- Palazzo Baldassare: In this splendid palace built between the 16th and 17th

centuries, an itinerary has been created that has as its theme the evolution of man, the times, and ways in which it occurred, with the support of various instruments. Of course, special attention is given to the "Man of Altamura," so much so that in the palace, there is a full-scale reconstruction of the place where the skeleton was found and where it is still preserved today.

- National Archaeological Museum: here, the temporal experience is broader in the sense that the historical path covered goes from the Stone Age to the Middle Ages. Thanks to various computer and multimedia aids, prehistoric men's mentalities and ways of life are explained. So, again starting from the "Altamura Man," we go on an incredible journey to discover the life of hundreds of thousands of years ago.

THE PULO OF ALTAMURA

Not far from the area of the incredible discovery of prehistoric man, there is another special place: the Pulo of Altamura. As already mentioned, we must consider that being an area of essentially limestone origin, the whole of Murgia is full of caves, sinkholes, and all those phenomena typical of such an area.

Compared to Molfetta, the Pulo di Altamura presents a maximum depth of 75 meters with a diameter of 500 m. Along its walls are several caves that help to understand how water erosion works and reveal much about local history, as these caves have been inhabited since prehistoric times.

The place is truly enchanting, and if you wish, you can descend thanks to some trails with proper precautions.

Several agencies organize excursions and treks to discover the wonders of the Pulo area.

For climbing lovers, climbing the steep walls of the Pulo is also possible. However, it is only possible to do so between September and December. This is because the kestrel falcon nests here, and from January to August, climbing is prohibited, precisely to protect the broods of these birds.

THE BREAD OF ALTAMURA

Finally, we cannot talk about Altamura without considering what its crowning achievement is from a gastronomic point of view and beyond: its bread, famous and exported worldwide.

To understand why this bread is so good, you have to do only one thing: taste it.

This bread has a crispy crust, while inside it is soft and fluffy. A simple flavor, but one that warms your heart, accompanied perhaps by a drizzle of oil, also produced locally, or made into bruschetta, a slice of toasted bread seasoned with oil, salt, and a light rub of garlic, maybe accompanied by a good glass of wine.

The recipe for this bread has been unchanged for centuries: durum wheat flour, sourdough starter, salt, and water. These ingredients are enough to bring to life what is considered the best bread in the world. While it is baking, after a processing and rising phase, it must take place in a wood-fired oven on a stone base. Hundreds-years-old ovens still operate in the city and follow the ancient recipe.

A bread museum is available today to understand what bread represents for Altamura and the context in which it was created. This has been set up in one of the old ovens in the town, where through a multi- media and sensory journey, one will realize the strong connection of bread production with the surrounding area.

GRAVINA AND THE RUPESTRIAN CIVILIZATION

A short distance from Altamura is another incredible village where it seems that time has stopped: Gravina in Puglia.

In fact, the entire village rises on a "gravina," one of those typical canyons of the Murgia, which contributes to creating a fairy-tale land- atmosphere, a sort of gateway to an enchanted world.

Human presence in this area has been attested since prehistoric times; in fact, there are sev-

eral archaeological sites surrounding the Gravina area.

For a long time, the niches distributed along the canyon were used as houses or shelters in case of danger, most of which can be visited today.

Many of these cave environments are carved deep into the rock, such as the cave of the seven chambers. These include precious rock churches such as the crypt of San Vito Vecchio and the church of San Michele delle Grotte.

A symbol of the city is the aqueduct bridge, famous as it appeared in the latest film in the Secret Agent 007 saga, which connects the two banks of the Gravina and is 37 meters high.

UNDERGROUND GRAVINA

Underground Gravina is a beautiful treasure hidden from the surface: a sequence of environments, spaces, rock churches, and narrow meanders that develop under the city, completely excavated by hand. An incredible spectacle. If you happen to be in these areas, all you can do is leave the sunlight behind and enter this "alternative" world to the surface, where time seems not to exist.

To visit underground Gravina, you need to make reservations and choose which route to follow. Several options are available, with different routes and times. This is the website for all the information:

https://www.gravinasotterranea.it/

Coming back up, a visit to the magnificent old town is to be noticed. Consisting of three wards, it represents the old part overlooking the canyon end, with a panoramic tour as beautiful as any.

Having been over time a town with some importance (there was even a pope originally from this hamlet), the historic center of Gravina is teeming with noble palaces and churches, buildings constructed from white tuff, a typical local stone.

ST. GIORGIO'S FAIR

Gravina is also famous for hosting what is considered the oldest fair in the world, it has even been held since 1294!

Today the fair opens with a magnificent medieval re-enactment through which a precise ritual is retraced, as it took place centuries ago. Nothing could be more evocative and exciting. The fair itself involves the whole town. It is not only composed of exhibitors who intend to sell their wares or who want to showcase the latest news and trends of the moment but also presents concerts, and events of all kinds in which everyone, citizens and non-citizens, are called upon to participate.

The event usually takes place in the second half of April and lasts just under a week. Ready to throw yourself into an ocean of colors, sounds, and fun?

CASTELLANA CAVES

Caves and underground cavities are scattered almost everywhere in an area composed of limestone rocks, and it is no coincidence that the largest and most spectacular cave complex, spanning 3 km in length, is located in the very area we are about to talk about.

In the province of Bari, not far from Polignano, is the town of Castellana Grotte, which owes its name precisely to the presence of this cave complex candidate for UNESCO World Heritage status.

The Castellana Caves are among the most famous underground natural cavities in the world, and since they were opened to the public, more than 15 million people have visited them. Visiting the caves is a 3-kilometer route that takes visitors 70 meters deep into an extraordinary environment that no wildest imagination could imagine. Here canyons, deep chasms, fossilizations, stalactites, stalagmites, and concretions surprise children and adults alike. Therefore, these caves are an unmissable opportunity to admire one of Puglia's most extraordinary natural places.

To visit the caves, it is possible to make the ticket online and on-site. Of course, the walk in the caves is always under the guidance of experienced staff who know the place. A short and a long route are available, and it is also possible, by reservation, to visit the caves at night.

To further appreciate the beauty of the place, concerts, theater events, and exhibitions have also been organized inside the caves for the past few years.

One example is the show "Hell in the Cave," where a theatrical performance of the cantica of Hell from the Divine Comedy by Dante Alighieri, the supreme Italian poet, is put on.

Hell in the Cave is a theatrical performance that uses the Castellana Caves as a natural setting. The event combines dance, voices, sounds, and lights in a grand multimedia performance that transports the audience on an adventure into Hell as described by Dante. The natural environment of the caves is transformed into a stage of macroscopic dimensions, and the audience is captured by the innovative theatrical dynamics that lead them into a unique experience in Hell.

PUTIGNANO AND ITS CARNIVAL

If in Gravina we find the oldest fair in the world, the city of Putignano is home to the oldest carnival in Europe.

Here the carnival is a deeply felt event, the preparations for which last most of the year. It begins in December with the so-called offshoots and continues until "Shrove Tuesday," the day before "Ash Wednesday," with which the period of Lent begins.

The Putignano carnival (held according to tradition in the weeks preceding Lent), takes place through really special festivities and rituals, finding the highest and best-known expression in its four parades, three on Sundays, the last one corresponding to Shrove Tuesday.

When one thinks of the Putignano carnival, the papier-mâché giants immediately rush to one's mind: huge sculptures (called floats) made by the skilled hands of papier-mâché artisans, which are distinguished by their refinement, workmanship, and finish, the technique of which is handed down from master to master.

Carnival in Putignano has been celebrated as far back as 1394.

Those were years when foreign peoples carried out constant attacks and raids on the Adriatic coast. There was a particular fear of the theft of the holy relics in case of attacks.

It was then decided to transfer the remains of the protomartyr Stephen from Monopoli to the best-defended Putignano church, that of Santa Maria la Greca.

With a procession, the transfer of the remains took place on St. Stephen's Day itself. It is from this moment that history fades into legend:

Oral tradition has it that peasants performing grafts on vines, according to the technique known as "off-shooting," at the sight of the procession abandoned their activity and followed it with singing, dancing, and satirical verses. ❧

This is the best-known story about the origins of Europe's oldest and longest-running carnival and the festival from which it all began, that of the offshoots.

So, for a long time, the Carnival was a festival the preserve of the peasantry, in which ideally, roles in society were reversed, and the wealthier classes were somehow mocked.

It was not until the 1930s that the carts created with straw and rags began to give way to floats made of iron and papier-mâché, making the Carnival a celebration in which all walks of life participated. From the 1950s onward, thanks to new techniques and materials, floats took on the complexity and beauty that can still be admired today. Floats that are always related to current political and economic events intrinsically carry a message that never gets old.

The atmosphere of the Putignano carnival is incredible. The preparations of the costumes, masks, floats, parades and rituals repeated every year reinforce the sense of a community that welcomes everyone, inviting them to participate in a celebration of exaggerated fun.

PATHS AND TRAILS OF MURGIA

The Murgia is a wonderful territory. Therefore, the "Alta Murgia National Park" entity was established precisely to protect its flora and fauna and to best preserve all the treasures of the small villages. The goal is also to enhance all this magnificent territory offers.

For those who want to enjoy and get to know the Murgia in its most natural, wildest aspect, several itineraries can be followed, depending on your strength and desire to explore. Such itineraries can last from a few hours to several days, with development in stages, to be done for example, on foot or even by bike.

In these itineraries, you can get to know more closely what is the typical flora of the place, such as oaks or olive trees, but also wildlife, such as the birds of prey typical of these places, or the jazzi, those structures used by shepherds to aggregate their herds.

An example of an itinerary is the Jazzo Rosso-San Magno-Castel del Monte cycle route, which includes seven routes for a total of 65 kilometers, which can be done either on foot or by bike. At the same time, some of these stretches can also be done on horseback.

In recent years, many associations and groups have been organizing itineraries linking various cities in Puglia and beyond.

One such itinerary starts in Bari with a week-long route in stages along the Murgia Mountains to reach one of the unique UNESCO heritages in the world: the city of Matera and its world-famous Sassi.

THE CITY OF STONES: MATERA

Before talking about Matera, it is necessary to specify how it, despite being part of the Basilicata region, is located in a purely Murgia geographical territory, therefore with features in common with the area we have treated so far. Moreover, given the geographical proximity, it is impossible not to talk about a unique place in the world.

Matera is a city that leaves anyone who visits it speechless, attracting tourists worldwide thanks to its beauty and cultural heritage. Declared a UNESCO World Heritage Site, this city offers a lot to see, such as natural areas, museums, rock churches, and breathtaking landscapes.

But let's start with why Matera deserves so much attention. What are these Sassi?

By Sassi we mean an actual city totally carved out of the rock. Houses, churches, water wells, and any kind of structure or building have been carved out by digging everything by hand over time. In an overpopulated and very poor hygienic conditions, these environments were inhabited until a few decades ago, so much so that a nationwide scandal was created that forced the government to intervene and move those who lived inside these "caves."

Later, after a few years of total neglect, these environments were recovered and restored, showing themselves to the world in all their splendor and uniqueness.

The area of the Sassi is divided into two areas, that of the Sasso Caveoso, which houses the oldest part, and that of the Sasso Barisano whose original core has been gradually modified over time, with houses no longer dug into the rock but built.

It is difficult to explain the beauty of this city if you do not see it in person because it almost seems as if it has been transplanted to the present day directly from another era or even from another world.

Taking a walk through these ancient little streets, made up of stairs, narrow streets, blind alleys, and balconies overlooking nowhere, is an experience that gives emotions that, in terms of intensity and uniqueness, cannot be found anywhere else.

Among the many places in Matera to visit, there are a couple that are able to give an insight into the identity and authenticity of Matera:

- The church of Madonna of Idris: it is recognizable as being dug into a small mound with an iron cross on top, one of the most beautiful rock-hewn churches, partly dug into the rock, built, both because of its panoramic position and the fact that it is very ancient and has within its small environment frescoes of Byzantine origin.

- Vico Solitario Cave House: a cave-house showing how a peasant society lived until a few decades ago. It is not far from the Church of Our Lady of Idris.

The Cave House is furnished exactly as it would have been back in time. It allows us to understand how a poor, mostly peasant population lived here, with the space dedicated to animals, the water collection system, and all the everyday items used at the time. Something that seems incredible today.

Matera's treasures are countless; listing them all here would be impossible. However, among those that definitely remain in the soul of those who visit are:

- The church of St. Augustine was built on the top of a spur, on what is called the "Belvedere of the Murgia." Its style is typically Baroque, while inside, at 2 euros, it is possible to visit a cave church with several frescoes. A place steeped in history with a very characteristic setting, The cathedral of Matera, dedicated to the holy Madonna della Bruna and St. Eustace, a triumph of Baroque with stucco and decorations that make it a beautiful place. The cathedral is located at the city's highest point, and to reach it you will have to walk up climbs, stairs, and small paths... but both the walk and the view of both the church and the surrounding area will be worth it.
- Underground Matera, an actual city under the city. Composed of streets, houses, warehouses, stables, barns, lighting, and ventilation systems placed below the surface creates a mystical atmosphere which breathes the essence of ancient times and civilizations.
- The long Palombaro, a large cistern connected by canals to underground tunnels once used to collect rainwater, shows the capacity for ingenuity and adaptation to an often-hostile place of the ancient population of Matera. It descends to a depth of 17 meters to admire one of the largest stone-cut cisterns in the world.
- The many rock-hewn churches, hermitages, and small religious environments carved into the rock, for which tours are also provided.

As mentioned, these are just some beauties that await you in Matera.

For those who want to discover the history and traditions of Matera further, there are several museums in the city, both public and private, that can give you an understanding of the more than thousand-year history of this area.

FEAST OF THE MADONNA DELLA BRUNA

The last special feature to highlight is the patronal feast, which takes place in early July: on the evening of the feast, a huge cavalcade precedes a large papier-mâché float that carries the Madonna della Bruna, the saint patron of Matera, around the city.

At the end of the parade, there comes the moment that all the people of Matera look forward to with trepidation: the destruction of the float. Instead, everyone pounces on it to take home a piece of the choreography of the float as a symbol of good luck and blessing. Something in which the sacred and the profane merge, creating a completely incredible moment that is both wonderful and frightening at the same time.

There are several legends as to the reason for this tradition, one of which speaks of an attack by the Saracens and the decision by the people of Matera to destroy the effigy of the Madonna to keep it from falling into enemy hands, or another that speaks of disagreements between the local lord, Count Tramontano, hated by the people of Matera, who following a rebellion had made several promises to appease their tempers, including that of guaranteeing a new float every year for the patronal feast.

The citizens then destroyed the float to make the count keep his promise.

Whatever the truth may be, the patronal feast casts a charge of joy, colors, lights and fun over the town to which all are invited, where preparations are made to welcome all those who want to share an atmosphere of celebration and merriment.

FOODS TO ABSOLUTELY ENJOY IN THE MURGIA AREA

Except for fresh fish, the foods in the Murgia area are similar to those found in Bari environs. Also, in the Murgia, focaccia, panzerotti, fresh pasta, and many other products we have already mentioned are found everywhere.

This area is particularly characterized by the production of cheeses and dairy products, both fresh and aged.

Other elements of the local cuisine are legumes, such as chickpeas, chickling peas, and beans.

Essential for typical dishes are wild herbs such as chicory, sivoni, asparagus, and other plants that grow wild, used to prepare tasty and genuine dishes or as side dishes.

In each center of the Murgia area, it is possible to taste a specialty typical only of that particular center.

Altamura bread: we have already described Altamura bread, its authenticity, and the importance it has achieved.

Pallone of Gravina: pallone of Gravina is a semi-hard, spherical- shaped cheese made from raw cow's milk cheese. It has different aging times. it is considered one of the finest cheeses in southern Italy.

Andria's burrata: this is a fresh cheese made from cow's milk. It looks like a pouch whose interior is filled with a mixture of cream and shreds of the same paste used for the wrapping. The flavor is exceptional because of its softness and uniqueness.

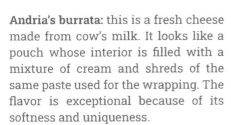

Pecora alla pignatta (cutturidd): a typical Matera dish, widespread throughout the Murgia area, where it takes on different names depending on where it is eaten. It is a lamb stew, simmered for hours in an earthenware pot with many ingredients, especially the wild herbs typical of the Murgia, such as chicory and asparagus.

Eating this lamb stew is a return to the flavors of yesteryear, those of the peasant civilization, to something extremely simple, but that has nothing to envy from more modern and emblazoned dishes.

Peperoni cruschi: these are another Matera specialty. The peppers are deep red and particularly prized for their sweetness. "Crusco" stands for crunchy, which is the typical characteristic of these peppers, which lend themselves to be cooked in many different ways, eaten as a snack or as a side dish for other dishes.

As for wines, we find many noteworthy products here as well.

Castel del Monte: this wine is one of the most famous in the entire Murgia area. It is a very popular wine in its white version and the other red and rosé versions. It is very dry and fresh on the palate.

Primitivo di Gioia del Colle: wine produced for centuries in the Murgia area. It presents a very intense ruby-red color, almost purplish.

Its flavor is very warm and enveloping, with a robust fruity component.

Gravina: White wine, suitable for mushrooms or fish. Its appearance is straw-colored, tending to soft green, while it is dry or sweetish on the palate. It is also produced in a sparkling version.

CHAPTER 4

ITRIA VALLEY AND THE TRULLI AREA

Located in the most southern part of the Murgia, the Itria Valley, also called the valley of the trulli, is located in the area roughly compressed between the chief towns of Bari, Taranto, and Brindisi.

The Itria Valley is, according to all, simply stunning. With its expanses of olive trees, towns characterized by the whiteness of the houses, ancient farms, and yet another UNESCO heritage site in Apulia, the trulli of Alberobello, it guarantees an unforgettable spectacle for all tourists who visit it.

All the elements that can be found in this succession of gentle highlands contribute to the fairy-tale atmosphere that is worth being surrounded by at least once in a lifetime.

The Itria Valley villages have long been considered among the most beautiful in Italy. They are places full of life, where events with international resonance take place, and where unique traditions and flavors can be found.

There are no more Instagrammable places than those in the Itria Valley.

But let's start on this journey by beginning with the most famous of these villages: Alberobello.

ALBEROBELLO

Despite being an increasingly popular destination, especially for mass tourism, this small village manages to retain all its charm and magic.

Its outline is delineated by quite distinctive dwellings, built with local stones and set together without cement or mortar, according to the technique known as "a secco." The conical roof is characteristic, composed of "chiancarelle" with the keystone surmounted by

a pinnacle, which can take different shapes, and according to tradition, serves to drive away bad luck. For the same reason, a religious or mythological symbol is painted on each of these roofs with white ash.

To wander into the trulli area, with its alleys full of flowers, artisans, restaurants, and with the smells of typical Apulian cuisine, is to end up in a fairy tale, in a labyrinth that is the result of some magician's imagination.

These are the must-see spots within the trulli area:

- Trullo Sovrano, located in the northern part of town, the only double-floor Trullo in Alberobello furnished with original furniture from the early 20th century;
- The Monti district, the largest area of trulli. Here are the two Siamese Trulli, two trulli with their cones fused centrally, which, according to an old tradition, are the symbol of a troubled history between two brothers;
- "Casa Pezzolla," where 15 communicating trulli constitute a museum that tells the story of the area, which can be visited free of charge.

Finally, if you want an unforgettable souvenir photo, go to Belvedere Santa Lucia for the best view of the whole trulli complex. The advice is to go there at sunset, because the view is very impressive.

LOCOROTONDO

While Alberobello is famous for the conical shape of the roofs of its houses, Locorotondo is renowned for its "cummerse." In short, the stone used is the same as that seen in Alberobello. However, the roofs are pitched and aligned with the walls of the fronts. Were it not for the difference in the materials used, the houses in Locorotondo would be quite similar to typical houses in northern European countries. The shape of these roofs is functional for rainwater collection.

The village of Locorotondo is distinguished by its circular layout (thus its name) and historic center, with white walls and colorful flowers everywhere, making the narrow streets a fairy-tale place.

SAN GIORGIO CHURCH

The Mother Church of St. George is the main place of worship in the village and is located in the heart of the historic center. With its 35- meter-high dome and bell tower standing above the other buildings, the church is easily visible even from a distance.

The church was built between 1790 and 1825 and is based on the remains of two older churches dating back to 1195 and the 16th century, respectively. The facade of the church follows a majestic and elegant 16th-century style. At the same time, the interior has a cross-shaped plan and is characterized by a fusion of elements of Baroque and Renaissance architecture. Inside the church is a painting of St. George and a magnificent marble altar.

ST NICOLA CHURCH

A more hidden and modest church, but one with a magnificently frescoed ceiling, is the Church of St. Nicholas, built in the 1600s. Inside there are also stone bas-reliefs found inside a cave, presumed, therefore, to be older than the church itself, depicting the crucifixion of Jesus.

Locorotondo also turns out to be magnificent because of the natural setting in which it stands: from its position, it dominates the entire Itria Valley, offering breathtaking views.

In this regard, it is a must to reach the viewpoint of Lungovalle - Via Nardelli - Lungomare. Many beautiful venues here allow you to have a few drinks while overlooking a magnificent view.

Of all the events that are organized in this beautiful village, the Locus festival is a music festival that hosts famous international artists every year, varying for multiple musical genres.

MARTINA FRANCA

The triumph of Baroque characterizes Martina Franca. We find this architectural style throughout the historic center, coexisting alongside the trulli, also present here.

Among the churches to visit, San Martino is considered an important example of Baroque architecture in union with local elements. It is precisely the appearance of this and other churches in the historic center and beyond that contributes to the visually spectacular appearance of this village.

Instead, in the splendid Ducal Palace, it is possible to visit two museums: one dedicated to a particular

theme, the forest (in the territory of Martina Franca falls the Pianelle forest, considered a nature reserve), while the other is an exhibition of contemporary art.

Finally, not far from Martina Franca, in its magnificent countryside, is the cave of Mount Fellone, inside which tools dating back to the Neolithic period have been found. It is certainly worth a visit.

ITRIA VALLEY FESTIVAL

For music lovers, Martina Franca has been home to the "Festival della Valle d'Itria," a major cultural event held every summer to promote music and culture in the Itria Valley region, managing to attract visitors from all over the world.

The festival, which takes place during July and August, as the title says, is held in Martina Franca and nearby towns such as Locorotondo, Cisternino, and Ostuni. The festival's programming mainly includes performances of opera, ballet, and classical music, with the participation of internationally renowned artists.

This festival has become famous due to its productions of rare and little-performed operas, such as some of the works of Gioachino Rossini, a native of the Itria Valley region. In addition to concerts, the festival also offers events such as art exhibitions, meetings with artists, film screenings, and other cultural events.

The Itria Valley Festival is a unique experience for music and culture lovers and offers the chance to discover the beauty of this area.

Especially classical music lovers cannot miss the opportunity to attend this important cultural event.

OSTUNI

Now let's talk about Ostuni, the "White City of Apulia," so called because of its historic center characterized by houses and buildings painted with white lime. The color was not chosen casually: first of all, white lime is very easy to find in the area, then the color gives more light to the narrow and winding streets of the historic center, and finally, it was a widespread belief that white lime was a natural disinfectant against the Plague.

Ostuni stands on three hills, and compared to other towns in the Itria Valley, it is close to the sea.

To visit it is to be thunderstruck by this village that, from its position, dominates the entire surrounding area.

Ostuni is graceful and wandering through its incredible historic center's narrow, white streets. So, you can understand how this small town annually attracts thousands of tourists from all over the globe.

Many routes can be followed within the historic center. However, the advice of those who have been there is to walk freely and marvel at every corner, every glimpse, every beautiful church that suddenly appears before you, and squares filled with craft stores and restaurants that will make your mouth water.

PIAZZA DELLA LIBERTA'

A must-see is " Piazza della libertà," the main square, where St. Francis Palace, a former monastery and now a city palace, stands out, with the beautiful St. Francis Church next to it. This square is always full of people, movement, and places to relax and enjoy the view. But its beauty does not end there.

In the center of the square stands a 21-meter-high obelisk with the statue of the city's patron saint, St. Oronzo, on top.

Finally, in this square, it is possible to observe the archaeological excavation that has unearthed part of the city's ancient fortifications, the construction of which predates 1500.

THE DEFENSIVE BELTS

There are 3 imposing defensive walls around the city, each referring to a particular historical period: the first was built by the Messapians, a very ancient population of the place; the second by the Byzantine emperor Basil the Macedonian; and the last, the most majestic is the one built by the Aragonese, whose archaeological excavation is visible in Piazza della Libertà.

THE COAST NEAR OSTUNI

Let's put aside the beauty of the historic center to head toward the sea. Ostuni is also famous for this.

The center is only 8 km from the Adriatic coast, where the sea is clean, transparent, and unspoiled, and the beaches and coves are a wonder of nature, particularly on the Costa Merlata. The Ostuni marina has 20 km of coastline with beautiful and distinctive landscapes. Among those to absolutely visit are:

BEACH OF TORRE Guaceto

This beach is located in the WWF-managed marine protected area of the same name in the municipality of Carovigno, just 8 km from the white city. It is one of the most beautiful in the entire region. The beach takes its name from the nearby Aragonese watchtower and is surrounded by centuries-old olive groves that produce extra virgin olive oil of exceptional quality. The sand on the beach is fine and clear, with golden shades, and the sea is crystal clear with a seabed rich in flora and fauna.

Since the Torre Guaceto area is a natural park, some parts of the beach are not accessible. However, there is plenty of bathing establishments, restaurants, bars, and free areas to relax and enjoy the sea and the scent of the Mediterranean scrub. In addition, there is also a sailing center that offers catamaran, sailing, and windsurfing courses.

Rosa Marina Beach

With its wide expanses of sand, this resort is perfect for families, couples, and young people looking for a dream vacation surrounded by fragrant Mediterranean scrub. Rosa Marina is home to a residential village built in the 1960s that attracts many tourists yearly.

The beach boasts the prestigious 5 Sails Blue Flag from Legambiente and is ideal for lovers of water sports such as windsurfing and kitesurfing. It also offers equipped lidos for renting umbrellas, sunbeds, deckchairs, and villas for rent near the sea for a relaxing stay. This enchanting place is a perfect choice for spending a relaxing vacation away from the hustle and bustle of the hottest resorts.

Santa Sabina Tower

Torre Santa Sabina, located in the so-called Alto Salento, is a beach that offers moments of serenity and relaxation, ideal for those who do not like crowded beaches.

The beach, among the most beautiful on the Brindisi coast, is characterized by cliffs, white sand, and crystal-clear sea, perfect for swimming, while the shallow waters are ideal for children. It is located 15 km from Ostuni.

Torre Santa Sabina, precisely because of the presence of both sand and cliffs, lends itself to the needs of all visitors, including free beaches for the adventurous and numerous bathing establishments for those seeking comfort. Popular beaches include:

- Gola, with high and cliffs, ideal for those who enjoy diving; Camerini, with shallow and sandy seabed ideal for families with children;
- Cavallo Beach, with a horse-shaped rock and the imposing presence of a watchtower;
- Mezzaluna Beach, which offers both free and equipped stretches.

Torre Santa Sabina is a beautiful location, often overlooked in favor of other locations, but able to offer an authentic experience to tourists.

Torre Pozzelle

Torre Pozzelle is a wild and little-known beach in the Ostuni area.

Accessible only on foot after walking along an unpaved path, it consists of several coves, some with sand and others with rocks.

The beach is characterized by its crystal-clear sea and the presence of a 16th-century coastal tower, now partially collapsed. There is little human hand in the Torre Pozzelle area, which is ideal for those who love the wilderness and want to spend moments of relaxation and tranquility.

Costa Merlata

Costa Merlata beach, located near Ostuni, is characterized by fascinating bays alternating sand and jagged rocks overlooking the deep blue Adriatic Sea. The beach's name comes from the jagged shape of the coastline, which is reminiscent of the battlements of medieval castles.

This area offers a peaceful corner away from the hustle and bustle of mass tourism.

Surrounded by Mediterranean vegetation, Costa Merlata is a natural gem perfect for those who love to experience the sea authentically, between rocks and soft sand. The beach is ideal for families and friends seeking relaxation and direct contact with nature.

Are you still there? What are you waiting for? Come immediately to discover these fantastic places!

FOODS TO ABSOLUTELY ENJOY IN THE ITRIA VALLEY

Like the rest of the region, the Itria Valley offers unique and genuine flavors.

The valley's best dishes are made with meat, cooked in wood-fired ovens, and seasoned with spices and herbs. Also of great value is the production of cured meats.

BOMBETTE DI ALBEROBELLO: also called bombette pugliesi, are an incredible treat. Small rolls of pork capocollo seasoned with salt, pepper, and, if needed, a small piece of caciocavallo cheese. Once you taste the first one, you won't be able to stop.

Gnummareddi: these are roulades prepared from mixed offal of lamb and suckling kid, tightened with their own casing along with a parsley leaf. They have a very intense flavor, especially when grilled with bay or olive leaves. They are also found in other areas of Puglia, in different variations and with different names.

Capocollo di Martina Franca: typical cured meat from the Itria Valley, one of the most popular. It is made by subjecting the pig's cervical area to salting, smoking, and then curing. It is a product in high demand everywhere and with extraordinary flavor.

As for wines, we also have a fairly important production here. They stand out in particular:

Vino Locorotondo: is a white wine to be served fresh, ideal as an aperitif.

It is bright greenish in color, with a slightly fruity but intense bouquet. On the palate, it is smooth and with great finesse.

Vino Terra d'Otranto: produced in 3 variants, white, red and rosé.

It is a very versatile wine that goes well with different dishes of Apulian cuisine. It is fresh and light on the palate with a fruity aroma.

Vino Ostuni: Ostuni wine has an intense ruby red color, a complex, and pronounced bouquet, with notes of berries and spices. The palate is full-bodied and tannic, with good structure and long persistence.

CHAPTER 5

SALENTO

With Salento, we have come to the extreme part of Puglia, the southernmost, a peninsula that witnesses the contact between the Ionian and Adriatic Seas.

Salento, because of its traditions, its local languages (in some inland areas, a dialect very similar to ancient Greek, called "Griko," is spoken), and its characteristics is almost considered a different region from the rest of Apulia.

It is an exceptional territory, which almost seems to be born from the union of the sea and the countryside. Yet, despite the strong passion for the sea of the area's inhabitants, even its inland part with the countryside, centuries-old olive trees, vineyards, rhythms, and traditions, has left a strong imprint on the identity of Salento.

From the ancient "masserie", places of dwelling and agricultural production, to the many but very small seaside villages, each with its own story to tell, Salento is ready to leave a part of its magic in the hearts and minds of those who visit it.

A saying in Salento dialect goes like this: "Salentu: lu sule, lu mare, lu ientu" (Salento: the sun, the sea, the wind).

These are the first 3 elements ready to welcome the tourist, seen as a guest to be welcomed and pampered. The sun, ready to embrace its warmth, the sea with its crystal-clear waters like few other places in the world, and the wind that brings with it the typical smells and flavors of these areas.

LECCE

The most important city in Salento is Lecce, the capital of the province and a magnificent example of Baroque architecture.

Starting in the XVII century, architects and artists gave the city that triumphal and majestic appearance that has come down to the present day.

The Baroque physiognomy that characterizes the city today is also made possible by 'the use of local stone, known as "Pietra leccese." This material of limestone origin is easily worked, and over time tends to take on a typical yellow color, as well as hardening. This stone makes the entire historical center a triumph of putti, twisted elements, garlands, and all that is whimsy and irregularity, making Lecce Baroque an architectural style with clearly recognizable peculiarities.

ST. ORONZO PLAZA

Piazza Sant'Oronzo, one of the most fascinating places in Lecce, fully expresses the city's thousand-year history. Here it is possible to see elements of different eras overlapping and coexisting. The square is an exclusively pedestrian area, so much so that it has become a place where events and manifestations take place, as well as a meeting and entertainment place for the inhabitants of Lecce.

Among the first elements that stand out and characterize Piazza Sant'Oronzo is a portion of the Roman amphitheater brought to light in the 1900s. It is estimated that it could hold up to 25,000 people in its heyday.

Just as in Ostuni, here we have a 29-m column topped by a bronze statue of St. Oronzo, the city's patron saint.

To further embellish the square's beauty and centrality, we have several splendid civil and religious buildings:

- The Sedile (once the seat of the municipality)
- The small church of San Marco
- The church of Santa Maria delle Grazie and Palazzo Carafa

All this view should be considered the "antechamber" to the historical center, the main focus of which is Piazza Duomo, with its magnificent cathedral, bell tower, episcope, and seminary.

PIAZZA DUOMO AND CATHEDRAL

The square hides a series of incredible peculiarities: one of the few squares closed on three sides, with a single entrance. This can be explained by the fact that where there is now access with the presence of propylaea, surmounted by statues depicting three church fathers on one side and St. Irene, St. Oronzo, and St. Venera on the other, there was actually a wall with doors that were locked at night. The whole area of the

cathedral constituted a citadel under religious control, autonomous from the rest of the town.

As it appears today, the square with the cathedral and the other buildings is one of the highest expressions of Lecce Baroque: an entire complex of buildings that are harmonious as a whole.

Thanks to the use of yellow-colored Lecce stone for both the buildings and the paving, the square gives back a strong sense of warmth, resulting in a welcoming place for anyone who spends time admiring it.

The greatest wonder, however, comes during sunset: in fact, the sun's rays hitting the protrusions, recesses, and decorations of the façades provide a majestic spectacle of light and shadow, of astounding beauty.

The cathedral has a peculiarity: its façade overlooking Piazza Duomo, which immediately catches the attention of those who arrive, is actually a secondary façade, as it is located on one of the long sides of the church. The main facade, on the other hand, is hidden from the square.

If outside the cathedral presents this bizarre character, entirely "normal" within a Baroque context, the church's interior is no less so.

Decorations and ornaments will leave you breathless, as the whole church is decorated whimsically, with ornaments, architectural solutions, and other devices in front of which one cannot remain indifferent. There are as many as 12 altars besides the main altar, each dedicated to a saint and richly decorated with different motifs.

BELL TOWER IN PIAZZA DUOMO

The architectural complex of Piazza Duomo culminates in the majestic Bell Tower, one of the tallest in Europe, located on the left side of the square. Standing 68 meters tall, the Bell Tower looms lightly in the Lecce sky, dominating the entire historic center with its soaring bulk. It has a square plan with five floors that decrease in height as you ascend, each of which is decorated with a richly ornamented balustrade and a round-arched window. Each floor has a commemorative epitaph at the top. In addition, the top floor features four floral spires on angular obelisks, which correspond to the pinnacles with flowering baskets on the octagonal dome that harmoniously concludes the building.

The bell tower also offers one of the most beautiful views imaginable.

Indeed, you can climb to its top to embrace in a single glance the entire surrounding area all the way to the Adriatic, and on clear days you can even spot the lands of Albania - an incredible sight.

To enjoy this view, walking up many uphill steps was necessary. Today, however, an elevator has been installed that makes it possible to climb to the top of the building effortlessly, subject to ticket payment.

Little trivia: the bell tower is not perfectly straight, but due to a small subsidence of the foundation, it has a slight curve to the left.

EPISCOPE AND SEMINARY

The other two buildings contributing to the harmonious spectacle of Cathedral Square are the bishop's seat, the episcope, and the seminary, which has a highly decorated facade arranged in three orders. Once inside, after passing among 12 statues depicting doctors of the church, a small masterpiece of Baroque art is located in the atrium: a beautifully sculpted " baldachin " well.

A small but very precious treasure to be discovered.

Inside the palace, there is also a museum of sacred art and a small private church dedicated to St. Gregory the Wonderworker, a small treasure chest of Baroque art, unfortunately unknown to many but absolutely worth visiting.

THE CHURCH OF SANTA CROCE

Not far from Piazza Duomo stands a church considered among the masterpieces of all Baroque art: the church of Santa Croce. Built on a pre-existing structure, the church is notable for its intricate decoration both on the facade, with statues, balustrades, indentations, projections, and symbols of various kinds, and on the interior, which is also richly decorated and apt to enrapture anyone who enters.

UNDERGROUND LECCE

An excellent environment that few people know about is the underground Lecce. Like many other Apulian cities, we have discussed, Lecce has its own underground part.

The discovery was accidental, thanks to a private individual who, to carry out pipe replacement work, discovered by chance this hidden world under his house.

Exploration and restoration works have wrested from the oblivion of time incredible places, such as houses, or ancient monasteries, and even tanks in which the Jewish community of Lecce performed their rituals.

To learn more, one can visit and inquire at the "Pheasant Archaeological Museum," housed in that very house from where the discovery started.

OTRANTO

Otranto is the city referred to as the "Gateway to the East" since among the Italian countries, it is the one that is located most eastward, overlooking that part of the Adriatic Sea placed between Apulia and the Balkans called the Otranto Channel.

Precisely because of its location, every year at the turn of the year, the event "Dawn of Peoples" is organized, which we will talk about later.

Otranto is a small village of just 5,000 inhabitants, but in summer, it turns into a sort of "melting pot" of people from all corners of the globe.

Its ancient importance is evidenced by the fact that the Turks tried several times to take Otranto, succeeding only in 1480 and maintaining control for only one year, a year remembered by the population as terrible.

At the end of the long siege, after looting, violence, and killing, there remained only 800 survivors on whom conversion to Islam or death was imposed. These 800 survivors did not convert and were all killed. After the invaders were driven out, their bodies were moved to Otranto Cathedral.

A few centuries later they were declared martyrs by the church and became objects of worship because of this.

CATHEDRAL OF OTRANTO

The cathedral of Otranto is extraordinary. First of all, in terms of size, it is the largest church in Apulia, 54 meters long and 25 meters wide.

Suppose you pay attention to the columns that subdivide the cathedral space. In that case, you will notice something quite unusual: they are different in material type, color, and workmanship (some are smooth, others fluted). And the same goes for the capitals; no one is the same as another.

But what is most surprising is that instead of creating an environment composed of different pieces, the skillful arrangement of the columns managed to marry perfectly with the other elements of the cathedral, creating a just as much as surprising balance, both with the gilded coffered ceiling of the nave and with one of the most beautiful and mysterious mosaics ever created, dating back to the 12th century.

That mosaic occupies the entire length of the cathedral, with an interweaving of symbol motifs on whose interpretation scholars still disagree.

The mosaic is considered a true encyclopedia of medieval life; several events and characters are represented, all arranged in a balanced and unified whole. The sight of it cannot help but leave one amazed and incredulous. It also imparts a sense of disquiet precisely because of the mysteries concealed in it, along with a sense of horror vacui precisely because of its decorative fullness. An incredible treasure of Puglia's historical-artistic heritage.

Among the apses, the left one preserves in some cases the remains of those who the Turks killed in 1480.

HISTORIC CENTER AND HARBOR

The old town, where the harbor is included, is a maze of small streets and lanes with craft stores and restaurants. This was once one of the most important harbors and landings for ships from the east. You have to imagine the constant comings and goings of goods and people from all over the known world, with merchant ships leaving and arriving, the various sighting and defense systems (the towers), given the constant threat from the Turks.

THE CASTLE

Because of its strategic location, Otranto has a castle with a system of ramparts and defensive walls that, if they once served to repel enemies, today lend themselves to being places where visitors can touch history and enjoy the beauty and atmosphere of this magnificent seaside village.

The cartel's moats have also become venues for demonstrations and events, while ancient bombards are preserved and can be observed in its courtyard.

BAUXITE QUARRY

Before talking about the beautiful Otranto coastline, just a few kilometers from the city, there is a unique place, the bauxite quarry.

Bauxite was extracted from this quarry for several decades, until the activity was later discontinued. So far, nothing special.

With time, however, thanks to the limestone terrain and the presence of groundwater, the quarry is transformed into a small lake environment in front of which you cannot remain impassive. The spectacle is given by the strong contrast between the deep red of the quarry walls and the emerald color of the water, to which is added the green of the surrounding nature, has slowly reclaimed the territory.

An exceptional place, where at times it seems to be on another planet, a must-visit.

THE BEACHES OF OTRANTO

Let us now talk about what can be considered a paradise on earth: the beaches of Otranto. Actually, the entire Salento coast, both Ionian and Adriatic, can be considered a paradise.

However, let us start with Otranto and its beautiful beaches:

BAIA DEI TURCHI

The name comes from the Turks landing here during the siege OF 1480.

The beach is ideal for those who love contact with nature, which can be reached by walking along the paths of a dense pine forest. The beach is free and characterized by very white sand;

BEACH OF ALIMINI

The name of this beach, not far from the Bay of Turks, is due to the nearby presence of the Alimini lakes.

The sand here is golden, and in addition to the free beach, there are also lidos and kiosks;

BEACH OF MULINO D'ACQUA

The main feature of this beach is the different shades of blue of the waters. In addition, the entire beach is surrounded by caves and rocks.

The best-known cave is Grotta Sfondata, inside which it forms a natural basin that can be accessed from the sea;

BEACH OF RINULE

Fifteen meters of totally unspoiled, primeval beach surrounded by white limestone rocks. Crystal clear waters. You get there after some walking, but the beach spectacle is worth the effort.

BEACH OF PORTO BADISCO

A very renowned place in Otranto, where tourists can find beautiful coves with breathtaking views and wonderful SAND, with rocks plunging into the water. According to a legend, this is the landing place of Aeneas after escaping from Troy;

BAIA DELLE ORTE

This place is for lovers of calm, silence, and nature. Here glimpses of greenery and the presence of rocks give the idea of a wild place;

BEACH LA PUNTA

This area has well-equipped facilities to make the most of the deep blue sea. There are also renowned eateries ready to surprise your taste buds with typical local dishes;

BEACH TORRE DELL'ORSO

The beach is especially ideal for families with children. This place has won several awards for its waters and beauty. A pine forest surrounds a typically sandy beach with shallow waters.

L'ALBA DEI POPOLI

The event that takes place every year in Otranto is translated with "the dawn of the peoples."

It is now well known that Otranto is the easternmost city in Italy, and throughout its history, Otranto has always been a bridge between West and East. That is why a series of cultural events, concerts, art and film exhibitions, sports competitions, and many other events are organized between the months of December and January, in which all the cultures of the Mediterranean are called upon to participate in a mixture of history, culture and traditions.

This glorious event attracts thousands of tourists every year. The highlight is the event in front of the Punta Palascìa lighthouse on the evening of December 31 to bid farewell to the old year and welcome the new one with the best of luck.

SALENTO COASTS

This is where the real problem of Salento arises: when we decide we want to go to the sea, having to choose the seaside location from more than 200 km of beaches, bays, inlets, coves, and cliffs is difficult. Nevertheless, no coastline can be said to be less beautiful or attractive than the others.

Before starting this trip to the Salento peninsula, the advice is to rent a car so you can move comfortably from one beach to another, even over several days.

THE SALENTO ADRIATIC COAST

We begin with the Adriatic coast, which we have already talked about with Ostuni and Otranto, so let us continue southward to the furthest edge, Santa Maria di Leuca, from which we will then ascend along the Ionian coast.

THE MARINAS OF MELENDUGNO

Halfway between Lecce and Otranto, a series of beaches are part of the Marina di Melendugno, which offer real postcard views: Torre dell'Orso, San Foca, Roca, Torre Sant'Andrea and Torre Specchia Ruggeri constitute a mind-blowing spectacle.

1. San Foca is first in order, where in the harbor, you can admire an ancient watchtower dating back to the 1500s, and the Grotta degli Amanti, where according to legend, two lovers sought shelter. Then, especially on a clear day, it is possible to catch a glimpse of the Albanian mountains on the horizon. A sight not to be missed.

2. Roca Vecchia is another area that exerts a strong attraction for tourists, where nature and history come together: here, in fact, we have the enchanting Cave of Poetry, around which revolves the legend of a princess who loved to dive right here and where poets used to come to look for the girl to make her the muse of their poetic compositions.

3. Torre dell'Orso is among the most popular destinations in Salento, with white beaches and a crystal-clear sea embraced by a fragrant pine forest. In Torre dell'Orso, you can visit the Grotto of San Cristoforo, where graffiti is of considerable archaeological value. Making this beach famous are two stacks called "The Two Sisters." **Legend tells of two sisters who were enchanted by the beauty of the place; however, they drowned there while bathing. They were precisely turned into stacks so that they could admire the beauty of Torre dell'Orso for eternity.**

4. Torre Sant Andrea, on the other hand, is a popular destination for younger people who can enjoy concerts and find many clubs here.

The coast here is rocky and rugged, with caves and ravines interspersed with coves, with clear water that sometimes takes on cobalt-colored features.

SANTA CESAREA TERME

A visit to Santa Cesarea Terme is not to be disdained at all. In fact, although there are no beaches here, it is possible to admire the many villas and aristocratic palaces built by wealthy bourgeoisie as vacation spots. Since the early 1900s, this has been a bathing and vacation destination.

In addition, as the name of the village says, there is a spa, where I am sure you will appreciate a stop.

They are located inside an old building, now equipped with all modern conveniences. From four underground caves flow these waters, whose beneficial qualities have been known for 500 years.

ZINZULUSA CAVE

Continuing further south, halfway between Santa Cesarea Terme and Castro, there is one of the most scenically and geologically beautiful and interesting caves in the world: the Grotta Zinzulusa.

It can be accessed by sea. It is 160 meters long and is divided into three environ-

ments: the first is the "Conca," from which you access the "Corridor of Wonders," so called because the stalactites and stalagmites that characterize it with their different shapes have caused the inhabitants of nearby places to give each of these elements a name that recalls various objects and figures. In the corridor, there is also a small lake, called "Trabocchetto," followed by the most spectacular environment of this small geological complex: the "Crypt," a 25-meter-high room where the large and mighty columns give the place the appearance of a cathedral. Added to this environment is the Cocito Pond, which offers the sight of pure water on the surface and brackish water on the bottom, inhabited by microorganisms.

The name of the cave comes from an old legend:

Apparently, near the cave lived a very evil rich man, the Baron of Castro, who required his daughter to dress only in rags (zinzuli in the local dialect). One day, a fairy brought the little girl a new dress while the old rags were carried away by the wind and petrified on the cave walls, which took precisely the name Grotta della Zinzulusa . On the other hand, the Baron was thrown into the Cocito Lake, where the crustaceans remained blind forever after witnessing the scene. ༈

Visiting the cave only with an authorized guide and after paying a ticket is possible.

A little tip: exactly where you start to visit the Zinzulusa Cave, there is a mooring with boats to visit the other nearby caves as well. Of particular beauty is the Blue Cave, where there is a great play of light.

CASTRO

Not far away is the small town of Castro, once an episcopal seat and with some importance, as evidenced by the presence of a mighty castle and a large cathedral in the historic center located in the upper part.

The lower part, or Castro Marina, has a very cozy little harbor where you can let the gentle breeze sway you while sipping a cool drink.

Castro has no beaches, the coast is rocky, and its waters are particularly high. Therefore, it is not a suitable place to visit with children with you. However, a small gem not far

from Castro is the "Cala dell'Acquaviva." It is inland thanks to lush vegetation surrounding the small beach, ready to show itself in all its beauty. A steep cliff bounds it, creating an exceptional environment, where the presence of cold water makes one think of a Norwegian fjord.

Despite its wild yet enchanting appearance, the Acquaviva cove is well equipped, and it is highly recommended to stop for a few hours to relax in this superb place.

CIOLO BRIDGE

We are now at the most extreme part of the peninsula, and before we reach the final point, we can pause at another interesting place, the "Ciolo Bridge."

There is a breathtaking view from this 60-meter-high bridge: the area is a canyon created by the erosive action of water and wind and is a wonderful example of Mediterranean scrub vegetation.

A few daredevils have even dived from the 60-meter height of the bridge, which is recommended not to do, both because of the danger of jumping into the void below which the seabed is rocky, and because it is forbidden.

This area is full of caves, used by many birds that find shelter there. Below the bridge, there is also a small beach you can access by a flight

of steps nearby, from where you can see the bridge and the rocks on which it stands from below.

SANTA MARIA DI LEUCA

Finally, we come to the far end of Puglia and the Salento peninsula, Santa Maria di Leuca.

The southernmost point of the entire region (the common belief is that the Ionian and Adriatic seas touch here; in reality, such contact occurs near Otranto), where according to some sources, St. Peter landed from Palestine to begin evangelization of the local peoples.

Santa Maria di Leuca is wonderful for its coastline, where sand and rocks alternate, and its splendid caves and seabed, attracting thousands of divers every year.

Conversely, the hinterland sees a continuous succession of villas and palaces reflecting different styles, which gently slope down to the sea.

On the highest and most scenic point rises a shrine, which can be reached from below by walking up 184 steps.

Along the steps runs a 120-meter waterfall, a reminder of the great feat of constructing the Apulian aqueduct (a critical infrastructure for a water-poor region like Apulia). Here are the terminal works of this impressive structure that spans the entire area.

Having taken the 184 steps, one arrives at the Santa Maria Finibus Terrae shrine, according to tradition blessed by St. Peter himself, and a gateway to paradise. The sanctuary stands on an ancient temple dedicated to the goddess Minerva, so much so that some evidence is still visible inside the church.

The lighthouse stands not far from the shrine, nearly 50 meters high and rising 102 meters above sea level.

For an unparalleled panoramic view, one must climb the 254 steps. But the strenuous climb is worth it: once at the top, a magnificent 360- degree view is there, ready to amaze anyone. To add to the fascination, watching the sunset from the top of the lighthouse is one of the most beautiful experiences you will ever have in your life. The play of light created by the interaction between the sun's rays as it sets on the horizon and the sea steals the beholder's heart.

Both with respect to the east and west of Santa Maria di Leuca, there are several caves, which you can visit with guided boat excursions: Grotta Porcinara, Grotta del Diavolo, Grotta dei Giganti, Grotta del Bambino, Grotta delle Tre Porte, and many others, each with unique stories and anecdotes that are well worth a visit.

WEST COAST OF SALENTO

After enjoying the beauty of the extreme tip of Puglia, we continue to its east coast, the Ionian coast.

MARINA DI PESCOLUSE

Going up, you immediately come across the area that has been dubbed the "Maldives of Salento," the marina of Pescoluse.

A blue and calm sea, very white beach dunes and thick vegetation surrounding the 4 km of beach make this location a real corner of paradise on earth. Here portions of free beaches alternate with private lidos, plus the resort is particularly suitable for families with children.

The town of Pescoluse is not very big, but it has all the necessary services for vacationers, while in the evening it is transformed thanks to an extremely lively movida with bars, restaurants, clubs where you can dance and have fun.

Pescoluse is absolutely one of those destinations that you cannot forget after you have been there.

GALLIPOLI

Among the most popular places in recent years, especially by younger people, is Gallipoli.

With its clubs, nightlife, events, and beaches, Gallipoli fills up with thousands of vacationers every summer, who cannot help but be amazed by this location.

Gallipoli is not only beaches and fun, but like many other places in Salento it is also culture, history, traditions. So here is that a visit to the old part, located on an island, is an excellent idea. The stars of the old town are the Angevin castle and the basilica of St. Agatha.

In all the old part there are as many as 17 churches and monasteries, connected by secret tunnels, some of which lead outside the walls of the old town.

Also here, as in other areas of Salento, the Baroque has characterized the physiognomy of churches and towns.

One example is the church of Santa Maria della Purità, where along- side the rich Baroque ornaments and precious paintings, a beautiful majolica floor can be admired.

GALLIPOLI BEACHES

Spiaggia della purità

There is one at the foot of the old town, called the purity beach, a quiet place to relax, with imposing defensive walls behind it;

BAIA VERDE

A trendy beach in Gallipoli, where private lidos to stretches of free beach meet everyone's needs.

The beach is characterized by wonderful sand, surrounded by Mediterranean scrub, ready to inebriate the senses with its colors and smells. Adding further value to the place is the placid sea with its crystal-clear waters, which at every sunset offers a dreamlike spectacle.

The beach is only 3 km from the center and is easily accessible both on foot and by public transportation;

SPIAGGIA DEGLI INNAMORATI

Further south of Baia Verde is "Lovers' Beach," in the "LI Foggi" area. One is within the Regional Natural Park of the Island of St. Andrew and Punta Pizzo coastline. The beach's name comes from the fact that the place is quiet and uncrowded.

The beach is characterized by fine, cream-colored sand with a turquoise sea. It is truly a heavenly place where you can leave behind the daily hustle and bustle of the city and enjoy a moment of total relaxation together with a few intimates with whom to share peace and serenity.

The beach is reached after a short walk through the Mediterranean maquis, with its smells and aromas.

It is worth mentioning that the lovers' beach, or as the locals call it, "Foggi" beach, is located within a protected area known as the "Regional Natural Park of Sant'Andrea Island and Punta Izzo," considered the green lung of Salento. From a biodiversity point of view, the area is held in very high regard. The protected area has large expanses of woodland, with very special flora and fauna. At least ten species of oak trees have been counted in this area.

The area closest to the sea turns into a lush pine forest with rare plants and shrubs.

PUNTA DELLA SUINA

If with the marina of Pescoluse we were talking about the Maldives, with the beach of Punta della Suina, we are talking instead about the Caribbean.

So-called because of the particular projection of the shoreline towards the sea, this stretches alternate between sand and areas with rocks where you can dive.

What is wonderful are the crystal-clear sea, able to hypnotize you with its reflections, and the hinterland with its pine forest full of scents and smells.

A little further on is Punta Izzo, another must-see destination.

PORTO SELVAGGIO

Continuing further, there is a hidden place, one of the most beautiful in Italy and one of the most magical in all of Apulia and the Salento coast: Porto Selvaggio.

This enchanting place is located within the natural park of the same name, where out of 432 hectares of coastline, as many as 268 are composed of wooded area due to reforestation of the area.

The small cove that gives its name to the whole area is surrounded by a frame of rocks and ravines from which it is possible to dive, while the beach looks like pebbly sand. Because of the nearby presence of a spring that can be reached by swimming, if you do not fear the cold, a stream of fresh, cold water has been created in the cove.

Walking along one of the forest paths that protects this little gem, we arrive at Uluzzo Bay, where there is a Paleolithic deposit with stone artifacts and even the remains of large animals that once inhabited this area.

Continuing along such paths, one comes across several caves, such as "Capelve-nere," a name given to a fern seedling, within which ancient evidence from different eras has been found.

Among the many routes, one leads up to the "Torre dell'Alto," an imposing Aragonese fortification now home to the marine biology museum. This museum fortification stands on a point where its tip, which is 50 meters overhanging the sea, is called "Dirupo della Dannata." Here, a young woman sought death to escape the evil Count Giangerolamo Acquaviva.

The whole area of Porto Selvaggio is full of treasures and beauties, emotions to be discovered and experienced. Even the place that seems most mundane hides priceless treasures.

PORTO CESAREO

On the journey along the Ionian coast, a next stop is a place whose beaches are reminiscent of the Caribbean: Porto Cesareo. This destination is also among the most popular in Salento.

Porto Cesareo's beaches run uninterrupted for 17 km, with a calm sea with shallow sandy bottoms.

In front of the town's beach, about 200 meters offshore, are several islets, the largest known as "L'isola dei Conigli," which can be reached by boat or walking. The seabed, never more than a meter deep, allows this original "walk" to the islets. It should be remembered, however, that these strips of land are protected areas, and it is necessary to respect the laws for the protection of these natural environments, should one decide to visit them.

- Two hamlets of Porto Cesareo deserve to be mentioned: "Torre Chianca" and "Torre Lapillo."
- Torre Chianca is considered ideal for going diving. Its seabed is incredible. Moreover, it is also possible to observe some columns from the Roman era "anchored" to the seabed following the shipwreck of the ship that transported them.
- Torre Lapillo, on the other hand, is characterized by free beaches alternating with private beaches. Thanks to the presence of services and facilities, it is possible to carry out one of the many activities offered.

Also part of the municipality of Porto Cesareo is the beach of Punta Prosciutto.

This beach, precisely because of its beauty, is known worldwide, and tourists come from everywhere to enjoy the unique beauty of this place.

It is composed of 2 km of a very white beach, with the sea touching all shades of blue and azure.

Precisely because of its beauty and to preserve flora and fauna, it became necessary to create an institutional body and give birth to the "Count Marsh Regional Nature Park."

SMALL JOURNEY INTO SALENTO'S PREHISTORY: DOLMENS

After exploring the majestic beauty of the Salento coast, let's see how the equally magnificent hinterland holds something very special: dolmens.

But what are dolmens?

Dolmens are structures dating back to prehistoric times, consisting of large stone slabs placed vertically to support a large horizontal slab. On their functions, it is speculated that they were probably tombs or structures to perform rituals. Apulia is among the regions with the largest number of dolmens, most of which are in Salento (it is estimated there were at least 100 at one time, today, there are many fewer).

So, while delighting in all that this land has to offer, why not set out in search of these ancient structures that have been here for millennia and seem to guard the land?

These are the main dolmens that can be visited:

- The "Megalithic Garden of Italy": in Giurdignano, a small town near Otranto, there is a large area to protect and preserve seven dolmens, each of them with their peculiarities. Local authorities provide a series of tours, even at night so that you can visit them by bike or if you want, even by carriage.
- Within the Cultural Park of the Dolmen "Li Scusi" is placed the eponymous Dolmen, among the largest in the region, 1 meter high and with as many as 8 boulders supporting the horizontal slab. It was the first dolmen found in Apulia in 1879.
- The "Argentina" and "Così Così" dolmens, a few kilometers from Santa Maria di Leuca: the former is in an excellent state of preservation. At the same time, the latter is known because fragments of terracotta and bone remains have been found. The two dolmens, "Plau Grande Caroppo I" and "Plau Piccolo Caroppo II," located in Corigliano d'Otranto, are fascinating. The former has a gallery structure consisting of nine pillars supporting the horizontal slab, while the latter is smaller.
- The dolmen "Chianca Santo Stefano" in Carpignano Salentino has a structure that differs considerably from other dolmens in Salento, similar to those in northern Europe and consisting of three slabs.
- The dolmens "Placa" and "Gurgulante" are located along the road to Calimera in Melendugno. The former features seven vertical pillars and a roof, while the latter has a height of 90 cm.
- The dolmens "Stabile" and "Ore" are in Giuggianello. The structure of "Stabile" is still strong and consists of 2 monoliths and 7 columns, formed by overlapping boulders. On the other hand, that of the "Ore" dolmen consists of a monolithic and 2 stacked masses of stones, all resting on a rocky base.

MELPIGNANO AND THE TARANTA FESTIVAL

The event that every self-respecting Salento resident waits for at the end of August is the Night of the Taranta. A riot of celebration, dancing, music, and sounds where a small town, Melpignano, becomes the meeting center of cultures from all over the world. Hundreds of thousands of people meet to dance to the rhythm of the "pizzica," a typical Salento dance, under a huge stage. International artists participating in this event of celebration and communion between cultures.

But where does all this come from?

The "pizzica" is a type of dance that probably has its roots in the festivals honoring the Greek god Dionysus, in which moral restrictions were relaxed, and people threw themselves into wild singing and dancing.

Following the advent of Christianity, the Greek god was replaced with St. Paul, a healer saint who was often invoked in the various songs accompanying the traditional music, mainly performed with tambourine, accordion, violin and violin and guitar.

But what were the song and music supposed to heal from? From the bite of the tarantula, "taranta" in the local dialect.

Working in the fields it was easy for peasants to be bitten by the tarantula, which is why it was believed that such songs had the thaumaturgic power to nullify the power of the spider's venom.

Born therefore from a local belief, part of the traditions of Salento, today the pizzica finds its highest expression on the night of the Taranta of Melpignano, where it is reworked and combined with other musical genres to give life to an

incredible spectacle, in which for a whole night people sing and dance throughout the town in an almost surreal atmosphere, where ancient and modern merge, where the reverence for tradition also coexists with the impetus towards the future, with the awareness and the desire to never leave behind the history of this wonderful tradition.

FOODS TO ABSOLUTELY ENJOY IN SALENTO

Pasticciotto leccese: a small oval pastry cupcake filled with custard. In Salento, it is traditional to eat it for breakfast, probably because there is no better way to start the day.

There is also an alternative version, called "fruttone," where the pasticciotto is filled with almond paste and jam, all covered in dark chocolate.

Rustico leccese: two puff pastry disks between mozzarella, béchamel, and tomato. Some variations also include pepper and nutmeg. Best enjoyed hot if possible. A joy for the palate.

Friselle: made from durum wheat, frisella is cooked twice to obtain a porous and firm appearance. It is very hard, so before being seasoned with salt, oil, and tomatoes, it must be softened by "soaking" it in water.

When you bite into a frisella, you feel Salento in your mouth and all of Puglia.

Pettole: small globs of leavened dough, fried in oil, crispy outside and soft inside. Accompanied by different side dishes depending on the area: vincotto, salted anchovies, pieces of cod, or half-cooked broccoli - a delight.

Fish: Fish is also very good in Salento, in whatever way you cook it, whether fried or roasted, with sauce or in soup. In particular, mullet is to be tasted.

The wine production of Salento is also characterized by the excellent, whose demand is constantly expanding.

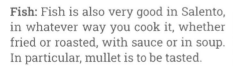

Primitivo di Manduria: it is believed that it was the Greeks who brought this type of wine over 2000 years ago, and today it is among the most famous wines of Puglia.

Its color is very deep red, almost purplish, with a sustained aroma of red fruits with a full and harmonious flavor.

Negroamaro: perhaps the best-selling Apulian wine in the world. Negroamaro red has a very dark color, and a lingering taste with a slightly bitter aftertaste. Excellent with meat and aged cheeses.

Negroamaro rosé, on the other hand, is widely used to give substance to other local wines.

Leverano: white wine with a straw yellow color, very delicate and dry. Perfect for appetizers. Its grapes are harvested in the early morning hours and undergo decanting and fermentation at low temperatures.

CHAPTER 6

TARANTO AND PROVINCIA

With the last beaches mentioned earlier, we arrived near one of the most import-ant cities in the region, Taranto. Here we are at the point where Murgia and Salento territories meet. A few kilometers from the magnificent beaches here, it is possible to find rock churches and dwellings carved into the rocks in canyons. It is no coincidence that here we have the "Parco delle Gravine," a protected area where it is possible to see entire settlements and villages built in the ravines, in territories that are impervious and beautiful at the same time.

TARANTO

Taranto is a city of Greek origin, more precisely it was founded by Spartan exiles (the only colony founded by the Lacedaemonian population). Because of its strategic location, the fertility of its soils, and its propensity for trade, Taranto has always been an important city that has had its own influence on all of southern Italy and beyond.

Today the city is home to one of the largest steel mills in Europe.

Taranto is also called "the city of two seas" as it precisely overlooks two seas, the "Mar Grande" and the "Mar Piccolo," which form the Gulf of Taranto.

"MarTA"

To learn about the history of Taranto and beyond and to understand its prestige in past centuries, one must visit the "MarTA," Taranto's museum, one of the most important in Italy. In this museum one can trace the entire history of the area from the Stone Age to the city's splendor during the Hellenistic age.

The museum is well organized and interesting, combining fun with knowledge. It is not only limited to introducing the history of Taranto, but depending on the period in which you visit it, you can see valuable paintings from different periods. In addition, temporary exhibitions and activities are often organized that can actively bring the museum experience to life.

HISTORIC CENTER

Another feature of Taranto is its historic center, which sits on an island. Were it not for two bridges (one revolving, another thing to see), it would be detached from the modern part of the city.

It is precisely this "isolation," according to those who have seen it and experienced it, that makes the old part of Taranto a world apart, where every stone seems to have so much to tell, and where around every corner there is either an incredible glimpse or a wonderful view.

The streets here are so narrow that one person can only walk some at a time. One street that perfectly testifies to this peculiarity is called "Street of the Kiss" because two people cannot pass without touching each other.

This narrow conformation of the streets in the old town is due to essentially defensive reasons, given the constant attacks by Saracens in the

Middle Ages, which led at one point to the destruction of the city and its necessary reconstruction.

CATHEDRAL OF SAN CATALDO

Entering the historic center, you must recognize the Cathedral of San Cataldo, the oldest in Apulia. Built about the middle of the 10th century, it was built on the ruins of a pre-existing religious building, possibly dating back about two centuries earlier. The building has undergone several changes over time: the original Byzantine-style layout underwent some renovations in the 11th century, while the Baroque-style facade was added in the 1700s. The old Norman bell tower no longer exists, having been destroyed by an earthquake around 1450. The church's interior consists of three naves, one central and two side aisles, and holds the tombs of some of the most important figures in Taranto's history.

THE ARAGONESE CASTLE

Along with the cathedral, also dominating the historic center, is the Aragonese castle, called "Castel Sant'Angelo," located at the far corner of the historic center island. Built-in Byzantine times around 900 AD, the rectangular-plan castle was originally designed to repel attacks by the Venetians and Syracusans, with tall, soaring towers to hurl arrows, stones, and boiling oil at enemies. In the late 1400s, King Ferdinand of Aragon II had the castle enlarged and modified, adding seven towers, including the Rivellino- a tower separated from the main part of the structure to allow a protected exit route in case of siege-giving it the appearance that can be seen today.

THE GREEK COLUMNS

Among the few remaining vestiges in the historic center of Greek Taranto are the two columns left standing in the ruins of an ancient temple. As soon as you cross the swing bridge from the modern city, these columns seem to be there waiting for the tourist to tell of millennia of history and the great prestige that Taranto held in antiquity.

Old Taranto is teeming with ancient hidden treasures that deserve to be discovered, hoping to avoid getting stuck in the narrow streets.

REMAINS OF GREEK TARANTO

Throughout the city, several sites testify to its Greek origins: from the necropolis, where 160 tombs can be visited, to the archaeological park of Collepasso, a true open-air museum, where it is possible to see the remains of a wall defending the city and a necropolis with different types of burials.

THE GULF OF TARANTO AND THE LEGEND OF THE SIRENS

Walking along Taranto's waterfront and observing its beautiful gulf, in some stretches, one cannot help but admire statues depicting mermaids built of marine concrete to resist the water's erosive action. The presence of these mermaids, which further embellish an enchanting landscape in itself, conceals an exciting romantic story.

In the days of Greek Taranto, sirens were so captivated by the beauty of the gulf that they decided to build their underwater castle here.

A young couple lived in the village: she was a beautiful girl who, due to his constant absence from her job as a fisherman, succumbed to the flattery of a local nobleman.

Gripped with guilt, she confessed everything to her husband, who decided to take her to sea and drown her in the gulf waters. However, the mermaids saved the girl, who, given her beauty, crowned her their queen with the name Skuma (Foam).

The young man, however, regretting what he had done, returned after some time to the scene of the misdeed, weeping all his tears. Here the sirens brought him before their queen. She forgave her husband and convinced the sirens not to kill him and bring him back to the surface.

The boy, however, decided he wanted his wife with him again, and with the help of a fairy, he managed to take her away from the mermaids' castle. ⚭

At this point, the legend has two different endings: in one, the Jovans returned to shore and lived happily ever after; in the other ending, a gigantic wave swept over the boy and the mermaids, disappearing into thin air, while the beautiful girl out of grief became a nun and locked herself up in what is now called "Monacella Tower" in the Aragonese castle.

THE PROCESSION OF THE MYSTERIES

After this brief legendary interlude, I want to talk about a particular event held during Holy Week, the procession of the mysteries.

The procession of the mysteries is a type of event designed to commemorate the passion and resurrection of Jesus. It is generally celebrated on the evening of the Thursday or Friday before Easter, somewhat throughout southern Italy. However, in Taranto, it takes on special connotations: in its procession through the city center it even lasts 15 hours!

The whole event follows its particular iteration, where the brethren of the order of the Church of the Carmine wear a series of special garments: a white smock, a black belt, the rosary, the scapular (the symbol of the devotees of the Virgin of Mount Carmel), the cream- colored mozzetta, the black hat edged in blue lowered onto the shoulders, and the white hood lowered onto the face. They are all barefoot and carry on their shoulders a series of statues depicting the last hours of Jesus' life.

What stands before one's eyes is something unique, where one cannot help but be fascinated and disquieted simultaneously. Participants in the procession walk at a very slow pace, called "nazzicata."

Attending this kind of religious event is a mystical experience, regardless of whether one is a believer. It isn't easy to describe what one can experience in this example of popular devotion that has its roots several centuries back.

RAVINES NATURAL PARK

Traveling through the beauty of the Murgia territory, we saw how entire complexes of caves were used as dwellings and more, how these cavities within the limestone lent themselves to human activity, and how more than one civilization flourished in these areas that at first glance may appear impervious and inhospitable.

The greatest concentration of ravines is in the province of Taranto, so much so that a few years ago, the "Gravine Natural Park" was established, an area that involves several inhabited centers and aims to protect and promote knowledge of this territory, where the wildest nature with its very rich biodiversity and human ingenuity coexist, capable of building centers clinging along the ridges of these ravines, which resist modernity and keep intact the charm of past civilizations.

As many as 13 municipalities located in the province of Taranto are part of this area: Castellaneta, Massafra, Crispiano, Palagianello, Ginosa, Grottaglie, Palagiano, Laterza, Martina Franca, Montemesola, Mottola, San Marzano di San Giuseppe and Statte; one municipality, however, Villa Castelli, is in the province of Brindisi.

Most of these centers are located not coincidentally not far from Matera, where we have the city carved out of stones par excellence.

The surprising thing is that each of these villages preserves priceless relics related to the rock civilizations that inhabited these canyons carved by the erosive action of water.

The village of Grottaglie already has in its toponym the idea of a multitude of caves in its territory. In particular, outside the center, it is possible to take a walk in the Riggio ravine, where there is a natural waterfall at the foot of which a truly impressive lake forms. In the Fantiano quarries, on the other hand, it is possible to walk among towers of tuffs excavated by the hand of man thousands of years ago, with nature taking over these places once abandoned by man. To date, the area has undergone reclamation to the extent that shows and events are organized.

Massafra has a canyon known as the Gravina of San Marco, which even cuts the town in two, inside which you can see the ancient caves inhabited by man since ancient times.

There are some perfectly preserved cave churches here, such as the church of San Leonardo (with frescoes dating back to the 11th-12th centuries), or the church of Candlemas, topped by domes, each with its particular shape. The columns still have their decorated capitals, while a Madonna painted in a typically Byzantine style stands out among the frescoes.

It is also possible to observe the hermit monk's cell near the church.

Very spectacular is the ravine of the "Madonna della Scala," which can be accessed after descending a long flight of steps immersed in the most impervious nature. Continuing, one arrives instead at another mystical and magical place: the pharmacy of the Magician Greguro, no less than 12 interconnected caves with over 200 niches in which the magician is believed to have prepared medicinal herbs.

From the magnificent medieval village of Mottola, one can visit an entire rock village called "Petruscio," built apparently in the 9th century AD by inhabitants fleeing from the Saracens. The peculiarity of Petruscio is the 600 caves arranged on several floors as if they were skyscrapers.

The element that stands out the most, so much so that it has been called the "Sistine of rock civilization," is the church of San Nicola, so called because of the valuable paintings contained inside, some of which, such as the crucifixion on the facade, is among the oldest in the entire region.

Perhaps the most striking ravine is that of Castellaneta: it is up to 300 meters wide, reaches 140 meters deep and stretches for 10 km. It can be seen in its entirety from the belvedere in the town's center. Something majestic, in front of which you cannot help but remain mute and appreciate its beauty.

An experienced guide is required to visit it, as accessing it is not easy.

The other ravine that must be visited is that of Laterza: the special place is the "Cantina Spagnola," an underground church. It is attested that a chivalric order was born in the 1600s, traces of which are on the walls, where a whole cycle of stories related to this order is frescoed, with still many obscure points. Finally, the church of San Lorenzo also has some very interesting elements.

FOODS TO ABSOLUTELY ENJOY IN AND AROUND TARANTO

Like the other areas of the region, Taranto and its province have a lot to offer from a gastronomic point of view. One is spoiled for choice between what the sea offers and what the hinterland offers.

Tarantine-style mussels: one of the specialties of Taranto, a major center for mussel farming.

Taranto-style mussels have a strong, bold flavor. Cooked in a pan with chili pepper and tomato and a crouton of bread to dip in the sauce. An incredible delicacy.

Clementine: in the province of Taranto are grown these very sweet mandarins, in whose segments, unlike other types of mandarins, there are no seeds.

Clementines are also considered a prized quality because of the area's sunny climate. They are still harvested by hand (between September and December) to avoid spoiling the fruit. The authenticity of these products of the earth never goes out of style.

Roast meat: throughout the province of Taranto, there are rotisseries ready to let you taste an incredible variety of meat specialties. Roulades, chops, ribs, sausages, you name it.

The meat is cooked over wood in stoves fit for the purpose, thanks to the skill of the rotisserie workers, who are adept at understanding how strong the fire is and how to place the different varieties of meat on the stove to ensure that they cook to the right point and do not burn.

The roasted meat that arrives on the table is an absolutely indescribable explosion of flavors. All are accompanied by local bread and wine.

As for the wines of Taranto and the province, one wine in particular should be mentioned.

Le Colline ioniche tarantine: a white wine, straw-yellow in color of varying intensity, sometimes with amber highlights; it has a very delicate and pleasant aroma with floral and fruity notes. This wine is also produced in red and rosé versions.

FINAL WORDS

My dear reader,

I hope this book has given you a foretaste of the beautiful trip you may be taking to Puglia very soon.

After reading about all the wonders this region has to offer, I think you will now fully agree with what I anticipated at the beginning of this book: it is indeed a tough task to choose what to visit in the short time of a stay in Puglia!

To help you in this, I would like to remind you that I am at your complete disposal in case you need help in planning your trip. If you wish, you can visit my website and contact me.

I will be very happy to meet you and help you create a perfect tour for you!

I thank you for reading this guidebook that I have created with the intention of telling the story of Puglia to those who do not yet know it, and I hope to meet you soon to experience beautiful Puglia adventures together!

A warm hug,
Francesco, your Apulian friend.

FOLLOW ME
ON SOCIAL MEDIA

@petru.life

@petru.life

@petru - Francesco Giampetruzzi

A FREE BONUS GUIDE
FOR YOU!

- ✓ THE BEST HIGH-LEVEL RESTAURANTS
- ✓ 7 ITINERARIES SELECTED BY A TRUE APULIAN
- ✓ THE MOST BEAUTIFUL EXPERIENCES
- ✓ THE 20 MUST HAVE ITEMS YOU MUST PACK!
- ✓ THE TASTIEST WINES

Scan this QR and download
now your FREE BONUS!

LEAVE A 1 CLICK REVIEW

Customer reviews
★★★★★ 4.9 out of 5
223 global ratings

5 star		93%
4 star		7%
3 star		0%
2 star		0%
1 star		0%

˅ How customer reviews and ratings work

Review this product
Share your thoughts with other customers

Write a customer review

SCAN THIS QR TO GET TO THE BOOK FASTER

I would be incredibly thankful if you could take just 60 seconds to write a brief review on Amazon, even if it's just a few sentences!

CAMPANIA

TRAVEL GUIDE

Set for a Historic Italian Journey?

Explore Campania's Unforgettable Sites and Savour the Depth of its
Renowned Gastronomy with Expertly Curated Recommendations

INTRODUCTION
TO CAMPANIA

A jewel nestled in the heart of the Mediterranean, where the sky and sea converse in hues of blue. It's a land that paints a sensory spectacle with its vibrant colors, the perfume of sea-salted air, and landscapes that could easily steal your breath away.

Campania, the charming southern Italy, stretches languidly along th southwestern coastline. Lazio winks from the north, Molise and Puglia from the east, and Basilicata stands to the south. Each border is a testament cultural mosaic that is Italy, yet Cam exudes its own distinct allure with a l untouched natural beauty, remnants of ered history, and a culture that pulses

The region is home to the provinces of Naples, Caserta, Salerno, Avellino, and Benevento, and nearly 5.9 million souls. Naples, the life-blood of Campania, beats as its capital. Here, the cultural heritage runs deep and the atmosphere dances to the vibrant tune of everyday life.

Campania's heart lies in its diverse landscapes. The west whispers stories of the sea with its series of gulfs, promontories, and islands as enchanting as a siren's song, such as Capri, Ischia, and Procida. The east, on the other hand, echoes with the majesty of the Apennines, their peaks reaching out to the heavens and valleys blooming with the bounty of the earth.

Campania also plays host to the world-renowned volcanoes, Vesuvius, and the Phlegraean Fields. Vesuvius, the sentinel over the Bay of Naples, is etched in history for its dramatic eruption in 79 AD. An event that buried Pompeii and Ercolano, yet paradoxically preserved the echoes of daily life in ancient Rome under its volcanic shroud.

But there's more to Campania than just its natural grandeur. It's a living testament to the march of history - the remnants of Greek colonies, ancient Roman cities, Bourbon palaces, medieval monasteries, and Renaissance art whisper tales of eras past.

The region also feasts on a rich tapestry of flavors. The essence of the sea and land weave together in the form of Campania's gastronomy. Recognized as a

UNESCO World Heritage, the Mediterranean diet here reveals its best in dishes like Neapolitan pizza, pasta alla Genovese, ragù, buffalo mozzarella, and the golden pour of limoncello.

In this journey, I'll be your guide. We'll traverse Campania's historic trails, drink in its natural wonders, and immerse ourselves in its vibrant cultural and culinary traditions. We'll get lost in its captivating cities and stumble upon quaint villages, uncovering places that will imprint themselves on your heart, places that will beckon you back.

Campania isn't just a spot on the map; it's a sensory extravaganza, a chronicle of beauty and history, a place where you can lose and find yourself again. So, lace up for a journey drenched in charm and pulsating with the passionate heartbeat of this captivating region. Welcome to Campania, my friend!

A GLIMPSE INTO THE HISTORY OF CAMPANIA

Before we venture deep into the heart of Campania, let's take a brief stroll down its historical lanes. Campania's history is a tapestry of cultures clashing and coalescing, invasions and transformations, rise and fall—a kaleidoscope of eras and peoples, each leaving an indelible mark.

Traces of human settlement in Campania lead us back to the Bronze Age. With the arrival of the Greeks in the 8th century BC and the founding of Cuma, the region's first Greek colony, Campania soon found itself at the epicenter of cultural revolution. Naples, originally christened Neapolis or "New City," owes its birth to the Greeks. The deep-rooted impact of Greek culture is evident in the art, philosophy, and day-to-day life of Campania, an influence that continued to echo through subsequent epochs.

As Rome's might expanded, it slowly drew Campania into its sphere of influence, first as part of the republic and then the empire. The aristocracy of Rome found the region's towns and countryside an irresistible charm, so much so that it was deemed "Campania Felix" or "Fruitful Countryside." Pompeii and Ercolano, in particular, flourished as luxurious holiday destinations for the noble class, until Vesuvius' fateful eruption in 79 AD cloaked them under a shroud of ash and debris. While the catastrophe snuffed out their vibrancy, it paradoxically preserved them in a state of incredible preservation, a phenomenon we'll explore further in upcoming chapters.

With the decline and fall of the Roman Empire, the Middle Ages and the Renaissance saw Naples and the broader region shuffled between ruling dynasties and shifting borders. The Byzantines, Angevins, Aragonese, Normans, and others left their distinct fingerprints on the territory, enriching Naples with an eclectic mix of artists, poets, and scholars.

The 18th century ushered in the Bourbon era, and Naples rose to the rank of Europe's third most populous city, trailing only London and Paris. After a brief brush with Napoleonic rule, the Bourbons reclaimed the throne until the Unification of Italy in 1861.

Campania, like the rest of southern Italy, grappled with significant social and economic issues post-unification, including organized crime and unemployment. Yet, the region clung tightly to its cultural identity and sense of pride, solidifying its reputation as one of Italy's key regions.

Fast forward to today, and you'll find Campania pulsating with life, where age-old traditions and innovation live in harmony. Its historic and cultural heritage, the allure of its landscapes, and the infectious energy of its people continue to captivate visitors worldwide, making it an unforgettable corner of the Italian landscape.

CAMPANIAN CUISINE AND TRADITIONAL FLAVORS

When the whispers of Campania echo, your taste buds spark into life. It's not surprising. You're venturing into a realm where each morsel savors of legends untold, every flavor pens its own sonnet, and each dish is a masterstroke of culinary art. The regional cookbook is a gastronomic adventure celebrating Italy's core: unpretentiousness, finesse, and ardor.

Campanian cuisine is a captivating tapestry, narrating passionate love stories for food through time-honored recipes from one generation to the next. This culinary wealth recounts tales of seafarers and tillers, of kinships around abundant dining tables, of languid Sundays dedicated to the craft of delectable dishes. Campanian cuisine is all this and more: sincere, original, and irresistibly tasty.

The pulse of this epicurean tradition lies in the peerless purity of its ingredients. Picture the vermilion richness of San Marzano tomatoes, basking under the bountiful sun, nourished by the mineral-rich soils of Mount Vesuvius, or the buffalo mozzarella, unmatched in texture, tantalizingly fresh and Buffalo mozzarellasweet. Imagine the effervescent zest of Sorrento lemons or fresh pasta, slow-dried under the shade of the towering Lattari Mountains. The Campanian culinary maestros wield these gifts of nature into dishes that ensnare the senses and strike a chord with the soul.

However, Campanian cuisine is also a badge of honor, a banner of Italian ingenuity and supremacy. Think of the Neapolitan pizza, granted the prestige of UNESCO's Intangible Cultural Heritage, or the baba, a fragrant delight that has won over global gourmet hearts. These emblematic dishes reflect an artisanal expertise that continually evolves, yet never severs its deep-rooted ties.

Indulging in Campanian cuisine is like embarking on an unforgettable odyssey through awe-inspiring landscapes, rich traditions, and fervent flavors. It's a welcome embrace that thrills and amazes, an adventure that imprints your memory. Trust me, it's a journey that will linger on your palate, long after the last bite.

So, as you make yourself comfortable at a Campanian table, bear in mind: you're not merely dining. You're embracing a slice of history, tasting a culture's quintessence, saluting a zest for life that only scrumptious food can truly embody. Welcome, my friend, to Campania, a place where every meal is a jubilee, each dish a treasure trove of unforgettable moments.

A culinary expedition through Campania isn't just about the food - it's about tradition, love, and a dash of adventure! Here's your guide to the must-taste delights of this vibrant region:

Neapolitan pizza

The journey commences with the iconic Neapolitan pizza. A culinary master-piece born in the historic pizzerias of Naples; it's been recognized as a UNESCO Intangible Heritage. This pizza isn't just about the melt-in-your-mouth mozzarel-la, the succulent tomatoes, or the fresh basil that dances atop. It's about the cen-turies-old art passed from generation to generation, each pie a testament to timeless tradition.

Campania buffalo mozzarella

Next, meet the Campan-ia Buffalo Mozzarella, an emblematic delight of this gastronomic won-derland. Picture this: cheese crafted in the marshy heartlands of Campania, delightfully creamy and subtly sweet. Whether you sa-vor it solo or nestled in a vibrant Caprese salad, it's a taste of Campania you can't miss.

Neapolitan Pastiera

Craving something sweet? The Neapolitan Pastiera is here to whisk you off your feet. This Easter-time delicacy is a symphony of flavors: the soft shortcrust pastry, the aromatic mix of cooked grain, ricotta, eggs, sugar, and candied fruit, the faint perfume of orange blossoms, and a whisper of cinnamon. A single bite is a flavorful journey through the vibrant Campanian culture.

Pasta alla genovese

The Pasta alla Genovese, despite its name, is pure Naples. Imagine onions and meat, slow-cooked for hours into a rich and flavorful sauce, a tribute to the heart-warming home cooking of Campania.

Limoncello

For an uplifting end to your meal, let the Limoncello be your guide. Crafted mainly on the sun-drenched Amalfi Coast and Capri, this lively lemon liqueur is a refreshing splash of the Italian coast in a glass.

Neapolitan sfogliatella

 And what about breakfast? Neapolitan Sfogliatella is the answer. Whether it's the crispy, multi-layered "riccia" or the soft, smooth "frolla", both filled with a sweet concoction of ricotta, semolina, sugar, candied fruit, and aromatic essences, these beloved pastries are a burst of joy to kick start your day.

Gragnano pasta

Let's talk about the famed Gragnano pasta. Made in the shadow of the Lattari Mountains, this pasta encapsulates the essence of Campania. The sustainable methods employed in its production result in a pasta of superior quality, with a unique flavor profile and perfect texture that expertly cradles sauces.

San Marzano tomato

This kind of tomato is the heart and soul of many Italian dishes, the San Marzano tomato. Grown in the fertile volcanic lands near Mount Vesuvius, its sweet taste and rich aroma are pivotal to the true Neapolitan pizza and the traditional Neapolitan ragù.

Friarelli

If you're seeking greens, meet the Friarielli, Campania's quintessential broccoli rabe. Traditionally sautéed with garlic and chili, they make a delightful side dish or a unique pizza topping. The slight bitterness enriched with a heady flavor profile is a delight to the palate.

Campania's bounty doesn't end here, though! Besides San Marzano tomatoes and friarelli, the region also gifts us precious fruits like Boscoreale strawberries, Marostica cherries, Sorrento walnuts, and Cilento white figs. These fruits are a testament to the biodiversity that Campania proudly maintains.

Taurasi

Washing down our tomato-infused delights, we find Taurasi, a robust red wine hailing from Avellino. Fondly known as the "Barolo of the South", it's an exquisite companion to meat dishes and aged cheeses.

Babá

Can't forget the sweet tooth? We've got you covered with the legendary Baba. Known and loved worldwide, this iconic Neapolitan dessert is a petite, mushroom-shaped leavened cake soaked in rum or another liquor. It is so soft and juicy that it practically melts in your mouth - a heavenly indulgence to complete any festive meal in Campania.

Frittata di maccheroni

For comfort food lovers, Fried Pasta or "frittata di maccheroni", is a must-try. A beloved dish hailing from the traditional Neapolitan cuisine, it is a delicious blend of leftover pasta, eggs, and cheese, fried to crispy perfection on the outside and soft on the inside.

Cuzzitiello

Feast your eyes (and your taste buds) on Cuzzitiello, a typical Sunday dish in Campania. Picture a pig intestine pouch stuffed with a variety of mixed meats, cheeses, and eggs, slowly cooked for several hours. The result is a flavorful, textured delight where each ingredient harmonizes perfectly.

The parigina

Craving a quick bite? The Parigina, a stuffed pizza typical of Naples, comes to the rescue. Imagine tomato, mozzarella, ham, and mushrooms, all tucked into a crispy thin pizza dough. This pizza "sandwich" is perfect for a quick lunch or an outdoor picnic.

Pasta with provola and potatoes

Another hallmark of Campanian tradition is the Pasta with Provola and Potatoes. This hearty rustic dish is a delightful marriage of short pasta, smoked provola cheese, potatoes, and sometimes pancetta. Every bite takes you back to the authentic flavors of the Campanian countryside.

Casatiello

Casatiello is a traditional Easter cake in Naples, adorned with cubed cheese, salami, and hard-boiled eggs embedded into the crust. This ring-shaped bread is a festive nod to the joys of Easter.

Lemon delicacies

Last but not least, let's end on a sweet note with the Lemon Delights, a classic treat from the Amalfi Coast. Soft pastries bathed in lemon glaze, they perfectly balance the tartness of the lemon with the sweetness of the cake - a light and delicious finale to your meal.

These culinary jewels are just a glimpse of Campania's gastronomic heritage. Each recipe tells a story of love, creativity, and dedication to the art of food. Be it humble comfort food or sophisticated cuisine, every dish pays tribute to the beauty and abundance of this enchanting land.

Each Campanian product is a story that has been nurtured over centuries, shaped by a unique landscape, and fueled by an unrivaled passion for food. It's not just about nourishment, it's about preserving and elevating a rich cultural and gastronomic heritage. Eating in Campania goes beyond the mere act - it's an immersive experience, a celebration of life in all its facets.

Indeed, as an ancient Neapolitan proverb states, "At the table, one does not age." In Campania, this rings particularly true. So come, let's embark on this journey together, exploring, tasting, and celebrating. Bon voyage and buon appetito!

NAPLES UNVEILED: ECHOES OF HISTORY AND THE SONG OF THE STREETS

As an experienced guide and seasoned guidebook writer, allow me to whisk you away on a journey through the pulsating heart of vibrant Napoli, a city that teems with remarkable beauty, history, art, and culture. With its rich legacy spanning over 2,800 years, the city boasts a captivating array of architectural treasures and artistic wonders.

Our expedition begins at the city's nerve center - Piazza del Plebiscito. Counted among Italy's most expansive squares, it is a tapestry of historically significant edifices. On the eastern flank rests the commanding Basilica di San Francesco di Paola, its imposing columns and majestic dome echoing the grandeur of Rome's Pantheon. Facing the basilica, the Palazzo Reale unfurls its story. Once home to Naples' Bourbon royalty, this palatial masterpiece now stands as a museum - its opulent interiors whispering tales of Neapolitan history.

In close proximity to Piazza del Plebiscito, the ancient Teatro di San Carlo makes its presence felt. As the world's oldest active opera house, its neoclassical facade and sumptuous interiors make it a must-see for art and music enthusiasts.

Treading towards the sea, the ancient Castel dell'Ovo emerges, nestled on an islet in the Gulf of Napoli. The castle, the oldest in the city, offers breathtaking views of the sea and the cityscape. Its name, meaning "Egg Castle", originates from a legend that poet Virgil hid an egg within its foundations. It's a joy to explore the historical halls, courtyards, and towers, all while taking in the panoramic vistas of Naples' waterfront.

Further north, towering over the port area, stands the imposing Castel Nuovo, also known as Maschio Angioino. This medieval castle, punctuated by five cylindrical towers, rules the Neapolitan landscape. It houses the Civic Museum, a treasure trove of sculptures, paintings, and artworks narrating Napoli's storied past.

Continuing our discovery, we find the National Archaeological Museum, one of Europe's paramount cultural institutions. It shelters an extraordinary array of ancient Roman artifacts, many unearthed from the excavations at Pompeii and Ercolano. The Farnese Collection, among the world's richest assemblages of ancient art, is a must-visit.

For contemporary art lovers, the MADRE, Museum of Contemporary Art Donnaregina, offers an encompassing view of recent artistic movements. Located in the historic center, the museum showcases works by international and Italian artists, presented within a captivating architectural space.

Napoli's array of attractions would be incomplete without its churches, each a masterstroke of art and spirituality. From the cathedral dedicated to San Gennaro, boasting its treasure chapel, to the unique diamond-point facade of Gesù Nuovo, to the majolica cloister of Santa Chiara - each structure tells its own tale.

A stroll along Napoli's enchanting waterfront, reputed as one of Italy's finest, is an absolute must. With Vesuvius in sight, the azure sea lapping at the shore, and the islands of Capri and Ischia on the horizon, this seaside promenade is the perfect bookend to your journey through this captivating city.

Napoli ceaselessly surprises with its bounty of historical sites, bustling streets, natural beauty, and unparalleled cultural and culinary traditions. To visit Napoli is to dive into a world of breathtaking beauty and passion - an encounter that will leave an indelible mark on every traveler's heart.

The Historic Center and Underground Naples: A Journey Through the Depths of Time

I invite you to join me on a mesmerizing journey through Naples' historic center and the enigmatic depths of Napoli Sotterranea. With an alluring tapestry of narrow lanes, churches, historic buildings, and monuments, every corner of Naples' historic center echoes tales from ages past. Recognized as a UNESCO World Heritage Site in 1995, this historic center, the most extensive in Europe, is a living testament to the centuries that have sculpted Naples' character.

The lifeblood of the historic center is none other than Spaccanapoli, a street that, as its name implies, splits the city in two. Strolling along this vein, you'll

encounter some of the city's most significant churches. Stand in awe before Chiesa del Gesù Nuovo, walk within the cloistered serenity of Chiesa di Santa Chiara, and soak in the splendor of the Duomo, home to the resplendent Cappella del Tesoro di San Gennaro.

Wandering through the quaint alleys of the historic center, your senses will be captivated by the rich heritage of art and culture. Do not miss an opportunity to step into Cappella Sansevero, where the enigmatic Veiled Christ — one of the world's most astonishing sculptures — awaits. And why not pause at Piazzetta Nilo, and marvel at the statue of the Nile god, an ancient testament to Naples' Greek lineage?

Yet, Naples conceals its greatest surprise beneath the surface. Venture into Napoli Sotterranea and traverse a labyrinth of tunnels, cisterns, and catacombs carved into the bedrock. The gateway to this subterranean wonderland is tucked within Piazza San Gaetano in the historic center. Here, a staircase whisks you 40 meters underground, where you'll tread through nearly 2,400 years of history. Explore ancient Roman aqueducts that once quenched the city's thirst, marvel at the tuff walls etched over the centuries, and experience spaces that provided refuge during the tempest of World War II.

One of the crown jewels of Napoli Sotterranea is the Greco-Roman Theatre, an ancient theater, partially carved into the underground, whose existence remained shrouded in mystery until recently.

Naples' historic center and its subterranean expanse weave a breathtaking tapestry of history, culture, and everyday life that is quintessentially Neapolitan. Embarking on this extraordinary journey through the depths of time will render your sojourn in Naples an unforgettable chapter in your life's travelogue.

Distinctive neighborhoods and their peculiarities: a mosaic of stories and colours

Every city possesses a unique personality, a collective expression of its vibrant neighborhoods, and Naples is no exception. Imagine the neighborhoods of Naples as pieces of a mosaic, each with its individual charm and distinctiveness, coming together to paint a lively and captivating tableau of a city rich in contrasts and surprises.

Quartieri Spagnoli

Our exploratory journey commences at the Quartiere Spagnoli, one of Naples' most popular and authentic districts. Founded in the 16th century as a Spanish military quarter, thus deriving its name, the Quartiere Spagnoli today throbs as the beating heart of Naples. Its narrow, winding streets, vibrant buildings, artisan shops, animated squares, and bustling open-air markets craft an unparalleled and incomparable atmosphere. Here, Naples reveals its true face, where everyday life is an open-air theatre, and every corner tells a tale. The district's pizzerias are renowned for their genuine Neapolitan pizza, and it's not uncommon to see locals savoring a 'cuoppo' of mixed fried seafood while strolling through the streets.

Vomero

From there, we journey towards Vomero, Naples' hillside neighborhood. Known for its more relaxed and genteel ambiance, Vomero offers a fascinating contrast to the energy of Quartiere Spagnoli. Its streets are

lined with elegant buildings and villas, fashionable boutiques, and cozy cafes and restaurants. Here, you'll find Castel Sant'Elmo, an ancient military fort offering a breathtaking panoramic view of the city and the gulf. A short distance away lies Villa Floridiana, a graceful neoclassical villa surrounded by extensive parkland, home to the National Museum of Ceramics Duca di Martina. The Antignano, the ancient heart of Vomero, with its narrow, winding streets, offers a captivating glimpse into the Naples of yore.

Chiaia

Our tour progresses towards the Chiaia neighborhood, situated along the waterfront. This is the district of luxury shopping, with its high-fashion boutiques along Via dei Mille and Via Filangieri, and historic antique shops of Via Tasso. But Chiaia is more than just shopping: it's also culture. Here, you'll find Villa Pignatelli, a splendid neoclassical villa housing the Museum of Historic Carriages, and the PAN, the Palazzo delle Arti Napoli, one of the city's primary contemporary art centers.

Quartiere Sanitá

Heading back towards the center, the Sanità district offers another world to discover. Once a vacation spot for the Neapolitan aristocracy, today it's a vibrant blend of history and modernity. Its streets serve as an open-air museum, showcasing baroque churches, ancient catacombs of San Gaudioso, and artisan workshops that continue the centuries-old tradition of creating Neapolitan nativity scenes, particularly along Via San Gregorio Armeno.

Each district of Naples represents a stop in a journey through centuries of history and culture, a unique experience of everyday life and traditions. Naples is not merely a city to see; it's a city to live, breathe, and savor. By exploring its neighborhoods, you'll dive into the beating heart of Naples, uncovering the soul of a city that never ceases to surprise and charm.

Recommended Itineraries for Visiting Naples: Beauty Through Routes

Naples is a city brimming with wonders and captivating places, and the best way to uncover them is by following thoughtfully crafted itineraries that allow you to explore the city in all its facets. Here are some recommended routes you might find intriguing.

Historical and Artistic Route

This journey starts at Piazza del Plebiscito, home to the Royal Palace and the Basilica of San Francesco di Paola. From there, you move on to the imposing Maschio Angioino, one of Naples' hallmark symbols, and then towards the historical center, a labyrinth of churches, historical buildings, and evocative streets. Don't miss out on visiting the Cathedral, the Sansevero Chapel with its famed Veiled Christ, and the National Archaeological Museum, housing one of the world's most extensive collections of ancient art.

Gastronomic Route

Kick off at Quartiere Spagnoli, where you can savor genuine Neapolitan pizza and the renowned 'cuoppo' of mixed fried seafood. Then, head towards Pignasecca, the city's oldest food market, and finally to the Sanità neighborhood, where you can taste the famous sfogliatella pastry. Remember to make a stop at Scaturchio, in Piazza San Domenico Maggiore, for a delicious babà dessert.

Panoramic Route

This trail begins at the seafront, where the breathtaking view of the Gulf of Naples and Mount Vesuvius will spellbind you. From there, ascend towards Vomero and make your way to Castel Sant'Elmo: the view over the city and the gulf from this point is simply spectacular.

Shopping and Fashion Route

Start from Via Toledo with its trendy shops, then continue towards Piazza dei Martiri and Vìa dei Mille in the Chiaia neighborhood, where boutiques from top Italian and international fashion brands await you. Don't forget to visit Galleria Umberto I, a masterpiece of 19th-century architecture.

Nature and Relaxation Route

Begin at "Villa Comunale" and stroll along the seafront to Mergellina. From here, take the funicular to "Parco Virgiliano", where you can enjoy a breathtaking view and a bit of tranquility, away from the city's hustle and bustle.

Remember, Naples is a city to be lived and discovered leisurely, without haste. Take your time to explore it, get lost in its streets, savor its flavors. Naples is not just a city to visit; it's a city to live.

DISCOVERING THE ISLANDS OF THE BAY OF NAPLES

The Gulf of Naples, with its crystalline waters mirroring the blue of the Mediterranean sky, is a vision of immeasurable beauty. Resting at the foot of majestic Mount Vesuvius, with the city of Naples clinging to its slopes, the gulf is a mesmerizing tapestry of colors and moods, a natural masterpiece enriched by indelible human imprints.

The view of the gulf is an experience that touches both heart and soul. From the seafront of Naples, your gaze sweeps over the expansive seascape, bordered by the silhouette of Vesuvius on one side and the Sorrentine Peninsula on the other. The city lights dance on the calm gulf waters, creating a luminous tableau that shifts in hue with the changing hours of the day: from the soft colors of dawn to the deep blue of midday, to the fiery red of sunset.

And then there are the islands, like gems nestled in the gulf: Capri, Ischia, and Procida. Each with its unique character and beauty, they form a world unto themselves, a refuge far from the city's clamor, a place where time appears to stand still.

Capri, with its breath-taking views, cliffs plunging into the sea, cobblestone streets, high-fashion boutiques, and the famous Piazzetta, is an island of enchanting elegance and sophisticated allure. The Faraglioni, three imposing rock formations emerging from the sea, are the island's emblem, offering an unforgettable spectacle.

Capri: A Dream Island in the Heart of the Mediterranean

Capri, an enchanting island in the Gulf of Naples, is a globally renowned tourist destination, celebrated for its extraordinary scenic beauty and its rich cultural and

historical heritage. This Mediterranean gem, with its clear waters, cliffs dramatically descending into the sea, breath-taking vistas, and narrow cobblestone streets, emanates a captivating elegance and sophisticated allure.

The unmistakable icon of Capri is the Faraglioni, three towering rock formations jutting out from the sea, providing an unforgettable spectacle. However, the island holds much more to discover: the Blue Grotto, a natural wonder famous for its intensely colored blue water; Villa Jovis, the residence of Emperor Tiberius, which offers panoramic views over the entire Gulf of Naples; the Church of San Michele with its exquisite majolica-tiled floor depicting Eden; the Augustus Gardens with its flower-laden terraces overlooking the Faraglioni.

Capri is also an island of fashion and worldliness. The Piazzetta, the island's beating heart, is an open-air salon where celebrities and tourists from around the world convene. Via Camerelle, with its high-fashion shops, is the perfect spot for luxury shopping.

For the more adventurous, Capri offers the opportunity for hiking along its panoramic trails, like the renowned Path of the Forts, which connects the island's ancient fortifications and offers breath-taking views of the sea.

Capri is readily accessible with hydrofoils and ferries departing regularly from Naples and Sorrento. The journey takes about an hour from Naples and 20 minutes from Sorrento. Once on the island, you can use the bus system or the distinctive open taxis to get around or choose to explore the island on foot or by bike.

Staying in Capri means living a unique experience amid nature, history, culture, and glamour. A place where time seems to stand still, where each corner conceals a surprise, where the blue of the sea and sky merge into a panorama of immeasurable beauty. Capri is not just an island; it's a dream nestled in the heart of the Mediterranean.

Ischia: The Green Island of beauty and Wellness

Ischia, the largest of the islands in the Gulf of Naples, is a slice of paradise renowned for its extraordinary natural beauty and therapeutic hot springs. Referred to as the "Green Island" due to the abundant vegetation that cloaks it, Ischia presents a variety of experiences, from exploring its captivating landscapes to visiting its historical sites, and relaxing in its famed thermal baths.

The island is celebrated for its hot springs, considered among the richest in the world for their diversity and concentration of mineral salts. The thermal resorts on the island, including the famous Poseidon Gardens, offer a wide range of treatments and therapies for the wellness of body and mind. One experience not to be missed is a dip in the fumaroles of Sorgeto beach, where the sea water mingles with the hot waters of the thermal springs.

But Ischia isn't just about the baths. The island offers many natural and cultural attractions. Mount Epomeo, the highest point on the island, affords breath-taking views over the gulf. The Aragonese Castle, an ancient fortress commanding the sea, is one of the most enchanting and photogenic spots on the island. The picturesque villages of Ischia, such as Sant'Angelo and Forio, with their cobblestone streets, colorful houses, and small churches, are a joy to explore.

Ischia is also a haven for food lovers, with a variety of local dishes based on fresh fish, seasonal vegetables, and the island's famous wines, such as Biancolella and Per'e Palummo.

The island of Ischia is reachable by hydrofoil and ferry from Naples in about an hour. There are also connections with Capri, Sorrento, and the Amalfi Coast.

Ischia is an island to be lived, a place where nature, culture, and wellness blend in perfect harmony. A visit to the Green Island is an experience of beauty and relaxation that leaves an indelible imprint on the heart and soul.

Procida: A Hidden Treasure in the Bay of Naples

Procida, the smallest and least known of the islands in the Gulf of Naples, is indeed a hidden treasure. Far removed from mass tourism, the island retains an authenticity and charm that render it truly unique. With its colorful houses, narrow alleys, tranquil beaches, and serene, genuine ambiance, Procida serves as a haven of peace and simplicity.

An iconic image of Procida is the fishing village of Corricella, with its pastel-colored houses overlooking the tiny harbor, its seafood restaurants, the fishermen's boats, and cats basking in the sun. This picture-perfect locale seems like a scene from a painting, where time appears to have stood still.

Procida's allure doesn't stop at Corricella. The island presents a range of attractions to explore, such as the striking historic center of Terra Murata, the Chiaiolella beach, the Abbey of San Michele Arcangelo with its ancient seminary and museum, and the Pizzaco viewpoint that offers a panoramic vista over the entire gulf.

Procida is also famous for its traditions and cuisine. The Sagra del Mare, an annual festival dedicated to the sea and its people, is an event not to be missed. The local cuisine, featuring dishes with fresh fish, garden vegetables, and typical sweets like lingua di bue, offers a gastronomic experience worth discovering.

Procida, the smallest and least known of the islands in the Gulf of Naples, is indeed a hidden treasure. Far removed from mass tourism, the island retains an authenticity and charm that render it truly unique. With its colorful houses, narrow alleys, tranquil beaches, and serene, genuine ambiance, Procida serves as a haven of peace and simplicity.

An iconic image of Procida is the fishing village of Corricella, with its pastel-colored houses overlooking the tiny harbor, its seafood restaurants, the fishermen's boats, and cats basking in the sun. This picture-perfect locale seems like a scene from a painting, where time appears to have stood still.

Procida's allure doesn't stop at Corricella. The island presents a range of attractions to explore, such as the striking historic center of Terra Murata, the Chiaiolella beach, the Abbey of San Michele Arcangelo with its ancient seminary and museum, and the Pizzaco viewpoint that offers a panoramic vista over the entire gulf.

Procida is also famous for its traditions and cuisine. The Sagra del Mare, an annual festival dedicated to the sea and its people, is an event not to be missed. The local cuisine, featuring dishes with fresh fish, garden vegetables, and typical sweets like lingua di bue, offers a gastronomic experience worth discovering.

The island of Procida can be reached in approximately 40 minutes by ferry from Naples. There are also connections with Ischia and the mainland.

Procida is an island that captivates and wins hearts with its understated beauty, its peaceful atmosphere, and its authenticity. It's a place where you can enjoy a travel experience far from the beaten tourist tracks, immersed in an atmosphere of genuineness and serenity. A hidden treasure in the heart of the Gulf of Naples, a tiny paradise waiting to be discovered and cherished.

EXPLORING THE AMALFI COAST

An Encounter Between Sea and Mountain

If you believe Campania's beauty is exhausted with Naples and its gulf, well, you are greatly mistaken. There are other areas, resplendent with allure and wonder, that can easily rival these well-known sights. One such place is the Amalfi Coast. As a UNESCO World Heritage Site, this stretch of coastline along the southern edge of the Sorrentine Peninsula in Campania is nothing short of magnificent.

The Amalfi Coast is a natural wonder marked by captivating landscapes where steep mountains plunge directly into the crystalline sea, creating an image of unmatched beauty. The initial impression that greets visitors is a rugged coastline, featuring coves, promontories, caves, and stacks. The narrow, winding roads climb rocky outcrops amidst olive groves, citrus orchards, and terraces cultivated with vines and lemons, offering breathtaking views at every turn. The deep blue sea forms a striking contrast against the vibrant colors of houses and villas clinging to the cliffs, set amidst the intense green of the Mediterranean vegetation.

Famed for its small, charming villages such as Positano, Amalfi, Ravello, Praiano, and Furore, the Amalfi Coast is truly enchanting. Each village has its own distinctive character and unique beauty. Positano, with its hillside houses cascading down to the sea, is one of the most photographed places in Italy. Amalfi, once a powerful maritime republic, mesmerizes with its splendid cathedral and a labyrinth of paved alleys. Ravello, with its historic villas and suspended gardens, offers unforgettable vistas.

The Amalfi Coast is also a rich tapestry of history, art, and culture. Churches, Saracen towers, historic villas, artisan shops, centuries-old lemon groves, and ancient paper mills all bear witness to the richness and vitality of this land.

Above all, the Amalfi Coast is a place of sensations, emotions, and flavors. The scent of the sea and lemons, the taste of fresh fish and local desserts like Delizia al Limone, the sound of waves breaking against the rocks, the sight of stunning landscapes, the feel of handcrafted ceramics – every element contributes to an unforgettable experience.

Visiting the Amalfi Coast means immersing oneself in a world of beauty, simplicity, and authenticity. It's a place where harmony between humans and nature is evident in every corner, every stone, every tree. It's a place that captures the heart and soul, enchants and bewitches, inviting one to return again and again. A journey along the Amalfi Coast is a journey into the heart of beauty. It's a trip to be experienced with all senses, savored slowly, and remembered forever.

A Journey Among the Most Fascinating Villages

The Amalfi Coast, a gem of captivating beauty in southern Italy, never ceases to amaze its visitors. This blessed strip of land, with its breathtaking natural beauty, is a kaleidoscope of colors, scents, and sounds. It offers a fusion of seascapes and mountainous landscapes, picturesque villages, and lesser-known but equally enchanting spots.

Positano

Positano, likely the most famous village on the Amalfi Coast, is renowned for a good reason. This vertical city, with its pastel-colored houses clinging to the steep slopes descending towards the sea, is a sight to behold. The narrow, winding streets, endless stairways, fashion boutiques, artisan shops, sparkling tiled churches, and sea-view restaurants all speak of elegance and charm. The relaxation on the sun and sea at Spiaggia Grande and Fornillo beach is unparalleled, separated by the Madonnina promontory. But Positano is also a launchpad for hikes along the trails winding through the surrounding hills, like the famed Path of the Gods.

Amalfi

The ancient maritime republic is the beating heart of the Amalfi Coast. Its emblem is the Cathedral of Saint Andrew, with its imposing staircase and splendid facade adorned with golden mosaics. Amalfi's old town, with its paved streets and blooming courtyards, is a labyrinth of beauty. The town is also renowned for its ancient paper mills and the Paper Museum, which narrates the story of handmade paper production. A visit to the Valle delle Ferriere, a nature reserve featuring waterfalls and remains of old factories, should not be missed.

The nature reserve Valle delle Ferriere, near Amalfi, offers hiking trails through lush forests, waterfalls, and ruins of ancient iron factories.

Ra vello

Ravello is a veritable balcony on the sea, with its historic villines and suspended gardens. Beyond the famed Villa Rufolo and Villa Cimbrone, Ravello offers the tranquil allure of its old town and the magic of its 11th-century cathedral. Ravello is also synonymous with music, with its renowned Ravello Festival animating its squares and terraces with classical music concerts each summer.

Praiano e Furore

Praiano and Furore are two hidden gems of the Amalfi Coast. Praiano, with its beautiful Church of San Gennaro and breathtaking panoramas, is a haven of peace. Furore, with its intriguing fjord, is an art village, with murals telling tales of everyday life and work.

Atrani

Atrani, just a stone's throw from Amalfi, is a small fishing village that has preserved its authenticity. Don't miss the chance to explore its narrow streets, visit the Church of San Salvatore de' Birecto, and enjoy a relaxing break on its beach.

Minori and maiori

Minori and Maiori offer wide, sandy beaches perfect for families and relaxation lovers. Minori is known for the Villa Romana, an ancient Roman thermal complex, and its gastronomic delights, such as lemon pasta and the desserts of the famous pastry chef Sal De Riso. Maiori, with its lively seafront and Norman Tower, is a holiday destination beloved by locals and foreigners alike.

Scala

Scala, the oldest village on the Amalfi Coast and lesser-known, is an ideal retreat for those seeking peace and serenity, with its tranquility, ancient churches, and nature-immersed trails.

Cetara

Cetara is a charming fishing village that maintains an authentic and peaceful atmosphere, famous for its production of "Colatura di Alici," a traditional fish condiment.

Tramonti

Hidden among the Amalfi Coast's mountains, Tramonti is known for wine production. This location, full of terraced vineyards, offers a peaceful and relaxing atmosphere, far from the crowd of more touristic locations.

Conca dei Marini

Located between Amalfi and Positano, Conca dei Marini offers beautiful sea views. Don't miss the Emerald Grotto, a large cave filled with stalactites and stalagmites lit by emerald water.

Pogerola

Pogerola, this small village on the hills above Amalfi, is away from the crowds and offers stunning sea views. From here, you can hike along the "Path of the Gods," one of the most scenic trails on the Amalfi Coast.

Nocelle

Nocelle, a small village only accessible by foot or bus, is perched on the hills above Positano and is a perfect spot for trekking enthusiasts. It offers quiet charm and breathtaking views that will remain in your memory long after you leave.

Exploring the Amalfi Coast: Activities and Excursions

Immerse yourself in the myriad delights of the Amalfi Coast, steeped in deep-rooted tradition and the vibrant pulse of la dolce vita. This enchanting Mediterranean landscape presents a cornucopia of activities and excursions to explore its natural, artistic, and cultural wonders.

Walking trails

The Amalfi Coast beckons walkers and hikers with its extraordinary trails. The acclaimed "Path of the Gods," beginning from Bomerano and ending in Nocelle, unfurls stunning vistas of the sea and the quaint coastal villages. From the cascading waterfalls and tropical vegetation of Valle delle Ferriere to the fragrant lemon groves lining the path from Ravello to Minori, every hike is an experience in itself. For mountain lovers, the trail from Scala to Monte Sant'Angelo a Tre Pizzi, the highest peak on the coast, provides a unique adventure.

Boat rides

Take to the sea with captivating boat excursions, exploring secluded coves and intriguing caves such as the Emerald Grotto in Conca dei Marini. These trips also open the gateway to the magnificent Capri and its famous "Grotta Azzurra".

Gastronomy and wines

Food and wine connoisseurs will be in their element here. The cellars of Tramonti and Furore offer wine tastings that reveal the essence of the land, while gastronomic tours introduce you to regional delicacies such as Amalfi Limoncello, Agerola mozzarella, or Neapolitan pizza. Plus, cooking classes in select restaurants let you dive deeper into the regional cuisine.

Art and culture

Artistic and cultural treasures abound in the coastal towns. Explore historic paper mills in Amalfi, delve into the ceramic's museum of Vietri sul Mare, visit the Roman villas of Minori, or soak up the melodies at a concert in the atmospheric setting of Villa Rufolo in Ravello.

Relaxation and wellness

or those seeking relaxation, the coast's sun-drenched beaches provide the perfect backdrop. Additionally, the wellness centers on the island of Ischia and in Sorrento offer indulgent treatments and rejuvenating thermal water baths.

Your journey along the Amalfi Coast is bound to be an immersive experience, touching all your senses and leaving you with indelible memories. It's more than a destination; it's an exploration of the very soul of la dolce vita.

THE TREASURES OF SALERNO AND THE CILENTO COAST

Salerno: A Journey through History, Sea and Vibrant Life

Nestled between the winding allure of the Amalfi Coast and the breath-taking landscapes of the Cilento National Park, Salerno awaits - a jewel of Southern Italy where a millennial history gracefully dances with modern vivacity, creating a harmonious symphony of emotions. The city thrums with an intriguing blend of bygone echoes and contemporary buzz, lending Salerno an irresistible and unique charm.

Salerno's unforgettable silhouette unfurls along the coastline, a harmonious fusion of ancient towers, historical monuments, and new buildings glistening in the sun. Its bustling port, one of the Mediterranean's busiest, proudly cradles vessels, while green hills seem to embrace the city with a protective hug. Salerno's heart beats in its historical center, a complex maze of alleys that transport you back to medieval times when Salerno was a significant hub of exchange and culture.

Among the city's significant symbols is the Cathedral, a magnificent edifice dedicated to St. Matthew. Constructed in 1076, the cathedral guards the cryptoporticus of the ancient Church of San Matteo, remnants of an early Christian church, and most notably, the remains of the Apostle Matthew himself. Wandering Salerno's narrow streets reveals another hidden gem, the San Pietro a Corte complex, an ancient Lombard palace concealing an underground rock church, a fascinating and mysterious place of worship.

Nature lovers will find a slice of paradise in the Garden of Minerva. Established in the 14th century, it's believed to be Europe's first botanical garden, preserving ancient medicinal plants used by the Salerno Medical School. From the garden, you can climb to Arechi Castle, a Lombard fortress offering breath-taking panoramic views over the city and the sea.

But Salerno is not just a city to be seen—it's a city to be lived. Its seafront promenade is one of Italy's most beautiful, an ideal place to immerse in the local atmosphere. A stroll along its main avenue, Corso Vittorio Emanuele, unveils a wide variety of shops, restaurants, and bars—perfect spots to savor the exquisite local cuisine or indulge in some shopping. Don't miss a visit to the fish market, a vibrant display of colors and flavors that'll make you fall in love with Salerno's culinary scene.

Salerno's streets echo with music, laughter, lively conversations. Its squares come alive with cultural events, street performances, and concerts. And Salerno wouldn't be Salerno without mentioning its brightest event of the year, "Luci d'Artista," when the city illuminates with millions of lights, transforming into an enchanted dream.

For those with a sweet tooth, Salerno has a treat in store: its famous patisserie. The "Pan di Spagna," a fluffy and delicious confection, embodies all the warmth and sweetness of this captivating city.

Salerno isn't just a destination; it's an experience—a place that enters your heart and invites you to discover its essence among historic alleys, vibrant squares, sunlit beaches, and rolling hills. Here, amidst the waves of the sea and the scents of the earth, you'll uncover a corner of Italy that will awaken your senses and steal your heart. Salerno awaits, ready to share its story, its soul, and unforgettable moments.

The beaches and villages of the Cilento coastline

Welcome to the Cilento Coast, a splendid corner of Southern Italy, where the deep blue of the Tyrrhenian Sea tenderly kisses golden beaches, and picturesque villages perch on mountains in a riot of colors.

Stretching along Campania's coast from the Gulf of Salerno to the Gulf of Policastro, the Cilento Coast boasts a striking variety of landscapes. Here, nature unabashedly takes center stage with sandy beaches, towering cliffs, lush forests, and crystal-clear waters.

Agropoli

Let's commence our journey from the north, in the village of Agropoli. This ancient fishing hamlet, crowned by a majestic castle, is the gateway to the Cilento National Park. Here, you can relish breathtaking views of the sea from atop its walls and explore its narrow cobblestone streets lined with restaurants and shops peddling local products.

Castellabate

Heading south along the coast, our next stop is Castellabate, a UNESCO World Heritage site. This enchanting medieval village offers unforgettable vistas, with narrow alleyways and stone houses, and a spectacular view of the Salerno Gulf. Don't miss a visit to the main square, Piazza 10 Ottobre 1123, the village's beating heart.

Acciaroli

Further south, we encounter Acciaroli, an ancient fishing hamlet renowned for its lengthy sandy beaches and clear waters. Its quaint harbor is always brimming with colorful boats, and the promenade along the seafront is a visual delight. Remember to pause at one of the numerous seaside restaurants to taste fresh fish and Cilento cuisine.

Palinuro

Continuing our journey, we reach Palinuro, one of the most captivating locales on the Cilento Coast. Perched on a rocky promontory, this village provides a stunning view of the sea and its numerous marine caves, including the famous Blue Grotto. From here, you can arrange boat trips to explore the incredible caves and secluded beaches.

Marina di Camerota

Our path leads us further south to Marina di Camerota, another gem of the Cilento Coast. This fishing village, nestled between hills and sea, offers enchanting beaches like Calanca and Lentiscelle, and a fascinating historical center with narrow streets and colorful houses.

Scario

Finally, we arrive at Scario, the last pearl of the Cilento Coast. This small maritime village is known for its picturesque harbor and pebble beaches. From here, you can catch a boat to the pristine beaches of the Gulf of Policastro, including the renowned Baia degli Infreschi, deemed one of Italy's most beautiful.

Journeying along the Cilento Coast isn't just a feast for the eyes; it's a culinary delight as well. Cilento cuisine is renowned for its simplicity and authenticity, featuring fresh seafood, seasonal vegetables, olive oil, and local cheeses. Savoring a plate of pasta with sea urchin or buffalo mozzarella with fresh tomatoes while watching the sunset over the sea is a truly unforgettable experience.

The Cilento Coast is a hidden treasure of Campania, where nature and culture blend seamlessly. It's a place where time seems to stand still, and you can immerse yourself in a world of tranquility and beauty. Once discovered, it holds a place in your heart forever.

A journey to the Cilento Coast isn't just a holiday—it's a life experience. It's a voyage of discovery and exploration that will make you fall in love with this incredible land and its proud inhabitants. So, what are you waiting for? The Cilento Coast awaits, ready to gift unforgettable emotions and unveil its hidden treasures.

ART AND HISTORY IN POMPEI AND ERCOLANO

Nestled in the fertile lands at the foot of Vesuvius and touched by the blue of the Gulf of Naples are two ancient cities that promise an unforgettable journey into the past: Pompeii and Ercolano. These places are more than significant archaeological sites; they bear testament to a distant era and civilization that left an indelible mark on world history.

Pompeii and Ercolano were thriving cities of ancient Rome, situated in an area of extraordinary beauty, teeming with culture and commerce. Their strategic location, near the sea and the Sarno River, rendered them vital hubs for trade, spurring vibrant artistic and cultural growth. Inhabitants, merchants, and visitors from across the Roman world enriched the social fabric of these cities, contributing to their prosperity and vibrancy.

The fame of these places, however, is not merely a tribute to their ancient flourishing but primarily a remembrance of the tragedy that immortalized them. In 79 AD, one of the most violent eruptions of Vesuvius abruptly ended the lives of Pompeii and Ercolano. A downpour of ash, lapilli, and gases buried the cities and their inhabitants, preserving them in an unparalleled state of conservation.

From that moment on, Pompeii and Ercolano have become symbols of nature's destructive power, and simultaneously, unique windows into the ancient Roman world. Each street, each building, each object unearthed from their ruins tells us a story, providing a glimpse of daily life as if time stood still on that distant day of 79 AD.

Today, nearly two millennia later, millions of visitors from around the globe come to tread the ancient streets of these cities, drawn by the chance to explore a past that seems almost within touch. Pompeii and Ercolano are more than two archaeological sites; they are the link between our present and a distant, yet incredibly close past. A journey through their ruins is a voyage through time, an experience that imprints itself in the hearts of those who undertake it.

Pompei

Stepping into Pompeii is akin to embarking on a unique temporal journey, retracing the footprints of daily life in an ancient Roman city. Picture yourself strolling along the ancient basalt streets, encircled by time-faded frescoes and stone edifices. It's as though you can hear the echo of Pompeian footsteps, the hum of artisan workshops, and the aroma of ancient cuisines wafting from the old 'tabernae.'

Spanning 66 hectares, the archaeological site of Pompeii is one of the largest and best-preserved globally. The remarkable assortment and preservation of structures offer an astoundingly detailed picture of life in a Roman city. You can explore the homes, vibrant with their frescoes and inner courtyards, workshops

still housing their craft tools, thermal baths with their intricate infrastructures, and places of worship where ancient Pompeians paid homage to their gods.

The pulsating heart of this ancient city, the Forum, where political, religious, and commercial activities took place, is undeniably a must-visit. You wouldn't want to miss the Temple of Apollo, one of Pompeii's oldest sacred places, or the Temple of Jupiter, standing majestically with Vesuvius as its backdrop.

As you journey onward, the Grand Theater rewards you with a thrilling experience. Try seating on the ancient stone tiers and imagine witnessing a period drama or comedy. Also worth visiting is the "Lupanare," Pompeii's most famous brothel, notorious for its erotic frescoes.

Arguably one of the most poignant spots is the Garden of the Fugitives, where plaster casts of those who tried to escape Vesuvius's wrath are preserved. These casts, made by filling the voids left by decomposed bodies with plaster, depict a dramatic and intense image of the catastrophe that struck Pompeii.

I encourage you to take your time exploring Pompeii. Get lost in its streets, pause to observe the details, touch the time-worn stones. Let the city narrate its story, whisper its secrets to you. With every visit, you'll realize that Pompeii isn't merely a place to see but an experience to live—an enthralling journey into the heart of ancient Rome. And remember, Pompeii's charm never ends: every new archaeological finding adds another piece to the mosaic of this immortal city.

Beyond its well-known spots, Pompeii is also home to many hidden gems. Take the "House of Menander," for instance, one of Pompeii's most opulent private residences, celebrated for its intricate frescoes and sophisticated architecture. Or the "Villa of Mysteries," just outside the city walls, known for its enigmatic frescoes that seem to narrate a mysterious initiation ritual.

Your Pompeii experience wouldn't be complete without a visit to the Amphitheater, the oldest known Roman amphitheater, a venue for gladiatorial battles and hunting shows. The Forum Baths, with their cold, hot, and tepid bathing rooms, gymnasium, and laconicum for steam bathing, are an extraordinary example of Roman ingenuity and love for comfort.

While exploring Pompeii, don't forget to notice the small things: the graffiti on the walls narrating stories of love, politics, and daily life; the holes in the roads used for street signage; the menus etched on the walls of ancient eateries.

The marvel of Pompeii is that discovery is perpetual. Even though the site was unearthed over 250 years ago, archaeologists continue to dig, research, and uncover new treasures. For example, a recent excavation revealed a new thermopolium, a kind of fast-food establishment in ancient Rome, complete with an exceptionally well-preserved fruit basket fresco.

Lastly, remember that visiting Pompeii isn't just a journey into the past but a way to support the research and preservation of this invaluable heritage. Every ticket sold contributes to funding excavation works, fresco restorations, and the training of future archaeologists.

So, as you traverse Pompeii, stepping back in time, you will be part of a story that continues to unfold, a centuries-long archaeological adventure. Pompeii isn't just a place to visit—it's a place to live, where the past meets the present and casts a vision into the future.

Ercolano

Herulano, a captivating hub steeped in history, presents an unrivaled exploration experience. More compact and intimate than Pompeii, it stands out for the extraordinary quality of its structures and the preservation of objects that would have been lost at other sites.

Upon arrival, the breathtaking view of the archaeological site excavated beneath the modern ground level is the first to awe. Indeed, as you navigate the streets of Ercolano, you'll feel as though you're truly plunging into the past, entering a city frozen in time.

One of the first must-sees is the House of the Wooden Partition, named after a preserved wooden partition found within its spaces. Although wood structures often succumb to the ravages of time, the eruption of Vesuvius here caused the wood to carbonize, preserving it and offering a unique, intriguing glimpse into daily life in ancient Rome.

Perhaps the most moving site in Ercolano are the ancient beaches, where the remains of over 300 individuals trying to escape the eruption were discovered. The sight of these scenes, perfectly preserved, makes the dramatic impact of the eruption tangible and serves as a powerful reminder of nature's might.

Another gem of Ercolano is the House of the Stags, one of the city's most opulent villas, named for the two marble stag statues decorating its garden. With its intricate frescoes and colorful mosaics, it's a masterpiece of Roman art and architecture.

But Ercolano is more than just these iconic sites—it's also a city of streets, shops, and homes. A city of everyday life. As you walk its narrow streets, you'll spot the taverns where the inhabitants ate and drank, the workshops of artisans, the public baths with their sophisticated heating techniques.

Don't forget to explore the Women's Baths, one of Ercolano's most evocative sites, renowned for its fresco of the Cumaean Sibyl, a prophetess venerated by the ancient Romans. Its lofty walls and well-preserved rooms will transport you back in time in a way few places can.

Visiting Ercolano, coupled with a trip to Pompeii, represents a quintessential experience for anyone journeying through Campania—a venture into the heart of ancient Rome, a vibrant, living history lesson that will leave you speechless. Ercolano is more than an archaeological site—it's a time capsule, a place where the past comes alive.

Tips and other utilities

- Reaching Pompeii and Ercolano: These archaeological jewels lie close to the city of Naples. A train from Naples, using the Circumvesuviana line towards Sorrento, will take you straight to the "Pompei Villa dei Misteri" station. For Ercolano, simply ride the same line and alight at the "Ercolano Scavi" station.
- Opening hours: The archaeological sites of Pompeii and Ercolano welcome visitors throughout the year, excluding January 1st, May 1st, and December 25th. Typically, they open from 8:30 AM to 7:30 PM in summer, and from 8:30 AM to 5:00 PM in winter. Always cross-check the timings on the official website before your visit.

- Visit duration: Your visit's length can vary depending on your interest. As a rule of thumb, plan at least two hours for Ercolano and three to four hours for Pompeii. For history and archaeology enthusiasts, you might wish to allot more time.

- Tickets: You can procure tickets at the entrance ticket offices of both sites. An option is a combined ticket, providing access to both sites within a 3-day period—ideal for those wishing to delve deeper into these historical treasures.

- Guided tours: Guided tours are available for both Pompeii and Ercolano. They can be instrumental in better understanding the history and significance of the sites. Some agencies even offer tours in English.

- Practical tips: Do wear comfortable footwear and carry a water bottle, particularly during the summer months. Don't forget your sunscreen and a hat for sun protection. Lastly, check the weather forecast ahead of your trip as most of your visit will be outdoors.

- Preparation: Before stepping onto these historical grounds, it can be rewarding to understand their history and context. This knowledge will enrich your experience and make your visit much more meaningful.

- Available facilities: Both sites feature amenities such as restrooms, refreshment points, and picnic areas. However, options can be limited, so packing a picnic might be a good idea.

- Naples Archaeological Museum: If time permits, a visit to the Naples Archaeological Museum is highly recommended. The museum houses a vast collection of artifacts from Pompeii and Ercolano, including frescoes, mosaics, and everyday objects. A visit here will provide a more comprehensive view of life in ancient Pompeii and Ercolano.

- Documentation: Remember to bring a valid ID. It may be required for ticket purchase or access to specific site areas.

- Photographs: Feel free to capture the beauty of these archaeological sites, but do respect any rules and restrictions. For instance, the use of flash is often prohibited inside certain structures to preserve ancient frescoes.

- Best time to visit: If you have the luxury to choose, spring and fall are often deemed the best times to visit. The temperatures are milder during these periods, and the sites are generally less crowded.

- Safety: Always keep an eye on your belongings and heed any directions provided on the sites. Some areas may be unstable or dangerous, so it's crucial to respect all signs and restrictions.

Remember, visiting Pompeii and Ercolano is not merely seeing ancient ruins—it's stepping back in time to discover how people lived in ancient Rome. Take your time, soak in the unique atmosphere, and let yourself be enthralled by the history.

ADVENTURES IN THE NATURE OF CAMPANIA

The region of Campania, known for its rich history, culture, and gastronomy, also presents a treasure trove of natural experiences. From the majestic allure of Mount Vesuvius to the hidden gems within a network of parks, reserves, and caves, Campania stands as a paradise for nature enthusiasts, hikers, explorers, and anyone seeking a taste of adventure.

At the heart of the region, Mount Vesuvius towers as a living testament to nature's might. This active volcano, eternally tied to the ancient history of Pompeii and Ercolano, offers a unique experience that combines breathtaking vistas with an open-air geology lesson. Its slopes and trails beckon anyone who wants to challenge themselves while taking in the incredible panoramic views stretching out to the shimmering Mediterranean Sea.

A journey further south uncovers another natural treasure: the Cilento, Vallo di Diano, and Alburni National Park. This expansive territory safeguards one of Europe's most biodiverse areas, where one can explore ancient forests, spectacular coastlines, vibrant rivers, and sky-defying mountains. It's a place where time seems to stand still, and visitors can lose themselves in numerous trails, discover enchanting villages, or simply enjoy the tranquility of the natural environment.

But the adventure doesn't end there. Campania conceals countless nature reserves and caves, where nature has sculpted landscapes of extraordinary beauty. These lesser-known but equally captivating spots offer the chance to see Campania from a different perspective, tread less beaten paths, and immerse yourself in pristine nature rich in biodiversity.

This chapter will guide you through the incredible natural beauty of Campania. From hiking volcanic mountains and leisurely walks through lush forests to exploring mysterious caves and wildlife-rich nature reserves, Campania offers a wide array of outdoor experiences that will make your visit unforgettable.

Vesuvio national park

For those who love to immerse themselves in nature and experience thrilling adventures, Campania provides an experience like no other. The region is wonderfully diverse with its captivating coastlines, charming islands, and imposing mountains, but one of its most shining jewels is the Vesuvius National Park.

Established in 1995, the Vesuvius National Park spans an area of about 135 square kilometers and is dominated by Mount Vesuvius, one of the most well-known and extensively studied volcanoes in the world. Situated east of Naples, the park presents a breathtaking landscape that blends the stark charm of the volcanic terrain with lush Mediterranean vegetation.

Hiking on Vesuvius

Walking along the trails of Vesuvius offers an unforgettable and unique experience. The most popular route is the trail leading to the crater's summit. This is a moderately challenging hike that takes approximately two hours. Upon reaching the top, you'll be rewarded with a spectacular view sweeping from the Gulf of Naples to the islands of Capri, Ischia, and Procida, extending to the Sorrentine Peninsula.

The park offers numerous other trails, suitable for all difficulty levels, winding through forests of pine and chestnut trees, vineyards, and fields of wildflowers. The trails are well marked and provide ample opportunities to discover the park's flora and fauna, along with beautiful views of the surrounding landscape.

Visit to the Volcanology Museum

For those who wish to delve deeper into their understanding of volcanism and the history of Vesuvius, a visit to the Volcanology Museum is highly recommended. The museum hosts a series of interactive exhibits that explain the mechanisms of volcanoes and tell the story of Vesuvius' eruptions, including the infamous one in 79 A.D. that buried Pompeii and Herculaneum.

Picnic Areas and Visitor Centers

The Vesuvius National Park is equipped with several picnic areas where visitors can take a break and enjoy an outdoor meal, surrounded by unspoiled nature. Additionally, there are various visitor centers scattered throughout the park, where detailed information about the park's attractions, trail maps, and guided tours can be obtained.

What to Bring

If you're planning a hike in the Vesuvius National Park, it's essential to be prepared. Bring plenty of water, a snack, sunscreen, and wear comfortable hiking shoes. Don't forget your camera to capture the breathtaking views!

A visit to the Vesuvius National Park is a must-do for nature lovers and those wanting to experience the heart of one of the world's most famous volcanoes firsthand.

Cilento, Vallo di Diano and Alburni National Park

In the heart of Campania, amidst landscapes varying from mountains to the coast, one of Italy's largest and most captivating parks extends: The Cilento, Vallo di Diano, and Alburni National Park. This natural jewel, recognized as a UNESCO World Heritage Site, covers an area of over 1,800 square kilometers and is a must-visit destination for outdoor enthusiasts.

Nature and Sites

The park's diverse ecosystems make every stroll a journey through biodiversity. From lush holm oak forests in the inner areas to rocky cliffs overlooking the crystalline sea, every corner of Cilento offers breathtaking panoramas. Visitors can explore the ancient Rosa Stone forest with its centuries-old trees or admire the beauty of the Venus Hair Waterfall, a refreshing oasis on hot days.

The park also encompasses numerous historical and cultural sites. Among these are the ruins of the ancient Greek city of Paestum, with its well-preserved temples, and the Charterhouse of Padula, a remarkable example of baroque architecture.

Park Activities

The Cilento National Park offers a vast range of outdoor activities. Trekking enthusiasts can follow numerous trails that meander through the hills and mountains, with paths suitable for all skill levels. Some trails lead to hidden historical sites, like the Hermitage of San Giovanni all'Orfento, a place of peace and meditation.

For those who prefer the water, there are many opportunities to enjoy the sea. Along Cilento's coast, you'll find numerous charming beaches and secluded bays, ideal for swimming, snorkeling, or simply basking in the sun. Additionally, the park offers canoe and kayak routes along the rivers, an exhilarating way to explore Cilento's wild nature.

Making the Most of the Park To fully enjoy the Cilento National Park, it's advisable to plan your visit in advance. You can download trail maps from the park's website and book guided tours or organized excursions. Remember to bring water, a snack, and a hat to protect yourself from the sun. And, of course, don't forget your camera to capture the beauty of this extraordinary corner of Italy.

Don't miss out on visiting the small villages that dot the park's area, rich in history and traditions. These are places where time seems to have stood still, offering visitors an authentic immersion in local culture. Cobblestone streets, ancient churches, local produce, and warm hospitality will make your visit unforgettable.

Remember, the Cilento Park is a protected area: respect nature, don't leave litter, and don't harm flora and fauna. In doing so, you'll help preserve this special place for future generations.

Beyond parks and historical sites, Campania also offers a series of hidden wonders beneath the surface and in extraordinarily beautiful nature reserves. These include fascinating caves and nature reserves that offer a unique and memorable experience for nature lovers and adventurers alike.

Caves and Nature Reserves to Explore

Pertosa-Auletta Angel's Cave

The Pertosa-Auletta Angel's Cave, nestled in the heart of the Cilento National Park, is one of Italy's most expansive and spectacular cave complexes. This karstic cave provides visitors the opportunity to delve into a mesmerizing subterranean world of stalactites, stalagmites, and underground lakes. A boat trip along the underground river stands as an experience not to be missed.

Castelcivita Caves

Near Salerno, the Castelcivita Caves form another cave complex of significant scientific interest. Here, you can meander between enormous chambers and narrow corridors, admiring millennia-old rock formations illuminated by evocative lighting. The guided tour tells the geological story of this place, making it an educational as well as adventurous experience.

Gole del Calore

State Nature Reserve Located between the municipalities of Felitto and Magliano Vetere, the Gole del Calore State Nature Reserve is a protected area of incredible beauty. The Calore River, with its clear, cool waters, has carved deep gorges and canyons over time, creating a stunning landscape. This reserve offers numerous opportunities for hiking, climbing, canyoning, and rafting amidst untouched scenery.

Persano WWF Oasis

Located in the Sele Plain, the Persano WWF Oasis is a haven for birdwatching enthusiasts. The area is one of the most critical wetlands in southern Italy, home to numerous migratory birds. Here, you can observe flamingos, white storks, herons, and many other species in a serene and relaxing environment.

Monte Nuovo

Oriented Nature Reserve In the heart of the Protected Natural Area of Campi Flegrei, you'll find the Monte Nuovo Oriented Nature Reserve. This reserve is unique for its youngest volcano, Monte Nuovo, born from an eruption in 1538. It offers the chance to explore a unique volcanic environment with a crater lake and distinctive flora and fauna. Well-marked hiking trails provide an excellent way to explore the area.

Bosco Faito Oasis

Located on Mount Faito, the Bosco Faito Oasis offers a refreshing escape from summer heat. The dense forest of white fir trees is ideal for hiking, and the elevated position offers breathtaking views over the Sorrento Peninsula and Amalfi Coast. Don't forget to visit the "Valle delle Ferriere", a natural park where you can find the Woodwardia radicans, a rare type of prehistoric fern.

Astroni Nature Reserve

The Astroni Nature Reserve, located near Naples, is one of the three remaining craters in the Campi Flegrei area. This natural park, managed by WWF, features three lakes surrounded by lush Mediterranean forest. In addition to being a protected area of ecological importance, the Astroni are also known for their rich biodiversity, including many bird species.

Caserta Lipu Oasis

The Caserta Lipu Oasis, located near the famous Reggia di Caserta, is a small but vital wildlife refuge. The area is home to a wide variety of birds, mammals, and insects and offers well-maintained trails for wildlife observation and outdoor walks.

The Royal Palace of Caserta: An Italian Masterpiece

Welcome, dear traveler, to a journey across time and art into the heart of Italy's grandeur. Here, in the fertile land of Campania, stands the regal testament to Bourbon ambition—the Royal Palace of Caserta, or Reggia di Caserta.

Conceived as a new Versailles, the palace was born of King Charles VII of Naples' desire to echo the European grand courts' splendor. Architect Luigi Vanvitelli, commissioned in 1752, brought to life this monumental vision blending baroque exuberance with neoclassical elegance.

At first glance, the palace's magnificence resides in its sheer size. A vast complex of 47,000 square meters, comprising more than 1,200 rooms, the royal residence encompasses royal apartments, theatres, chapels, libraries, each alive with tales of royal intrigues and luxuries. The walls whisper these narratives through their richly decorated frescoes, detailed stuccowork, and intricate sculptural reliefs.

As a jewel in its crown, the palace houses the San Leucio Complex, an intimate theatre echoing the grand Teatro San Carlo of Naples. A masterpiece in its own right, the theatre evokes a romantic nostalgia for the flamboyant performances of the past.

But, the palace's allure is not confined within its regal walls. The estate unveils a sprawling Italianate Garden, an expansive green canvas punctuated with elaborate fountains, sculptured figures, and water cascades—an Italian interpretation of the grand Versailles gardens. The English Garden, infused with a wild romantic charm, winds a delicate path through streams and lakes, showcasing a collection of rare botanical wonders.

As you tread these regal paths, remember that a visit to the Royal Palace of Caserta is not just sightseeing—it's stepping into an era of Italian history and artistic expression. Every fresco, every stuccowork, and every sculpted figure contributes to the story the palace tells—a tale of ambition, opulence, and architectural genius.

Planning your visit well can transform your experience. The palace's doors are open from 8:30 AM to 7:30 PM in the warmer months of April to October and from 8:30 AM to 5:00 PM in the cooler months of November to March, with the last admission granted an hour before closing. To capture the palace's full grandeur, reserve at least half a day for your exploration.

Tickets are available for purchase at the palace or online, with guided tours offering deeper insights into the palace's history and artistry. Though self-guided tours allow for personal freedom, the guided tours enhance your understanding with enlightening narratives and anecdotes.

The palace, being wheelchair-friendly, offers accessible routes and facilities, ensuring a comfortable experience for all visitors. If you choose to drive, paid parking is available at the palace. Alternatively, Caserta is well-connected by train, offering smooth transport options from major Italian cities.

In the Royal Palace of Caserta, you find more than a monumental building. It is an immersive historical journey, a dance with artistic grandeur, and a communion with royal opulence. Whether you are a history aficionado, an art connoisseur, or a casual traveler, the palace promises you a captivating journey filled with wonder and discovery. So, step in and let the grand narrative of Caserta unfold before your eyes.

Tales from the Royal Palace of Caserta: A Closer Look at Its Intriguing Stories

Journey with me through the remarkable Royal Palace of Caserta, as we unfold tales that go beyond its well-known architectural splendor. We are not just treading through an opulent palace but stepping back into a time rich with history, ingenuity, and tales waiting to be told.

- Start with a tale of a dream interrupted and later fulfilled. King Charles VII of Naples, the originator of the palace's idea, had to leave for Spain before he could see his dream take shape. His absence didn't deter his son, Ferdinand IV, who shared his father's vision and oversaw the palace's completion. A tale of ambition and tenacity indeed!

- Moving on, one cannot help but marvel at the inventive genius of Luigi Vanvitelli, the architect behind the palace's design. A vast network of fountains and cascades was woven into the palace's design, drawn from the water of Monte Taburno. This impressive hydraulic system didn't just serve an aesthetic purpose but was a climate control solution centuries ahead of its time.

- Let's step away from grandeur for a moment and walk towards San Leucio Complex, initially intended as a hunting lodge. It became an unconventional silk factory under the reign of Ferdinand IV. This community-driven silk production model blurred the lines between royal patronage and craftsmanship, demonstrating the king's progressive social vision.

- While the palace was primarily built for royal leisure, its role during World War II was starkly different. The Allies established their Supreme Command here, making strategic decisions amidst the palace's regal interiors. Imagine war maps unfurled on the ornate tables and military officials pacing the grand corridors, a far cry from its regular opulence.

- Speaking of divergent roles, the palace has had its share of fame in the cinematic world. Remember Queen Amidala's royal palace in Star Wars: Episode I - The Phantom Menace, or the backdrop for action-packed scenes in Mission Impossible III? Yes, that was none other than our own Royal Palace of Caserta, playing a starring role on the silver screen!

- As we stroll through the palace, the kitchen, though not as grand as the Royal Apartments, has its own charm. Picture rows of cooks preparing feasts for thousands using the original stoves and copper cookware, with majolica tiles adding a hint of art to this functional space.

Each tale from the Royal Palace of Caserta paints a unique picture of its history. Be it the innovative design, the dramatic war-time operations, or the flirtations with Hollywood, these stories make the palace more than just an architectural marvel. Each visit, therefore, becomes more than a tour; it's a step into a living, breathing narrative, enriched by centuries of captivating history.

CAMPANIA'S FOOD AND WINE ITINERARIES

Embracing the Wine Route in Irpinia: A Symphony of Flavors and Landscapes

If you're an enthusiast of wines and their stories, Irpinia - a region nestled within the lush heartlands of Campania - would unfold as an exquisite tale of flavors, cultures, and landscapes. Celebrated for its exceptional grape varieties, Irpinia is more than a wine route. It's a sensory voyage that traverses through vine-clad valleys, charming hillside towns, and a tapestry of traditions spun around its legendary wines.

Our adventure begins in the verdant countryside where rows of vines appear like stanzas in a wine lover's poem. It's in these rolling hills that you'll find the three DOCG (Denominazione di Origine Controllata e Garantita) wines of Irpinia - Taurasi, Greco di Tufo, and Fiano di Avellino, each bearing a distinctive personality of the terroir and the heritage of its vintners.

Named after a small town in the region, Taurasi is the 'Barolo of the South,' a noble red that draws its character from the Aglianico grape. Savoring a glass of Taurasi is like sipping a sonnet of Irpinia's spirit - intense yet elegant, bearing notes of dark fruit, spices, and often a hint of chocolate. A tour around vineyards like Mastroberardino, Feudi di San Gregorio, or Antonio Caggiano promises an intimate understanding of this cherished red and the care that goes into its making.

Veering our course towards Tufo, we encounter the second gem of Irpinia - Greco di Tufo. From the vineyards that surround the quaint town of Tufo, a delightful white wine, extracted from Greco grapes, is born. With an invigorating mineral-ity and a refreshing bouquet of pears, peaches, and almonds, it's a wine that pairs harmoniously with the regional cuisine.

As our journey continues through the undulating landscape, another outstand-ing white, Fiano di Avellino, graces our path. Fiano, a grape variety dating back to Roman times, now thrives in the vineyards around Avellino. As you raise your glass, savor the wine's honeyed texture, punctuated with notes of hazelnuts and subtle spices - a testament to the fertile volcanic soils and the vintner's artistry.

These wines are not just exquisite beverages but are part of Irpinia's cultural fabric, a fact evident as you meander through its charming towns like Taurasi, Tufo, and Avellino. A delightful harmony permeates the wine cellars, local trat-torias, and vibrant festivals, binding the community in a shared love for their cherished products. As you indulge in tastings, you'll not only savor the com-plexity of the wines but also absorb the warmth and hospitality that Irpinia generously offers.

The magic of Irpinia's wine route lies not just in its acclaimed wines but the people who pour their heart and soul into these bottles. Their stories intertwine with the vines, becoming part of the terroir, lending each sip a depth that is more than just taste. It's a sip that invites you into centuries-old traditions, a commit-ment to excellence, and a deep-rooted respect for the land.

Navigating the wine route in Irpinia is not merely an itinerary. It's an invitation to witness the region's evolving relationship with its vines, a testament to a leg-acy that has been meticulously tended and passed on from one generation to another. Whether you're a wine connoisseur or a traveler seeking novel experi-ences, Irpinia's wine route is sure to offer an immersive journey that engages all your senses and leaves you with memories as enchanting as the region's wines.

Distinguished Wineries and Wine Productions in Campania

Follow along as we uncork stories from Campania's most important wineries and their stellar productions. Our exploration paints a vibrant picture of the re-gion's vinous landscape, showcasing a mix of historic producers and ambitious newcomers, each contributing to the growing reputation of Campania's wine scene.

In the heart of Irpinia, the Mastroberardino family has been tending to their vineyards for over two centuries, steadfastly promoting native grape varieties such as Aglianico, Fiano, and Greco. Their persistence in preserving these an-cient varietals has sculpted the identity of Irpinia wines on the global stage. Mastroberardino's Taurasi Radici, with its bold structure and elegant depth, is a masterful ode to the Aglianico grape and Irpinia's terroir.

Feudi di San Gregorio, another beacon of the region, has redefined the potential of Campanian wines since its inception in the mid-1980s. Situated in Sorbo Serpico, Feudi is best known for their world-class interpretations of Fiano di Avellino and Greco di Tufo. In their capable hands, these varietals express a balance of power and finesse that keeps wine enthusiasts returning for more.

Venturing westward towards the slopes of Mount Vesuvius, we encounter Villa Dora, a family-run winery renowned for their Lacryma Christi wines. Made from Piedirosso and Aglianico for the reds, and Coda di Volpe and Falanghina for the whites, these wines reflect the volcanic soul of the soil and the unique microclimate of the area.

Nestled along the breathtaking Amalfi Coast is Marisa Cuomo. The winery perched precariously on the steep cliffs, facing the azure Mediterranean Sea, is famous for its unique and expressive wines. Their Furore Bianco Fiorduva, a blend of Fenile, Ginestra, and Ripoli, captures the essence of the sea breeze, citrus orchards, and mineral-rich soils in each sip.

Moving south to Cilento, we find Luigi Maffini, who has been instrumental in highlighting the potential of this beautiful coastal region. Maffini's wines, notably the Fiano-based Kratos and the Aglianico-based Kleos, exemplify the winemaker's commitment to expressing the distinct character of Cilento's terroir.

Lastly, we must not overlook Casa d'Ambra, the historic winery located on the stunning island of Ischia. Established in the late 19th century, Casa d'Ambra has championed the island's indigenous varietals, most notably the white Biancolella. Their Tenuta Frassitelli, a single-vineyard Biancolella grown on terraces at 600 meters above sea level, beautifully showcases the grape's delicate floral character balanced with a distinctive mineral edge.

These exemplary wineries, among others, have crafted a diverse and exciting narrative for Campania's wine industry. They invite us to dive deeper into their individual stories, to stroll through their vineyards, and to appreciate the subtleties of each glass of wine, understanding the passion, hard work, and tradition that go into their creation. Whether it's the bold Aglianico of Taurasi, the crisp Fiano of Avellino, the volcanic Lacryma Christi, or the island-grown Biancolella, each winery offers a unique lens to appreciate the richness of Campania's wine scene. So, pour yourself a glass, and let's toast to the allure of Campanian wines.

Tastings and culinary experiences

Embarking on a gastronomic journey in Campania is akin to opening a treasure chest brimming with vibrant colors, intense flavors, and authentic textures. You will find yourself caught in a sensory dance, an experience that tantalizes your taste buds and nourishes your soul. As each morsel melts on your tongue, you are offered a slice of Campania's culinary heritage, bringing you closer to its people and their traditions.

Picture yourself strolling down the narrow cobblestone streets of Naples, the birthplace of pizza. An aroma wafting from a bustling pizzeria beckons you.

Here, master pizzaiolos work their magic, skillfully kneading dough, swirling rich San Marzano tomato sauce, sprinkling creamy buffalo mozzarella, and finally baking it all in a wood-fired oven. The result is a pie so delectably simple yet profound, it's no wonder that UNESCO declared the art of Neapolitan 'Pizzaiuolo' as an intangible cultural heritage.

As you journey further, consider stepping into a pasticceria in Salerno to sample the sfogliatella. This iconic Campanian pastry comes in two main variants - 'riccia' (curly) or 'frolla' (shortcrust). As you bite into the flaky layers of a 'riccia', the filling of sweetened ricotta cheese, subtly perfumed with candied citrus, makes for a divine blend of contrasting textures. A 'frolla', on the other hand, with its crumbly shell, offers a harmonious play of the same flavors.

Venturing inland, the beautiful vineyards and olive groves of Irpinia offer an authentic farm-to-table experience. Join a local family for a hearty Sunday lunch, or 'pranzo della domenica'. Watch as Nonna stirs a pot of 'ragù', a slow-cooked meat sauce, to serve over fresh handmade pasta, or seasons home-grown vegetables for a refreshing 'insalata'. Pair this with a glass of full-bodied Taurasi wine, and you'll understand why Irpinians take such pride in their culinary and viticultural traditions.

Meanwhile, along the Amalfi Coast, let the seafood's freshness captivate you. The 'scialatielli ai frutti di mare', a dish of fresh pasta with shellfish and sea urchins, showcases the bounty of the Mediterranean Sea. Enjoying this, while overlooking the turquoise waters, is an experience that etches itself in your memory.

Your Campanian culinary journey isn't complete without participating in a traditional cooking class. Immerse yourself in the art of mozzarella-making in Caserta or the intricacies of crafting perfect 'gnocchi alla sorrentina' in Sorrento. These hands-on experiences don't just teach you recipes, but also the art of savoring life - the Campanian way.

In Cilento, become a part of the 'Mediterranean Diet', a UNESCO Intangible Cultural Heritage. Visit an organic farm, pick sun-ripened vegetables, savor DOP-certified olive oils, or indulge in the 'white figs' of Cilento - a delicacy that has been cherished since ancient times.

Imagine attending a 'sagra' - these are local food festivals that dot the Campanian calendar, each one dedicated to a specific product. From the 'Sagra della Castagna' (Chestnut Festival) in Montella to the 'Sagra del Carciofo' (Artichoke Festival) in Paestum, these events celebrate local produce with gusto. Participating in a 'sagra' means feasting on specialties prepared by locals, often accompanied by music, folk dances, and an infectious sense of camaraderie.

Have you ever tried the 'colatura di alici' of Cetara? This small fishing village on the Amalfi Coast is famous for its anchovy sauce, a modern descendant of the ancient Roman 'garum'. It's an elixir of the sea - intense, amber-colored, prepared through a centuries-old process of salting and aging anchovies. To watch the 'colatura' being made is to witness a timeless tradition. And to taste it, drizzled on spaghetti with a dash of parsley and garlic, is to discover an explosion of flavor that speaks of the Mediterranean in every drop.

In Campania, bread isn't merely a side dish, and the town of Altavilla Silentina is a testament to this. Here, the centuries-old ovens produce 'pane di Altavilla', a bread that's crispy on the outside, soft and airy inside, and carrying a distinctive aroma from the locally grown 'Cappelli' wheat. Enjoy it fresh out of the oven, smeared with a robust local 'ndunderi' cheese - it's the simplest yet most satisfying of pleasures.

Don't forget to explore Campania's liquid gold – its olive oils. In Salerno province, the 'Monocultivar Ravece' extra-virgin olive oil stands out for its unique spicy and bitter notes. Join a guided tasting at a local 'frantoio' (oil mill). You'll learn to discern the different aromas, flavors, and colors in olive oils, adding another layer of appreciation to your culinary exploits.

Campania also holds sweet surprises for chocolate lovers. In the Baroque town of Lauro, nestled at the foot of Mount Vesuvius, you'll find Gay-Odin. This historic chocolate factory, with roots in Naples, creates 'Vesuvio', a cone-shaped chocolate evoking the famous volcano. Made with high-quality cocoa and hazelnuts from the region, this delight promises a sweet ending to your culinary journey.

Unearthing Campania's culinary secrets is like engaging in a thrilling conversation with the region's soul. The experiences are varied and numerous, from rustic farmhouses to upscale restaurants, from vineyards to chocolate factories. This region offers a gastronomic symphony, where each note harmonizes to create a melody that lingers long after the journey ends. Savor the moment, cherish the memory.

Wish you the best trip to Campania.

3 IN 1 FREE BOOK FOR YOU!

✓ BOOK 1 – Everyday Italian Phrases
✓ BOOK 2 – Italian Slang
✓ BOOK 3 – Italian Traditions, Etiquette, and Curiosities

SCAN ME

SCAN THIS QR AND DOWNLOAD NOW YOUR FREE BONUS!

BASILICATA

TRAVEL GUIDE

Prepped to Navigate Italy's Best Kept Secret?

Delve into Basilicata's Unique Landscapes and Traditions, Plus a
Comprehensive Guide to its Distinctive Culinary Treats

INTRODUCTION
TO BASILICATA

Welcome to Basilicata, a region rich in history and tales, culture, traditions, and breathtaking landscapes. Here, the traces of a thousand-year-old past blend with the lively traditions of a warm and hospitable population. This book is not just a guide to the beauties of this territory, but also an invitation to explore and discover Basilicata, a hidden treasure in the heart of the Mediterranean, far from mass tourism.

Basilicata is a region that has much to offer: from its breathtaking land-scapes, made of towering mountains, wild coasts, and fascinating art cities, to its culture and traditions, deeply rooted in the history and lifestyle of its people. In Basilicata, time seems to have stood still, allowing one to find a slower, more authentic, more human pace of life.

Here, slow tourism is more than a simple trend: it's a way of life. It's the opportunity to discover places on foot or by bike, to taste local cuisine, to participate in folk festivals, to meet locals. It's the opportunity to live a holiday that is not limited to visiting places, but that transforms into an authentic experience, a journey into the culture and traditions of a people.

But it's not just about landscapes and traditions: Basilicata is also a region rich in history. From prehistoric remains and the ancient Greek and Roman civilizations, to perfectly preserved medieval villages, every corner of this land tells a fascinating story, a story that speaks of peoples, invasions, resistances, and rebirths.

Geographical and historical background

Basilicata (also known as Lucania), is a region in the southern area of Italy, bordering Puglia in its northern and eastern parts, the Calabria region to its south, and Campania to its west. It overlooks the Tyrrhenian Sea to the southwest (Gulf of Policastro), with a high and rocky coastline, and the Ionian Sea to the southeast (Gulf of Taranto) where the coast is low and composed of sandy elements. Apart from the flat expanse of Metaponto, the rest of the territory is divided between hills and mountains, with the mountain massifs of Pollino, Sirino and Maddalena, forming the Lucanian Apennines, where some elevations exceed 2000 meters in altitude. In the northwestern area, there is also an inactive volcano, the Vulture. Several lakes are present, although most are artificial (Lake San Giuliano, Grotta del Pertusillo, Monte Cotugno). Only the two wonderful lakes of Monticchio are of natural origin, located on the crater of Vulture. The other lakes are that of San Giuliano, Grotta del Pertusillo. Its regional capital is the city of

Potenza, while the other important city, famous worldwide, is Matera, capital of the homonymous province. It is inhabited, according to the last census, by 550,000 inhabitants, usually called Lucanians.

30% of the regional territory is considered an area subject to environmental protection: the Pollino National Park and the Lucanian Apennines-Val d'Agri -Lago-negrese National Park are the most important. Other protected areas are also reported such as the Murgia Materana or the natural reserve of the Lake Piccolo of Monticchio. The region has been inhabited since prehistoric times. Its coast, particularly the Ionian one, is known to have been colonized by the ancient Greeks (cities like Metaponto, for example), whose remains are still visible today. All the various historical epochs, with all the peoples that have passed through Basilicata, have left their imprint on the identity of the region.

PREPARING FOR THE TRIP: PLANNING AND LOGISTICS

Prepare everything to the best of your ability

Before we delve into the wonders of Basilicata, some advice on planning and logistics for your trip to this southern Italian region will surely come in handy. In fact, adequate preparation is the first step to ensuring that your full and captivating experience amid the beauty and magic of this stunning region isn't overshadowed by logistical or other issues.

Understanding how to organize your trip, being armed with essential information, will significantly enhance your experience and help tackle any potential hiccups.

As far as possible, I'll provide valuable tips and practical information to organize your journey and fully relish Basilicata, from choosing the best time to visit the region, to convenient commuting, or selecting the type of accommodation and itinerary.

Basilicata offers a variety of experiences to suit every type of traveller, and we'll start with choosing the ideal time to visit the region. I'll guide you through the different seasons and distinctive features of each, allowing you to select the most suitable time according to your preferences and interests.

I'll endeavour to illustrate the various transportation options available to reach Basilicata. I'll provide information on flights, trains, and car rentals, as well as how to get around within the region once you've arrived. I'll also suggest alternative modes of transport, such as cycling tours or hiking, for those seeking a more adventurous and immersive experience.

Accommodation options are also diverse: you can stay in characteristic rural farmhouses immersed in nature, or cozy bed and breakfasts in the heart of historical centres. Depending on your budget and desired experiences, there's always a solution.

Moreover, while it might not seem so, Basilicata harbours internal wonders and treasures that require itinerary planning. There are unique and surprising routes, through which iconic places like Matera and its Sassi, but also lesser-known yet equally fascinating destinations, will lead you to explore a territory that, although launched into modernity, has not forgotten its past. For this reason, I'll try to provide as much information as possible about attractions, points of interest, and activities you won't want to miss along your journey.

Finally, a series of tips on how to optimize your trip and your experience in Basilicata. From information on the climate and suitable clothing, to instructions on bookings and preventing tourist scams, I'll guide you so you can fully enjoy every moment of your trip in complete safety and peace of mind.

Basilicata is a unique, magical, and wonderful land. Suitable preparation before the trip will undoubtedly help you grasp its wonderful soul.

Flights, lodging and transportation to plan your trip to Basilicata

To start with, choosing your flights is a fundamental step. Basilicata doesn't have its own airports, but it's served by two significant airports, Bari-Palese and Naples-Capodichino. Whether by car, bus, or train, from these hubs, the main cities of the region are easily accessible.

How to arrive from Bari

From Bari-Palese airport, Basilicata is easily reachable by car, bus, or train. Matera, for instance, is located about 60 kilometers southwest of the airport.

By Car: The most direct route is the SS96 and the SS99, which leads straight to Matera in a journey of about one hour.

By Bus: There are bus services between Bari airport and various locations in Basilicata, including Matera and Potenza. These buses are managed by various companies, including Pugliairbus.

By Train: Bari Centrale railway station provides connections to various cities in Basilicata. From there, there are direct trains to Matera and other cities. To get to Bari Centrale railway station from the airport, you can take a train, a taxi, or a bus.

How to arrive from Naples

From Naples-Capodichino airport, Basilicata is also easily reachable by car, bus, or train. For instance, Potenza is located about 150 kilometers east of the airport.

By Car: By taking the A16 motorway, heading east, you can reach Potenza in about two hours.

By Bus: Various bus services connect Naples with various cities in Basilicata, including Potenza and Matera. Sita Sud is one of the main providers of these services.

By Train: From Napoli Centrale, there are direct trains to Potenza and other cities in Basilicata. To get to Napoli Centrale railway station from the airport, you can take an Alibus bus or a taxi.

Choosing the right accommodation, the right vehicle, and the right season

Once you've arrived in Basilicata, choosing your accommodation is an important aspect. The region offers a wide range of options, including hotels, bed and breakfasts, farm stays, and vacation homes. Choose your accommodation based on your preferences and budget, bearing in mind its strategic location for your points of interest. Advanced booking is recommended, especially during peak seasons.

For getting around within Basilicata, several means of transportation can be used. Renting a car is a popular choice and allows you to explore the region at your own pace. The roads are well-maintained and offer spectacular views along the way. However, you can also use public transportation, such as trains and buses, to reach different locations. Be sure to check the schedules and rates in advance to best plan your movements.

When planning your trip, always consider the time of year and season. Basilicata generally enjoys a Mediterranean climate, with hot summers and mild winters. However, temperatures and weather conditions can vary based on the specific area you wish to visit. Consult the weather forecast and organize appropriate clothing based on the season and planned activities.

Finally, it's always a good idea to find out about local events, festivals, and happenings that might take place during your stay. Participating in these celebrations can provide a unique experience to immerse yourself in Basilicata's culture and traditions. Check event calendars and plan your visits accordingly.

Tips for maximizing time and logistics during the stay

Here are some additional tips and suggestions from someone who knows these lands and appreciates how beautiful and important it is to experience them authentically.

First off, I would recommend making a list of the main attractions and places you want to visit. This will allow you to figure out how to organize your journey and related travel, considering the feasibility of the itinerary based on distance and opening hours of what you intend to visit.

Remember, however, to leave at least a little room for surprises and spontaneous discoveries along the way. After all, you never know what fantastic adventure or magnificent place you might stumble upon.

Basilicata is rich with hidden views, small villages, and breathtaking landscapes that you might discover en route. Don't be afraid to lose your way a little and follow your curiosity. Often, the most memorable experiences happen when you let the flow of the journey guide you. Here, curiosity is not a sin at all!

When you're in Basilicata, don't forget an important detail: interaction with the locals. They will all be ready to welcome you as if you were family. You'll have the feeling of being at home, of being with people you've always known and who will welcome you with open arms.

The locals are warm and welcoming, and you may discover many valuable secrets and tips about lesser-known places. Chat with merchants, restaurateurs, and locals. They will be happy to share their passion for the region with you and offer valuable insights.

Without belabouring the point any further, all that remains is to wish you the best of trips to this area, a treasure chest of treasures just waiting to be discovered.

BASILICATA'S ICONIC ATTRACTIONS: FROM THE SASSI OF MATERA TO THE LUCANIAN DOLOMITES

Matera: A Journey through History and Enchantment

Matera has already been discussed in the book about the Puglia region; however, the city is so beautiful, charming, and full of allure and magic that it cannot be ignored in this book, where I will attempt to capture its essence in words, as much as it is possible to do so.

Immersing yourself in the magical atmosphere of Matera, it feels like taking a leap back in time, transporting us to a past age, or rather, a succession of ages. The history of this city dates back over 9,000 years, with its ancient homes carved into the limestone rocks.

These extraordinary dwellings, known as the Sassi, have earned Matera a place on the UNESCO World Heritage List, as they represent a testament to human resilience and adaptation, showcasing a unique architectural heritage that, in its modesty, preserves something grand.

Exploring the Sassi is like getting lost in a fairy-tale village. The streets and labyrinthine alleys reveal an intricate maze of cave dwellings, churches, and underground cisterns.

As you journey through this ancient city, you will discover layers of history etched into the walls, from the Paleolithic period to the Roman era and beyond. The Sassi offer a glimpse into the everyday life of its past inhabitants, providing a fascinating window into the city's rich cultural heritage.

Although the Sassi are undoubtedly the jewels of Matera, there are other noteworthy places to explore. The stunning Matera Cathedral, dedicated to Santa Maria della Bruna, stands majestic in the heart of the city. Its intricate facade and beautiful interior showcase a fusion of Romanesque, Gothic, and Baroque architectural styles.

For those seeking hidden treasures, Matera unveils its secrets in the lesser-known corners of the city. By exploring off-the-beaten paths, you will find hidden churches carved into the rock, such as the Church of San Pietro Barisano and the Church of Santa Lucia alle Malve. These sanctuaries, which sometimes go almost unnoticed, guard breathtaking frescoes and intricate decorations carved into the rock, displaying the city's artistic skill and strong devotional sentiment.

Don't miss a visit to Casa Noha, a multimedia museum that tells the story of the Sassi and the people who once inhabited them. The immersive exhibits and audiovisual presentations provide a deeper understanding of Matera's history and the challenges faced by its inhabitants over the centuries.

Beyond the historical sites, Matera offers a vibrant cultural scene. The city has become a hub for artists, attracting creative minds from around the world. It's easy to stumble upon art galleries, craft workshops, and contemporary art installations that add a modern touch to the ancient streets. Matera's designation as the European Capital of Culture in 2019 further elevated the city's cultural offerings, with a series of events and festivals that celebrate art, music, and theatre.

To further appreciate the beauty of Matera, enjoy the panoramic view from the surrounding hills. When the sun sets and casts a warm light on the city, the Sassi come alive with an ethereal beauty that will leave you breathless.

One could talk endlessly about Matera. In reality, the only thing I can tell you is to visit it. It's a city that wins the hearts of all those who visit. Its timeless charm, its rich history, and its hidden corners make it an unparalleled destination. Whether you wander through its ancient streets, admire its splendid architecture, or immerse yourself in its vibrant cultural scene, Matera promises an unforgettable experience that will stay with you long after you have left.

The Lucanian Dolomites: A Natural Wonder to Explore

Let's momentarily leave the urban centers to immerse ourselves in the wilder part of Basilicata, where the majestic Lucanian Dolomites are located, a natural treasure worth discovering. These spectacular mountains, with their imposing peaks, enchanting valleys, and breathtaking landscapes, are a must-visit destination for nature lovers and adventurers. Here I want to guide you and introduce you to the discovery of the Lucanian Dolomites, revealing their unique beauty and the activities you can enjoy during your visit.

The Lucanian Dolomites extend into the Lucanian Apennines, embracing a vast area that stretches between Basilicata and Calabria. This mountain range offers pristine natural beauty, with peaks exceeding 2,000 meters in height and a variety of ecosystems that host rich biodiversity.

Their most iconic feature is the majesty of their summits, which emerge from the surrounding landscape like stone giants. While hiking along the well-marked trails, you will find yourself surrounded by breathtaking panoramas, with views ranging from green valleys to rocky cliffs. This enchanting beauty and the tranquility of nature will make you feel as if you are in a world apart, far from the hustle and bustle of daily life.

The Lucanian Dolomites offer a wide range of activities to suit all tastes and needs. Hiking enthusiasts will find a myriad of trails winding through ancient forests, lush valleys, and breathtaking landscapes. You can explore enchanting waterfalls, crystal-clear rivers, and lakes that reflect the splendor of the surrounding mountains.

For climbing enthusiasts, the Lucanian Dolomites offer vertical walls and cliffs that present an exciting challenge. You can test your skills by scaling these rocky walls, immersing yourself in an exhilarating adventure amidst the wild nature.

If you are birdwatching lovers, you will be happy to know that the Lucanian Dolomites host a rich variety of bird species. You can spot golden eagles, kestrels, and woodpeckers in their natural habitat, providing a unique and fascinating experience.

During winter, the Lucanian Dolomites turn into a paradise for ski and snowboard enthusiasts. Their pristine slopes, surrounded by enchanting landscapes, offer thrilling downhill runs for all skill levels. You can enjoy snow sports while immersed in the unspoiled beauty of the mountains.

Beyond outdoor activities, these mountains also offer rich culture and history. The entire area is indeed dotted with ancient villages and enchanting towns, where you can discover local traditions and savor delicious Lucanian cuisine. Be sure to visit the museums that tell the history of the region, offering a deeper perspective on life in the mountains.

The Lucanian Dolomites are a place of absolute beauty, worthy of discovery and admiration. Their unspoiled nature, spectacular views, and exciting activities make this region a true paradise for nature lovers and adventure enthusiasts. No matter which season you choose to visit, the Lucanian Dolomites will leave an indelible impression on the heart of anyone fortunate enough to explore them.

OFF-THE-BEATEN-PATH ITINERARIES: DISCOVERING BASILICATA'S HIDDEN GEMS

Basilicata is not only about Matera or the Lucanian Dolomites. There are various gems within its territory, off the beaten track, where timeless beauties await discovery. This captivating region offers much more than one might imagine, and nothing remains but to go and find them.

Ghost Town of Craco

We begin our off-road journey with a visit to the village of Craco. This small town has been uninhabited for decades and seems like something out of a movie. Nestled on a hill, Craco is a medieval village ready to provide a spectacular view of the surrounding countryside. Its narrow and winding streets emanate an almost surreal atmosphere, with a truly unique vibe that harkens back to a distant time. Despite being uninhabited for over fifty years, Craco has become a film location and a one-of-a-kind tourist attraction.

The Village of Tursi

We continue our journey to the charming village of Tursi, famous for its history and tradition. This small, magnificent village is an invitation to stop, to take some time for oneself, to savor tranquility. One of the most suggestive areas is located at the top of the village and is called "Rabatana": the name underlines how this place has long been inhabited by people of Arab origin, as demonstrated by the cultivation of oranges, a practice imported by the Arabs.

Inside this small jewel nestled between mountains and gullies, there is the magnificent church of Santa Maria Maggiore, which contains beautiful frescoes.

Tursi is also known as the birthplace of one of the most important contemporary poets of southern Italy: Albino Pierro (1916-1995), who was nominated for the Nobel Prize in Literature several times. His house has been transformed into a multi-level museum-house: it houses a series of personal memorabilia related to this poet who imprinted the rural life of these places into his verses, a museum dedicated to Lucanian poetry, and an art gallery with several pictorial works by local artists made on the tenth anniversary of the famous poet's death.

Pietrapertosa and Castelmezzano

Continuing, we reach Pietrapertosa and Castelmezzano, two picturesque villages situated among the mountains. These enchanting places are famous for their dwellings built on cliffs, overlooking the valley below, offering breathtaking views of the entire surroundings. Through these narrow streets, one can experience the authentic atmosphere of southern Italy's rural civilization. For the most daring, there is an unmissable opportunity, the "Flight of the Angel": a cable has been installed between the peaks of the two villages; attached to a sturdy harness, you can fly over the entire distance between the two villages suspended in the void at a height of 100 m. An incredible adventure. For those who want to immerse themselves in pristine nature, a visit to the Park of the Murgia Materana is indispensable: a spectacular landscape, with gullies, gorges and woods, among flora, fauna and ancient cave dwellings.

Acerenza

Another hidden gem worth exploring is the picturesque village of Acerenza, with its magnificent Romanesque-style cathedral. This charming village offers an authentic and tranquil atmosphere, with its cobbled streets and stone houses. This small village, built on a rocky ridge, offers a panoramic visit to the surrounding landscape of hills and cultivated fields.

The Charm of the Lakes of Monticchio

Lastly, one of the most fascinating destinations in Basilicata is the lakes of Monticchio.

This extraordinary natural site, located in the municipality of Rionero in Vulture, within the regional natural park of Gallipoli Cognato Piccole Dolo-mitiLucane, offers a unique scenario that combines the beauty of the landscape with geological and naturalistic interest.

The Lakes of Monticchio are no ordinary lakes: they are in fact two volcanic lakes, formed in the craters of the ancient extinct volcano of Mount Vulture, the youngest volcano of the Southern Apennines.

The Lago Grande, the largest of the two, is surrounded by lush vegetation, where oak, chestnut, and maple trees alternate. Here, one can take a pleasant walk along the shores of the lake, admiring the landscape or observing the numerous species of birds that populate the area. During the warm season, the waters of the lake beautifully reflect the surrounding vegetation, creating a fascinating play of colors. It is also possible to rent a small boat to navigate it.

The Lago Piccolo, located a little higher up, is less accessible but equally fascinating. Its banks are characterized by high tuff walls that rise directly from the water, giving the landscape an almost surreal appearance. From the banks of the lake, one enjoys a breathtaking panoramic view of the valley below.

But it's not only nature that makes this place special: on the shore of the Lago Piccolo, for example, is the Abbey of San Michele, an ancient Benedictine monastery dating back to the 8th century.

The abbey, built directly on the rock, is a perfect example of rock architecture and offers a fascinating slice of the region's religious history. For those who love wine, near the lakes is also the winery of a major producer of Aglianico del Vulture, one of the most appreciated wines of Basilicata. A visit to the winery is a great opportunity to discover the secrets of this fine wine and taste a glass overlooking the lakes.

The Lakes of Monticchio are a real jewel of Basilicata, a place where nature, history, and culture merge into perfect harmony. Whether you are a lover of hiking, passionate about history or simply a lover of nature, this place will certainly captivate you with its enchanting beauty and suggestive atmospheres.

CUISINE AND WINES OF BASILICATA: SAVORING THE FLAVORS OF AUTHENTIC ITALIAN TRADITION

If from a visual perspective, Basilicata offers unique and enchanting places, taste and smell also get the chance to encounter unparalleled experiences. The cuisine of Basilicata has preserved the intact and authentic flavors of the past, without closing itself off to modernity, able to enhance your palate with unique tastes.

Imagine enjoying traditional culinary delights while seated at an antique wooden table, covered by a white lace tablecloth, surrounded by the scent of garlic and olive oil dancing in the air, as the sun sets, painting the sky with strokes of pink and orange. Complement all of this with a local wine, a true liquid poetry that contains all the history and tradition of these enchanting places and their pristine corners, and the expert hand of those who live and continually work the land.

In the various dishes, wisely used seasonal ingredients, local products, recipes passed down from generation to generation, will bear witness to a deep and respectful love for the land. The crusco pepper, the extra virgin olive oil, the bread of Matera, the Podolico caciocavallo cheese, each bite will tell you about a place that has preserved the authenticity of its flavors over time.

Typical Cuisine of Basilicata

Let's begin our culinary journey exploring the very roots of Lucanian cuisine, a tribute to authenticity, simplicity, and love for the products of the earth. Traditional dishes of Basilicata are born from genuine, seasonal ingredients, handpicked under the blue sky and warm sun of Southern Italy. In every dish, you can perceive a humility and respect for nature that touch the heart as much as the palate.

Your initial encounter with Lucanian cuisine might occur through a dish of handmade pasta, like the famous "strascinati" or "orecchiette", served with a simple tomato and cruschi pepper sauce, dried in the sun and then fried until they become crispy. Every bite of this pasta reveals a symphony of flavors: the acidity of the tomato, the sweet and smoked cruschi pepper, the aromatic garlic, and the virgin olive oil. A dish like this, made with skilled hands, evokes the warmth of home kitchens, the joy of large family meals, the laughter of a grandfather telling stories of times past.

Later on, you might try the "pignata", an ancient dish of lamb cooked in a wood-fired oven, slowly, in a terracotta pot with potatoes, onions, peppers, and tomatoes. The meat, left to cook for hours, becomes tender and succulent, melting in your mouth, releasing its rich and profound flavor, awakening memories of special Sundays, festive moments, occasions when everyone gathered to celebrate.

In Basilicata, even vegetables hold a place of honor. Take the "lampascione", a bulb with a bitter taste that, after being boiled and flavored with oil, vinegar, and chili pepper, becomes a unique side dish or appetizer. Its strong flavor awakens the senses, stimulates the appetite, and leaves a sense of wonder at the earth's ability to create so much variety.

Basilicata is also famous for its bread, particularly that of Matera, a rustic naturally-leavened bread baked in wood-fired ovens that has an unmistakable flavor. Its scent of wheat, wood, and yeast evokes waking up in a country house, the warmth of the oven, the patient wait while the dough rises, transforming into bread that's crispy on the outside and soft inside.

And how can we not mention the "Podolico Caciocavallo", a stringy cheese made with the milk of a particular breed of cattle, the Podolic. Its intense and slightly spicy flavor fills the mouth, leaving a persistent and pleasant aftertaste. It is the taste of tradition, of respect for animals, of the patience of the cheesemaker who works the cheese with care and passion.

Each of these dishes brings forth an emotion, a sensory journey that puts us in contact with the earth, with its seasons, with its people. It's an experience that touches the soul, that makes us feel part of a long and rich history, that makes us appreciate the beauty and simplicity of life. It's an invitation to slow down, to savor each bite, each sip of wine, each shared moment around a table. Welcome to the world of Basilicata's flavors.

Recommendations on the Best Restaurants, Local Products, and Wines to Try

As we continue our journey through the flavors of Basilicata, we now delve into the heart of Lucanian hospitality, exploring the best restaurants, the finest local products, and the wines of this enchanting region.

If you're seeking a true culinary experience in Basilicata, "Re Santi" in Matera is a restaurant that deserves a visit. This welcoming place, carved into the caves of the Sassi city, masterfully combines traditional Lucanian cuisine with a modern reinterpretation. We recommend trying their strascinati with sausage and cruschi peppers, a dish that will make you feel the warmth and passion of authentic cooking.

In Potenza, the restaurant "Al San Rocco" offers gourmet Lucanian cuisine, where the excellence of the local product is married to the chef's creativity. Don't miss their version of "baccalà alla lucana", a riot of sea and land flavors that will leave you speechless.

For an unforgettable gastronomic experience, we recommend visiting "La Locanda di Alia" in Castelmezzano, one of the most beautiful villages in Italy. Here you can savor traditional dishes such as lamb alla pignata or sweet and sour lampascioni, all while enjoying a breathtaking view of the Lucanian Dolomites.

Lastly, a trip to Basilicata would not be complete without tasting its wines. Aglianico del Vulture is the undisputed king of Lucanian wines. We recommend visiting the "Cantine del Notaio" winery in Rionero in Vulture, where you can taste this full-bodied red wine rich in flavor and discover the art of winemaking.

If you are a lover of white wine, try the "Greco di Basilicata", an aromatic and fruity wine. A visit to the "Basilisco" winery in Barile will allow you to taste this amazing white wine and enjoy a panoramic view of the surrounding vineyards.

EVENTS AND FESTIVALS - CELEBRATING THE CULTURE OF BASILICATA

Basilicata is a land that vibrates with culture, traditions, and colorful celebrations. Every event and festival here tells a unique story, invites you to immerse yourself in its social fabric, and leaves you eager to discover more. Both religious and civil celebrations are open to everyone, ready to make you feel the hospitality and warmth typical of southern Italy, with its folklore and traditions.

Events you absolutely can't miss

Feast of San Biagio, in Maratea (February)

Maratea wakes up to the feast of its patron saint with a procession, fireworks, and an abundance of culinary specialties. A perfect taste of religious devotion and Lucanian celebration.

Carnival of Tricarico (March)

The vibrant Carnival of Tricarico welcomes you into a world of masks, dances, and traditional songs. With its parades and local culinary delicacies, Tricarico shows the most festive side of Basilicata.

Flight of the Angel, Pietrapertosa and Castelmezzano (Summer)

Prepare to fly among the peaks of the Lucanian Dolomites! The thrilling Flight of the Angel gives you an unforgettable experience and a breathtaking view of the natural beauty of Basilicata.

Matera Balloon Festival (Summer): Matera dresses up in colors during the Balloon Festival. With its hot air balloons flying over the Sassi, Matera transforms into a living masterpiece.

Maratea Jazz Festival (July)

Jazz makes its way through the narrow streets of Maratea during the summer. With internationally renowned artists and outdoor concerts, the Maratea Jazz Festival is a must for music lovers.

Feast of the Madonna Bruna, Matera (July 2)

The fervent celebration of the Madonna Bruna in Matera is a mix of religious devotion and popular festivity. The procession, the fascinating cart race, and the fireworks are not-to-be-missed events.

Aglianica Wine Festival, Barile (July)

The Aglianico del Vulture festival is a true homage to the wine heritage of Basilicata. Seminars, workshops, and tastings will take you into the heart of the Lucanian wine world.

Potentino Ferragosto, Potenza (August 15)

Ferragosto in Potenza is a vibrant and colorful summer festivity, with concerts, dances, and fireworks transforming the city into a center of celebration.

Feast of San Rocco, Senise (August 16)

Senise pays homage to its patron saint with music, dances, and local culinary specialties, including the famous cruschi peppers.

Living Nativity Scene, Matera (December)

Matera, with its Sassi, offers a unique setting for a living nativity scene. The ancient city of stone transforms into a living Bethlehem, bringing the Nativity to life.

But it's not just the ones listed above that are events in Basilicata, many others reflect the rich culture and traditions of the region:

Feast of San Giuliano, Melfi (May)

This is one of the oldest and most important patron saint celebrations in the region. It takes place in Melfi, a city rich in history, and sees a grand procession through the streets, with the statue of the saint carried on the shoulders by the faithful.

Sagra della Varola, Melfi (December)

During the Christmas period, Melfi hosts the Sagra della Varola, an ancient rite that involves the creation of a wooden candlestick adorned with dried fruit. The streets light up with these creations, creating a magical atmosphere.

Lucania Film Festival, Pisticci (August)

This international short film and documentary festival takes place in the picturesque setting of Pisticci. It's an opportunity to discover new talents and artistic visions, with a particular focus on social and environmental themes.

Rite of the Pappamusci, Ferrandina (Holy Week)

During Holy Week, Ferrandina hosts the Rite of the Pappamusci. This ancient tradition sees a group of hooded men, the Pappamusci, silently moving through the streets on a penitential journey.

Soup Festival, Potenza (April): This culinary event celebrates soup, a simple but delicious dish that is part of the Lucanian tradition. During the festival, visitors can taste different variants of soup and vote for their favorite.

International Folklore Festival, Potenza (July): This festival celebrates traditional dances and music from around the world. Folkloric groups from different countries perform in the streets of Potenza, creating an atmosphere of celebration and cultural sharing.

IMMERSIVE EXPERIENCES - LIVING THE LIFE OF BASILICATA

Basilicata, a place where life flows intensely, filled with stories, flavors, and images. This region, so deeply rooted in its past yet vibrant with a lively present, offers an authentic and unforgettable travel experience, far from the mass tourism routes.

The entire territory is an invitation to let yourself be embraced by a generous and authentic culture, to experience the sincere joy of everyday life. Basilicata is a journey through the colors of its traditions, the aromas of its laden tables, the whisper of its ancient villages, and the majesty of its untouched landscapes.

Living Basilicata means discovering its natural resources, set in a frame of beautiful landscapes among the Lucanian Dolomites (which we have already discussed), natural parks, and coasts washed by the Tyrrhenian and Ionian Seas. It also means immersing yourself in its rich traditions, in its popular festivals that mix the sacred and the profane, in its ancient craft practices, and in the culinary art that smells of earth and love for local products.

Here, every stone tells a story, every face reveals a trace of time, every dish celebrates the art of good food. Living Basilicata means listening to these stories, meeting these faces, savoring these flavors. And it means doing it slowly, with the same slowness with which fruits mature on the branches of its centuries-old olive trees, with which its gentle and fertile hills stretch out to the horizon.

Everything told so far and everything that will follow will open the doors to a series of immersive experiences that will allow you to live Basilicata in all its authenticity and intensity. They will be experiences that will leave a mark, that will become precious memories, that will make you say: "Yes, I have lived Basilicata".

Because living Basilicata is not just visiting it. It's absorbing it, understanding it, loving it. And, ultimately, it's leaving a piece of your heart among its gentle hills, its enchanted villages, its welcoming people. Thus, even when you are far away, you will still feel the call of Basilicata. And you will understand that a part of you has remained there, in that wonderful land, waiting for a new, exciting journey.

Living Basilicata in an authentic and participatory way is an experience that goes beyond the simple concept of tourism. This fascinating and welcoming land gives unforgettable emotions and experiences, making you an active part of its vibrant daily life. And every detail, every little ritual, every gesture, and every story lived here becomes a precious memory to keep and an indissoluble bond with this land of authentic beauty.

The rituals of food preparation, the ancient pastoral traditions, the exploration of Carlo Levi's literary landscape, the active participation in local festivals - all these experiences will make you deeply immersed in the essence of Lucanian life.

For example, if you are fortunate enough to witness the process in which bread is kneaded, you might feel the warmth of the hands of the master bakers, witnesses of an art that is passed down from generation to generation, or sense the smell of the wheat, the taste of the salt, the humidity of the water, simple ingredients that transform into bread, a primordial food, a symbol of sharing.

Aliano

In the village of Aliano, you will walk the paths tread by Carlo Levi (a writer exiled here during the Fascist regime), and you'll sense the atmosphere of introspection and discovery that pervaded his days of confinement. You can al-

most hear the echo of his words, the silences of his thoughts, the beat of his heart full of affection for a land and a people forgotten by time.

Maratea

At sea, with the fishermen of Maratea, you will learn the ancient art of fishing, the patience of waiting, the respect for the sea and its rhythms. You will feel the freshness of the wind, the taste of salt on your skin, the euphoria of a bountiful catch.

Participating in the local festivals and fairs we have already mentioned, you will let yourself be infected by the joy and cheerfulness of the people, you will lose yourself in the rhythms of the music, in the dances, in the colors. You will taste the authentic flavors of Lucanian cuisine, you will discover ancient dishes and recipes, you will celebrate the art of hospitality.

These are not just tourist experiences. They are fragments of real life, precious moments that put you in direct contact with Lucanian culture. They are experiences that touch the heart and soul, transforming every visit into a unique and unforgettable adventure. Basilicata will not only be a destination on your journey, but a lifelong companion that you will always carry with you, in your memories and in your heart. And every time you think back to these experiences, you will feel the call of this wonderful land, it will seem as though you can hear its breath, feel its warmth, and understand that a piece of you has remained there, among its mountains and its seas, in its streets and its squares, in the laughter of its people and in the silence of its stones. And it will seem to you, once again, like being home.

Opportunities to participate in artisanal, agricultural, gastronomic, or cultural activities

Basilicata's cultural, gastronomic, and artisanal heritage is a rich and varied mosaic of millenary traditions, age-old techniques, unique and refined flavors.

Visiting Basilicata also means immersing yourself in this reality, actively participating in the life of the area, learning its arts, savoring its products, getting to know closely the work of those who keep these traditions alive.

Artisanal workshops

An unmissable experience is the visit to the artisan workshops, where you can admire masters at work in their studios, transforming clay into valuable ceramics, wood into meticulous sculptures, iron into intricate artifacts. In Matera, the stonemasons' workshops are living laboratories of an art as ancient as humankind, where you can not only observe but also get your hands dirty, trying to carve tuff under the expert guidance of the artisans.

Visiting the farms

Agriculture in Basilicata is strongly linked to the land, its rhythm, its products. Visit a farm, participate in the olive harvest, smell the intense aroma of freshly squeezed oil, the bitterness of black olives, the sweetness of green olives. In spring, the hills turn red for the Melfi strawberry harvest, an experience not to be missed to immerse yourself in the colors and flavors of this land.

Cooking workshops

Lucanian gastronomy is a plunge into authentic flavors, a journey between ancient traditions and creative innovations. You can participate in cooking workshops, where you'll learn to prepare traditional dishes: from "orecchiette" with breadcrumbs, to "peperoni cruschi", from "scoratelle" to "baccalà alla lucana". You can also visit the cellars, where you can taste local wines, and understand the passion and dedication hidden behind every bottle.

The culture of Basilicata is a mix of stories, languages, art, and traditions. You can participate in tarantella lessons, the popular Lucanian dance, and let yourself be carried away by the overwhelming rhythm and contagious joy of the musicians and dancers. You can visit museums, where you can discover the region's rich artistic and historical heritage, from prehistory to contemporary art. And you can participate in the numerous cultural events that animate the region throughout the year: film festivals, art exhibitions, theatrical performances, poetry readings, concerts of traditional music, and much more.

Each experience in Basilicata is a piece of the mosaic of this region, a tile that will help you understand its soul, get to know its people, feel the warmth, colors, sounds, smells of this land on your skin. And each experience will be a precious memory, an indissoluble bond with Basilicata, a story to tell when you are back home, with the certainty of having left a piece of your heart in this wonderful land.

BASILICATA'S NATURAL TREASURES: NATIONAL PARKS, BEACHES, AND BREATHTAKING LANDSCAPES

Basilicata, nestled in the heart of southern Italy, is a land of extraordinary beauty, a varied landscape where nature has painted scenes of unparalleled splendor. From the Apennine mountains, through lush forests and fertile plains, to the coasts lapped by the Ionian and Tyrrhenian Seas, Basilicata offers a captivating ensemble of natural landscapes, ready to be discovered and admired. Imagine walking among the rocky mountains, in a silence only interrupted by the wind's whisper and the song of birds. To breathe the crisp air of the woods, to admire the flight of the golden eagle or to meet the gaze of an Apennine wolf. Or to stroll along the golden beaches, while the crystal-clear water gently laps the shore and children's laughter fills the air.

Every step, every breath, every glance reveals a hidden Basilicata, a Basilicata that speaks with the voice of nature, a Basilicata that will surprise you with its wild and untouched beauty. From the high peaks of Pollino, with its loricato pines and eagles, to the coasts of Maratea, with its small coves and azure waters, every corner of Basilicata is a treasure to discover.

In this chapter, we will delve into the national parks of the region, exploring the richness of its fauna and flora, the grandeur of its mountains, the tranquility of its lakes. We will explore its beaches, some of the most beautiful and untouched in the Mediterranean, and admire its breathtaking landscapes, where the human hand has perfectly integrated with nature, creating a harmonious and fascinating balance.

Through the paths of the parks, along the banks of the beaches, on the tops of the mountains, I invite you on a journey through the natural treasures of Basilicata, to discover a land that knows how to surprise and enchant, that knows how to speak to the heart and soul, that knows how to make you fall in love with its pure and wild beauty. A land that, once discovered, can never be forgotten.

Basilicata is a real paradise for lovers of trekking and outdoor activities, thanks to its untouched nature and its varied and exciting landscapes. From north to south, the region offers a series of routes and itineraries suitable for everyone, from beginners to more experienced hikers, offering unique emotions and breathtaking views.

Let's start with the Pollino National Park, a place that never ceases to amaze. With its imposing mountains, wild rivers and ancient woods, Pollino is a real paradise for hikers. The largest protected area in Italy, extending between Basilicata and Calabria for about 200,000 hectares. This wonderful park offers a diversity of landscapes, flora and fauna truly unique, combined with invaluable historical and cultural richness.

The Pollino Park is dominated by the homonymous mountain range, which includes the Pollino massif and the Orsomarso massif. Mount Pollino, at 2,248 meters, is the highest peak in the park and offers breathtaking views of the surrounding landscapes. During winter, these peaks are covered with snow, offering postcard-like scenes.

One of the symbols of the park is the Loricato Pine, a species of pine found only in a few other regions of the world. Its characteristic figure, with bark that seems formed by small plates, gives the landscape an almost prehistoric appearance.

The fauna of the Pollino Park is equally extraordinary: it is home to wolves, deer, golden eagles and many other animals, some of which are protected species or endangered.

The park offers countless opportunities for trekking and hiking lovers, with over 600 km of marked trails. Among these, the trail leadingto the source of the Lao river is one of the most suggestive. The Lao River is indeed one of the longest torrential rivers in Italy and its source is a place of rare beauty.

Among the most evocative routes, we mention the Loricato Pine Path, which leads to the Serra delle Ciavole, one of the highest points in the park, from where you can enjoy a breathtaking panoramic view. But the Pollino Park is not only nature: it is also a place rich in history and traditions. In the park territory, there are numerous ancient villages, such as Morano Calabro, recognized as one of the most beautiful villages in Italy, and Rotonda, famous for its Fauna Museum.

Another unmissable excursion is the discovery of the Lucanian Dolomites, in the heart of the Gallipoli Cognato Regional Park. Here, you can test your endurance with the exciting "via

ferrata" route that allows you to admire the fascinating rock formations up close. For climbing love(not by chance we have already devoted space to it in a previous chapter), the via ferrata routes offer a unique experience of adrenaline and spectacular views. If you are lovers of more tranquil nature experiences, the Pantano di Pignola Nature Reserve offers the opportunity for long walks on its well-marked trails, breathing fresh and pure air and observing the avifauna and typical flora of this area. Discovering the coast, we recommend a walk along the paths of the Policoro Pantano Forest Nature Reserve, where the forest meets the sea. Here, between swims, you can stroll among pine forests and dunes, admiring the flora and fauna of the reserve. finally, don't forget to explore the paths of the Murgia Materana Park, which offer panoramic views of the famous Sassi di Matera. Among the various options, the Path of the Rupestrian Churches will lead you to discover the numerous churches carved into the tuff that characterize the park. Remember, Basilicata is a place to explore slowly, taking the time to savor every moment, every landscape, every breath of fresh air. So pack your backpack, put on comfortable shoes and let the beauty of this region guide you, through mountains, woods, rivers, and coasts, for an outdoor experience you will not forget.

YOU WILL GET BACK HOME WITH A LOVING HEART: REFLECTIONS AND MEMORIES OF A TRIP TO BASILICATA

Every journey we take changes us in some way, adds a piece to the mosaic of our life, paints our memories with new shades. This is particularly true when we visit places like Basilicata, which have the power to touch the heart and soul, leaving us with an indelible imprint. When you say goodbye to Basilicata, it won't be a farewell, but a see you later.

Leaving behind the imposing peaks of Pollino, the characteristic Sassi of Matera, the coasts washed by crystal clear seas, you will feel a sense of melancholy, but also profound gratitude. You will have savored the genuineness of its cuisine, shared stories and laughter with its people, explored historical villages and breathtaking landscapes. And every place, every flavor, every smile, will stay with you, precious memories of an unforgettable journey. You will think back to the walks in the green of its parks, the emotions felt while admiring the Lucanian Dolomites from the ferrata path, the days spent along the golden beaches bathed by the waters of the Adriatic and Tyrrhenian seas. Images of Basilicata will accompany you as you return to everyday life, like a sweet and nostalgic melody.

You will find yourself smiling, thinking back to the evenings spent in typical restaurants, where you discovered the authentic flavors of Lucanian cuisine. To the discovery of local wines, which made you appreciate every meal as a unique experience.

To the typical products, brought home as treasures to prolong the journey experience a little. And, above all, you will think about the people you met. The inhabitants of Basilicata, with their warm and sincere hospitality, will have made you feel at home. They will have told you stories, shared traditions, opened the doors of their homes and their hearts. And you will have discovered that, beyond the wonderful places and unique experiences, it's the people who make a trip truly unforgettable. Returning home, you will carry with you not only souvenirs and photographs, but something much more precious: the experience of an authentic region, far from mass tourism, where traditions are still alive and where beauty is found in every corner. A place that, once discovered, remains in the heart. And so, even though you will be physically distant, a part of you will always remain in Basilicata, among the wild mountains of Pollino, the paved streets of its historical villages, the waves of its sea. And know that, wherever you are, Basilicata will wait for you, ready to give you more emotions, more discoveries, more stories to tell.

Every corner of this land will invite you to return. Perhaps it will be the memory of the taste of a traditional dish, the longing for breathtaking landscapes, the need to find that feeling of peace and authenticity that only Basilicata can offer.

Perhaps, without even realizing it, you will find yourself dreaming of its mountains, its villages, its coasts, and you will know that it is time to return to that region that, more than any other, will have known how to win you over. In summary, Basilicata is a land of intense beauty, rich and deep culture, authentic flavors, and genuine people. It is a land that invites discovery, exploration, sharing.

A land that leaves a mark, that enters the heart and stays there, a sweet memory of unforgettable moments. So, once home, while sharing stories and memories of this trip with friends and family, you will discover that Basilicata has changed you in some way. You will have a new appreciation for simplicity, for natural beauty, for art and culture. And, above all, you will have a new awareness: that of having discovered a special place, a place worth visiting again and again.

With these reflections and memories, we wish you a safe journey home. But know that Basilicata is waiting for you, always ready to offer you new adventures and unforgettable memories. And we, for our part, can't wait to welcome you back to this wonderful region, to guide you to discover its hidden treasures, to share with you its traditions, its flavors, its beauties. Because we are sure that, once you have tasted life in Basilicata, you will always want to return.

CALABRIA

TRAVEL GUIDE

On the Lookout for Italy's Undiscovered Southern Delights?

Traverse Calabria's Lesser-Known Gems and Relish the Authentically Rich
Flavors of its Regional Cuisine.

LEAVE A
1 CLICK
REVIEW

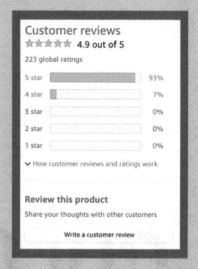

Customer reviews

★★★★★ 4.9 out of 5

223 global ratings

5 star		93%
4 star		7%
3 star		0%
2 star		0%
1 star		0%

⌄ How customer reviews and ratings work

Review this product

Share your thoughts with other customers

Write a customer review

SCAN THIS QR
TO GET TO THE
BOOK FASTER

I would be incredibly thankful if you could take just 60 seconds to write a brief review on Amazon, even if it's just a few sentences!

INTRODUCTION
TO CALABRIA

Picture the sun hanging lazily in the azure sky, its warm rays kissing olive groves and vineyards, while the rhythmic ebb and flow of the Ionian and Tyrrhenian Seas serenade the rugged coastline. Welcome to Calabria, the toe of Italy's boot, an untamed region waiting to be discovered, a land where ancient history and lively traditions are tightly woven into the fabric of everyday life.

To say that Calabria is rich in beauty would be an understatement. A joy to the senses, this southern paradise surprises at every turn. Rolling hills adorn the countryside, their verdant hues blending seamlessly with the endless blue of the skies. Century-old olive trees stand as sentinels, silent witnesses to the passage of time, while vines heavy with plump, juicy grapes promise the delicious, ruby-red wines the region is celebrated for.

Beyond the bucolic landscape, the craggy mountains reaching up to brush the sky create an exhilarating contrast. Here, the Aspromonte and Sila ranges offer adventurous souls trails that take them through verdant woodlands, past gushing waterfalls, and up peaks that provide breathtaking views of the region. Amid this natural splendor, the intrepid will find ancient villages nestled, each a time capsule preserving Calabria's fascinating past and vibrant culture.

Calabria is not just a haven for nature lovers. History buffs will marvel at the region's rich heritage that spans millennia, with remnants of Greek, Roman, and Byzantine civilizations etched into the Calabrian soil. From the Riace Bronzes, world-renowned Greek statues recovered from the sea, to the architectural wonders like the Aragonese Castle and the Norman-Hohenstaufen Castle, the history of Calabria is a captivating tale written in stone.

Moreover, no journey to Calabria is complete without savoring its gastronomic delights. Calabria is, after all, a place where meals are a celebration, where food is an expression of culture. Let your taste buds dance with 'nduja, a spicy, spreadable sausage, or be swept away by the robust flavors of Caciocavallo Silano cheese. Each dish is a testament to the region's culinary traditions, where simple, fresh ingredients are transformed into feasts for the senses.

Yet, what makes Calabria truly enchanting are its people. Calabrians, with their warm hospitality, create an atmosphere that makes everyone feel like family. They're proud custodians of their land and culture, always eager to share their stories, customs, and the joy of living.

Calabria awaits the curious traveler, those looking for authentic experiences and genuine connections. It offers a taste of the true Italian south, away from the tourist throngs that flock to Rome or Venice. It's a place to slow down, to relish in the sweet rhythm of life, to awaken the soul. This unpolished gem of southern Italy is more than just a destination—it's an immersive journey into a rich tapestry of landscapes, culture, history, and cuisine.

So come, explore Calabria—the region that Italy keeps for itself. Every twist and turn here holds a promise of discovery, where every moment becomes a cherished memory. From the rolling countryside and sandy beaches to the timeless villages and friendly locals, Calabria's allure lies in its contrasts and in its heartfelt hospitality. Come for the beauty, stay for the warmth and, when you leave, be prepared to take a piece of Calabria with you, etched forever in your heart.

Discovering Calabria:
Geography & General Information

Situated at the southernmost tip of Italy, Calabria is the captivating toe to the country's boot, straddled by the sparkling Ionian and Tyrrhenian Seas. The region is almost a peninsula within a peninsula, reaching out towards Sicily, with the Strait of Messina serving as a narrow divide. Its unique geographical position has not only shaped its vibrant history but also its diverse landscapes and the character of its people.

Calabria's geography is a stunning mixture of dramatic mountain ranges, lush forests, and breathtaking coastlines. The region is predominantly mountainous, with the rugged Pollino Mountains dominating the north and the austere Sila and Aspromonte Ranges occupying the central and southern areas, respectively. These highlands provide a refreshing contrast to the idyllic beaches and steep cliffs along the coast, painting a picture of a land where nature thrives in its most majestic forms.

The coastal areas offer an intoxicating blend of vibrant resort towns and quaint fishing villages, while the inland is punctuated by ancient hilltop settlements. The Ionian coast on the eastern side is adorned with long, sandy beaches, while the Tyrrhenian coast to the west presents scenic rocky coves and towering cliffs.

Calabria's climate, too, mirrors its varied geography. Coastal areas enjoy a Mediterranean climate with hot, dry summers and mild, wet winters. The mountains, however, experience a colder, alpine climate with heavy snowfall in winter - a testament to Calabria's delightful climatic duality.

The region is also home to several national parks, teeming with diverse flora and fauna. Among them, the Pollino National Park, Italy's largest protected area, stands out with its rugged landscapes, rare plants, and animals, offering an untouched wilderness for nature enthusiasts to explore.

Brief History of Calabria

Time travel isn't just a pipe dream in Calabria. Every cobblestone street, every weathered building, every towering monument is a window into the past, transporting you through a fascinating journey across the millennia. Calabria, cradled by the Ionian and Tyrrhenian Seas, has seen a multitude of cultures ebb and flow like the gentle waves that kiss its shores.

The story begins in prehistoric times when the first humans set foot on this land, leaving behind intriguing cave art as their legacy. The Bronze Age saw the flourishing of the Ausonian-Italic tribes, which marked the beginning of Calabria's journey into civilization.

As the wheel of time turned, the region became a hotspot for mighty civilizations. The Greeks arrived in the 8th century BC, establishing prosperous colonies and imprinting their profound culture onto the landscape. They named the region 'Italy', originally Italía, which extended to encompass the whole peninsula over time. The ruins of the ancient cities of Sybaris, Croton, and Locri bear testament to their grandeur and ingenuity.

The Romans, captivated by this sun-drenched land, arrived next, integrating Calabria into their vast empire. The Via Popilia-Annia, an ancient Roman road, still snakes its way across the region, a silent reminder of Roman engineering genius. Their reign too eventually gave way, and Calabria became a chessboard for the Goths, Byzantines, Lombards, and Saracens, each leaving their distinct mark.

The Middle Ages painted Calabria with a different brush. Feudal lords, Norman knights, and Spanish viceroys took turns to rule, leaving behind castles, fortresses, and stories of power struggles and conquests. The Aragonese Castle in Reggio Calabria and the Norman Castle in Cosenza, their stones imbued with tales of yore, stand as proud guardians of Calabria's multifaceted history.

More recently, the region bore witness to the tumultuous events of World War II before embarking on a path of renewal and growth in post-war Italy. Today, Calabria is a melting pot of cultures, its history echoing in the local dialects, folklore, architecture, and the spirit of its people.

As you wander through Calabria, remember, each footprint you leave behind treads upon a land that has been the canvas of human history for thousands of years. The echoes of the past live on in the present, making Calabria not just a place on a map, but a vibrant chronicle of the human journey. Step into Calabria, and you step into a living, breathing history book. Just remember to tread lightly, for in Calabria, history lies just beneath your feet.

Travel Information:When to Go, How to Get There, and Getting Around

When contemplating a journey to Calabria, one must consider not only the alluring destinations awaiting them, but also the logistics of the journey itself. From the best times to visit to the nuances of getting around, understanding these practical elements can help you fully immerse yourself in the captivating spirit of Calabria.

When to Go

Calabria is enchanting year-round, but each season carries its own unique charm. Summer, from June to August, is undoubtedly the peak tourist season, where sun-kissed beaches sparkle under a near-perpetual sun and the azure sea invites endless swimming and water sports. The highlands, meanwhile, offer a refreshing respite from the summer heat.

Spring (April to June) and Autumn (September and October) are equally enticing. The temperatures are milder, landscapes burst into a riot of colors, and local festivals bring the towns and villages to life. These are also ideal seasons for outdoor activities such as hiking and cycling.

Winter, though quieter, offers a unique perspective of Calabria. The mountains don snow-capped peaks, offering a range of winter sports. Plus, with fewer tourists around, it can be a great time to enjoy a more personal encounter with the region's rich history and culture.

How to Get There

Calabria, being the toe of Italy's boot, is well-connected by various modes of transport. Lamezia Terme, the region's main airport, serves both domestic and international flights. There are also airports in Reggio Calabria and Crotone.

If you prefer a scenic journey, train services connect Calabria with other parts of Italy. The 'boot train' from Milan or Rome to Lamezia Terme or Reggio Calabria is a popular choice.

For those who relish road trips, well-maintained highways and coastal roads offer breathtaking views along the journey. Ferries also operate between Sicily and Reggio Calabria for those venturing from the island.

Getting Around

Getting around in Calabria offers its own adventure. Trains and buses connect the main towns, although services may be less frequent to smaller villages. Renting a car provides flexibility and allows access to more remote areas. And for the coastal regions, nothing beats the romantic appeal of exploring by boat.

Biking is a popular option, especially in the hilly countryside where the pan-oramic views are a worthy reward for your efforts. Finally, remember that some of the best parts of Calabria are tucked away in narrow lanes or atop hills - areas best explored on foot.

For the mountainous hinterland and its unspoiled nature, the best option is to move around by car, which makes it possible to reach otherwise unreachable places and not risk standing still for hours waiting for public transportation.

This will also guarantee you direct contact with the meandering nature of this region, and its essence.

Armed with these travel insights, you're ready to embark on a journey that prom-ises rich rewards – an intimate encounter with the heart and soul of Southern Italy that is Calabria. Embrace the journey, and let Calabria reveal itself to you.

Calabria and the enchantment of its cities

In the heart of Southern Italy, a land steeped in rich history and dazzling beauty unfolds. Welcome to Calabria, the region where rugged mountains meet tur-quoise seas, where age-old traditions remain alive in bustling cities and tranquil villages. Here, five remarkable cities, each possessing its unique character, serve as jewels in Calabria's stunning crown. We are talking about Cosenza, Catanzaro, Reggio Calabria, Crotone and Vibo Valentia. Follow me and discover all these beautiful cities.

Cosenza

As you wind your way into Calabria, nestled amid the peaks and valleys of the Crati and Busento rivers, you'll find a city that is a beguiling mix of the ancient and the avant-garde - welcome to Cosenza, the vibrant beating heart of the re-gion.

Cosenza is a city of two worlds, a dynamic juxtaposition of past and present. Stepping into its Old Town, or "Cosenza Vecchia" (old Cosenza), is like turning the pages of a living history book. Its winding medieval streets and stone-cobbled piazzas transport you back to the days when this city was a Byzantine stronghold. A walk through these narrow lanes, lined with terracotta-roofed houses, is a delightful journey of explora-tion.

"Cosenza Vecchia" is crowned by the commanding sight of the Norman-Swabian Castle. From its elevated position, this silent sentinel overlooks the city in stoic majesty, preserving centuries of history within its stone walls. Its ruins, though worn by time, echo tales of knights, kings, and intrigue.

Below the castle, the Cathedral of Cosenza, a UNESCO World Heritage Site, is an-

other testament to the city's rich historical past. Its Romanesque architecture, coupled with the grandeur of its Baroque interior, creates a unique atmosphere of calm and reverence (we will discuss this more fully in the next chapters). The cathedral houses the tomb of Queen Isabella of Aragon, adding a touch of royal prestige to its charm.

Stepping out of the time capsule of "Cosenza Vecchia", the city unfurls into a modern, cosmopolitan metropolis. Contemporary Cosenza is a lively cultural hub, filled with modern art, music, and gastronomy. From the striking design of the Calabria National Library to the visionary sculptures of the open-air Bilotti Museum, contemporary art thrives in this city.

The Corso Mazzini, the city's main thoroughfare, is a vibrant hive of activity, dotted with boutiques, cafes, and bars. Here, the locals, affectionately known as cosentini, enjoy their evening promenade or 'passeggiata,' a delightful ritual of socializing and people-watching.

Beyond the city's artistic and architectural allure, Cosenza's rich culinary tradition is another captivating tale to tell. Its cuisine, a smorgasbord of hearty rustic dishes, reflects the bounty of its surrounding landscape. Whether it's the tantalizing 'pitta mpigliata,' a sweet Christmas pastry, or the savory 'soppressata,' a local cured sausage, Cosenza's gastronomy is an authentic expression of its cultural identity.

Every year, the city hosts the Feast of San Giuseppe, a spirited celebration that sees the streets come alive with music, processions, and traditional 'tavole di San Giuseppe,' tables laden with local delicacies dedicated to St. Joseph. The festival encapsulates the city's love for communal celebration, reflecting the warm and welcoming nature of its people.

Cosenza, with its duality, draws you in with its harmonious blend of antiquity and modernity. Its culture, deeply rooted in history, yet blossoming with contemporary innovation, mirrors the soul of Calabria itself - a region where traditions and progress interweave seamlessly to create a captivating tapestry of experiences.

As we continue our journey, allow the story of Cosenza, a city that seamlessly marries its past with the present, to linger in your thoughts. For it's a testament to the region's timeless charm and an ode to the Calabrian spirit of resilience and reinvention. Welcome to Cosenza, where every corner holds a new discovery, and every discovery is a cherished memory in the making.

Embracing Catanzaro: The City of the Three Hills

As we navigate through the varied tapestry of Calabria, our journey brings us to

Catanzaro, often hailed as the "City of the Three Hills." Perched atop a narrow ridge between the Ionian Sea and the Tyrrhenian Sea, Catanzaro captivates with its stunning panoramas, an intriguing blend of history, and a vibrant contemporary scene.

Catanzaro's distinctive geography is a central character in its narrative. The city expands over three hills, each unfolding its unique chapter of the Catanzaro story. The hills of Episcopio, Pancrazio, and San Rocco together sketch a dynamic topography that makes Catanzaro both a scenic delight and an exciting exploration.

As you wander around Episcopio, the oldest of the three hills, it's hard to miss the awe-inspiring sight of the Basilica dell'Immacolata. With its imposing façade and intricate interiors, the Basilica stands as an eloquent testimony to Catanzaro's deeply embedded religious heritage. The hill is also home to the Bishop's Palace and the Seminary, enhancing the ecclesiastical ambiance of the area.

Pancrazio, often considered the heart of the city, brims with life and character. The Piazza Matteotti, a bustling hub of activity, is surrounded by the city's key administrative buildings, including the Prefecture and the Town Hall. A short walk away, the Park of Remembrance offers tranquil retreats, where locals and visitors alike can unwind amidst lush greenery and sweeping views of the city below.

However, Catanzaro isn't just about stately buildings and panoramic vistas. San Rocco, the third hill, illustrates this perfectly. It's a vibrant, modern neighborhood teeming with shops, restaurants, and bars, each reflecting the effervescent spirit of Catanzaro's people.

A trip to Catanzaro isn't complete without a visit to the Bisantis Bridge. One of the highest bridges in Europe, it symbolizes the city's progress and innovation. Standing atop this architectural marvel, with the stunning Catanzaro skyline stretched out beneath you, is an unforgettable  experience that speaks volumes about the city's forward-thinking ethos.

Yet, at the heart of its urban vibrancy, Catanzaro holds tight to its traditions. This city is celebrated as the 'capital of silk.' Delving into the art of silk production at the Silk Museum is like retracing the city's journey from a humble trading post to an important silk hub in the Mediterranean. The city's annual Silk Festival, with its colorful processions and market stalls showcasing exquisite silk crafts, paints a vivid picture of this ancient craft's enduring legacy.

Catanzaro's food culture, like its silk heritage, is deeply rooted in tradition. Local specialities, such as the delectable 'tartufo di Pizzo', a sumptuous chocolate and hazelnut gelato, or the 'fileja', a unique pasta variety often served with spicy 'nduja sauce, promise a gastronomic experience that lingers long after the last bite.

Yet, it's not just the sights, history, or cuisine that make Catanzaro special. It's the infectious energy of its people, their warmth, and their enduring love for their city. Whether it's the passion of the silk weavers, the jovial conversations in the city's cafes, or the enthusiastic welcome from the locals, the spirit of Catanzaro is its defining feature. It's a testament to a community's unwavering commitment to preserving their heritage while embracing the new.

In Catanzaro, the city of the three hills, the journey is as enriching as the destination. As you meander through its history, savour its culinary delights, and get swept up in its vibrant modernity, you'll understand why Catanzaro stands as a unique testament to the enchanting diversity of Calabria.

Reggio Calabria: Between Majestic Mountains and Mesmerizing Seas

Unveil your senses as we journey through Reggio Calabria, a city standing boldly at the edge of the world, the soles of its feet dipped in the Ionian and Tyrrhenian seas, whilst across the shimmering Strait of Messina, the hulking mass of Sicily's Mt. Etna looms in the distance. A majestic spectacle that stirs a sense of awe and fascination, and one of the many reasons why Reggio Calabria is one of Italy's most evocative destinations.

Reggio Calabria's heart beats in rhythm with the ebb and flow of the sea, a reminder of the city's age-old connection with the Mediterranean and its people. The Lungomare, considered one of the most beautiful promenades in Italy, is a testament to this symbiotic relationship. Here, palm trees sway lazily in the sea breeze, couples stroll hand-in-hand, and families savor gelato whilst bathing in the warm glow of the setting sun.

If you can tear your eyes away from the sea, you'll be met with the allure of Corso Garibaldi, the city's main artery and shopping hub. This bustling street, brimming with boutiques, restaurants, and gelaterias, embodies the vibrant, joyful spirit of the Calabrese people. Venture further into the heart of the city and you'll discover the Duomo di Reggio Calabria, a magnificent cathedral that symbolizes resilience and faith, having been rebuilt multiple times after numerous earthquakes.

In the National Archaeological Museum, history whispers from every corner. The star attraction here is the Riace Bronzes, two stunningly detailed Greek warrior statues discovered off the coast of Calabria in the 1970s. These remarkable masterpieces, with their enigmatic expressions and finely detailed anatomy, are a testament to the ancient world's skill and sophistication.

Beyond the city limits, Aspromonte National Park beckons with its verdant forests, rugged peaks, and abundant wildlife. This green heart of Calabria offers an invigorating escape for nature lovers and adventure seekers. Whether it's trekking along mountain trails, discovering hidden waterfalls, or picnicking amidst a symphony of birdsong, Aspromonte is an oasis of natural wonders.

Reggio Calabria is also a culinary paradise. Let your taste buds revel in the symphony of flavors that Calabrese cuisine offers. From the fiery 'nduja, a spreadable salami that packs a spicy punch, to the delicate sweetness of the red onions of Tropea, every dish is a celebration of the region's bountiful produce.

As day turns into night, the city comes alive in a riot of color and sound. The pulsating beats from the beach clubs echo across the waters, while the city's bars and clubs teem with locals and tourists alike, creating a vivacious nightlife scene.

And as the dawn breaks over Reggio Calabria, revealing the city in a soft, golden light, you'll understand the magic of this place. It's not just about the stunning views, the ancient history, or the flavorful cuisine. It's about the spirit of the people, their warmth, and hospitality that truly encapsulate the soul of this enchanting city. So come, explore, and let Reggio Calabria leave an indelible mark on your heart.

Crotone: A Coastal Gem Rich in Ancient History

Crotone, a city adorned with the radiant colors of southern Italy, awaits the traveler's curiosity with a timeless tale that echoes the echoes of ancient civilizations. Sun-kissed by the splendor of the Ionian Sea, Crotone, Calabria's eastern coastal marvel, basks in the beauty of its archeological treasures, resplendent nature, and genuine hospitality.

The city's roots delve deeply into the realms of the ancient world, having been a significant settlement during Magna Graecia's golden age. This splendid era has endowed Crotone with a wealth of historical landmarks that still bear witness to its former glory. The Archaeological Museum of Crotone is a veritable time capsule that offers a captivating journey through the city's illustrious past. Here, one can gaze upon the famed Hera Lacinia helmet, an ancient bronze artifact discovered in the sacred site of Capo Colonna, and other significant pieces that resonate with the city's vibrant history.

As you stroll through the city's historic center, the allure of the past is ever-present. The enchanting medieval Castle of Charles V majestically overlooks the city and the sea, its imposing presence a testament to Crotone's strategic importance

through the ages. Wander through its rooms and courtyards and let the tales of knights and nobility fill your imagination.

Yet, Crotone is not only about history. The city's charming streets are lined with a myriad of local eateries and shops where you can relish the gastronomic delights of Calabrian cuisine. Savory nduja, tantalizing seafood, and refreshing local wines – the tastes of Crotone are as rich as its history.

But a visit to Crotone would be incomplete without enjoying its splendid coastline. The city's beaches, such as Capo Rizzuto and the Marine Reserve, offer a perfect retreat for those seeking tranquil turquoise waters and sun-drenched shores. As the sun sets, the coastal promenade offers stunning views, the perfect conclusion to a day of exploration.

Crotone's verdant surroundings offer an array of nature activities. Explore the Sila mountains for hiking and mountain biking adventures, or spend a day birdwatching at the nature reserve of Lake Soverato. Crotone effortlessly melds the past with the present, the man-made with nature, in a warm, sunlit dance of Southern Italian life.

So, come and step into Crotone's rich tapestry of history, cuisine, and natural beauty. Discover a city where ancient legends intertwine with modern-day life, where the warmth of the sun is matched only by the warmth of the people. Crotone invites you to experience its mesmerizing tale, etched in stone, whispered by the sea, and waiting for you in the heart of Calabria.

Vibo Valentia: The City of Sunsets and Scenic Splendors

Vibo Valentia, one of Calabria's most magnificent hidden gems, lies in waiting for the traveler ready to discover its sublime splendors. Perched upon a hill overlooking the mesmerizing turquoise waters of the Tyrrhenian Sea, Vibo Valentia offers a unique blend of history, culture, and stunning natural beauty, all bathed in the warm, golden hues of the Calabrian sun.

The city's history stretches back millennia to its founding as the ancient Greek colony of Hipponion. Evidence of this rich past can still be discovered within its charming streets. At the heart of the city lies the impressive Norman-Swabian Castle, a monument to Vibo's strategic importance during the Middle Ages. Wander within its walls and let your imagination be filled with tales of knights, nobility, and the city's steadfast resilience.

Descending from the castle's heights, Vibo's historic center unfolds with an array of beautiful churches, fascinating archeological sites, and picturesque streets that carry the rhythm of Calabrian life. Among them, the Church of Santa Ruba, a charming edifice dating back to the 11th century, stands out with its imposing bell tower and the echoes of its storied past.

Yet, Vibo Valentia is not simply a destination for history lovers. As you meander through the city's alleyways, you will encounter a variety of local eateries serving mouthwatering dishes that highlight the richness of Calabrian cuisine. Be prepared for an explosion of flavors as you savor Vibo's famed 'nduja, a fiery spreadable salami, or the region's delicious pecorino cheese.

Beyond the city's confines, Vibo's stunning coastal and mountain landscapes are a haven for outdoor enthusiasts. The Costa degli Dei, or "Coast of the Gods," is renowned for its enchanting beaches and crystal-clear waters that stretch beneath towering cliffs. Here, picturesque towns like Tropea and Pizzo offer breathtaking views of the Tyrrhenian Sea and sublime sunsets that set the sky ablaze.

The nearby Vibo Valentia Marina serves as a gateway to the idyllic Aeolian Islands. Reachable by boat, these volcanic islands are a dream for those who enjoy

snorkeling, diving, or simply lounging on beautiful black and white sand beaches. Back on the mainland, the surrounding hills and mountains offer spectacular hiking routes that offer panoramic views over the Calabrian landscape.

Vibo Valentia, with its compelling blend of history, gastronomy, and stunning landscapes, is a testament to the varied experiences that Calabria offers. So, come and embark on an unforgettable journey into a city where the past and present harmoniously intertwine, where stunning sunsets paint the sky, and where every corner unveils a new chapter of Calabria's enchanting story.

Major attractions and historical sites

Sila National Park: A Vast Expanse of Pristine Wilderness

Tucked away within the heart of Calabria, Sila National Park offers an exhilarating escape into Italy's less-traveled terrain. The park, often referred to as the "green lungs of Italy," spans over a vast 73,695 hectares, providing a breathtaking contrast to Calabria's sun-drenched coastlines and bustling cities.

The Sila is divided into three sections: Sila Grande, Sila Piccola, and Sila Greca, each presenting its unique characteristics and delights. The mountainous Sila Grande is home to the park's highest peak, Botte Donato, standing proud at 1,928 meters. A hike to its summit rewards the intrepid explorer with panoramic views of the diverse Calabrian landscape, from the azure expanse of the Ionian and Tyrrhenian seas to the snow-capped peaks of the Aspromonte Mountains.

Meanwhile, Sila Piccola's sloping hills and fertile valleys hold a wealth of picturesque villages, such as San Giovanni in Fiore, renowned for its beautiful Florense Abbey. Here, travelers can marvel at the grandeur of its historic architecture while delving into the region's spiritual history.

Yet, the beauty of Sila National Park extends beyond its breathtaking vistas and cultural treasures. The park boasts an astonishing biodiversity, with its verdant forests providing a sanctuary for a wide variety of wildlife. Among the dense populations of beech, pine, and fir trees, it's not uncommon to spot roe deer, wild boars, and even the rare Italian wolf. Birdwatchers, too, will be enchanted by the abundance of species that inhabit the area, from the regal golden eagle to the elusive black woodpecker.

The park's lakes further enrich this biodiversity. Of these, Lake Cecita, nestled within Sila Grande's highlands, is perhaps the most famous. Its mirror-like waters reflect the surrounding forests' verdant hues, while its shores provide a tranquil spot for relaxation or a picnic amid nature. The lake also serves as a haven for a host of bird species, making it a favored destination for ornithology enthusiasts.

Sila National Park caters to a wide range of outdoor activities, offering something for every nature lover. Adventure seekers can partake in mountain biking, horseback riding, or cross-country skiing during the winter months. The park's extensive network of well-marked trails makes it a paradise for hikers of all levels. One such route, the Path of the Giants, traverses ancient forests of towering trees, some over 500 years old. These trees, witnesses to centuries of history, add a touch of magic to the Sila's already captivating scenery.

Sila National Park caters to a wide range of outdoor activities, offering something for every nature lover. Adventure seekers can partake in mountain biking, horse-

back riding, or cross-country skiing during the winter months. The park's extensive network of well-marked trails makes it a paradise for hikers of all levels. One such route, the Path of the Giants, traverses ancient forests of towering trees, some over 500 years old. These trees, witnesses to centuries of history, add a touch of magic to the Sila's already captivating scenery.

Cosenza's Crown Jewel: The Cathedral, A UNESCO World Heritage Site

Whispers of our previous exploration of Cosenza's vibrant cityscape bring us back to a particular architectural gem, Cosenza Cathedral. A symbol of Calabria's enduring spirit, this magnificent structure is more than just an iconic landmark; it's a testimony to the region's storied past, intricately woven into its grand arches, towering spires, and elegant artwork.

Having proudly stood in Cosenza's historic center since the 11th century, the cathedral embodies the intricate dance between time and architecture. While some of its original Norman features remain, a succession of renovations and restorations have imbued the cathedral with a patchwork of styles. Romanesque, Gothic, and Baroque influences converge in an aesthetic tapestry as rich and varied as Calabria's own history.

Step inside, and you'll find the cathedral's beauty extends well beyond its enchanting facade. The grandiose interior brims with artistic treasures, from the lavish marble altar to the delicately carved wooden choir stalls. Perhaps the most striking is the 16th-century Byzantine icon of the Madonna del Pilerio, which greets visitors with a serene gaze from its position above the main altar.

However, it's not just the cathedral's aesthetic prowess that has garnered international recognition. In 2011, Cosenza Cathedral was named a UNESCO World Heritage site, an honor bestowed not only for its artistic and historical value, but also for its unique role as a place of 'testimonies of exchange' - a core theme of UNESCO's recognition criteria. The cathedral, through its layered architectural styles and collection of artworks, tells a silent tale of cultural interchange across centuries, marking it as a key site of global cultural heritage.

This recognition highlights the cathedral's unparalleled ability to take us on a journey back in time. Walking its hallowed halls, we can feel the echoes of history reverberate around us, from the high-pitched chants of medieval monks to the soft whispers of modern-day worshippers.

But the Cosenza Cathedral is not a relic frozen in time. It remains a vibrant part of the city's life, hosting religious ceremonies, cultural events, and attracting admirers from across the globe. Each visitor, whether touched by the spiritual aura or enthralled by the historical richness, forms a part of the cathedral's ongoing narrative.

Visiting the Cosenza Cathedral offers more than just an insight into Calabria's past; it's a journey into the heart of Calabrian culture, a monument to the region's resilience and enduring beauty. As you step out under the cathedral's towering arches and into the cobblestone streets of Cosenza, you carry a piece of this timeless legacy with you, a testament to the enduring allure of Calabria.

Aragonese Castle of Reggio Calabria: A Tapestry of History, Majesty, and Mystery

Our journey through the heart of Calabria now leads us back to the coastal city of Reggio Calabria, home to the Aragonese Castle. This imposing fortification, also known as the Castello di Reggio, crowns the city with a sense of majesty and mystery, whispering tales of the past within its age-old walls.

Perched on a rise overlooking the Strait of Messina, the castle's origins remain shrouded in mystery. Yet its commanding presence speaks to a history steeped in conquests, rebellions, and royal machinations. The castle, as we see it today, was primarily constructed in the 15th century under the reign of the Aragonese dynasty, hence its name. But its beginnings are believed to trace back to the Byzantine era, or possibly even earlier.

As you approach the Aragonese Castle, the first thing that strikes you is its robust architecture. The massive quadrangular structure, flanked by round towers, presents a stark contrast to the azure backdrop of the Mediterranean. Thick walls of hewn stone, built to withstand the most formidable attacks, now stand as silent sentinels guarding the city's storied past.

Once inside, the castle unveils a labyrinth of halls and chambers, each brimming with tales waiting to be discovered. One intriguing narrative revolves around the castle's infamous dungeon, the Castellan's Tower. It's said that during the 16th century, notorious pirate Barbarossa was imprisoned here, his haunting cries echoing through the castle's corridors.

Another anecdote hails from the turbulent era of the 1800s when the castle served as a stronghold during the War of the Spanish Succession. It's said that the castle's garrison held out for months, surviving on a diet of bread and olives. This tenacious spirit resonates through the castle, a reminder of the resilience of the Calabrian people.

The Aragonese Castle is not just a gateway to the past; it's also a testament to the city's vibrant present. Today, it serves as a cultural hub, housing the State Archives and the Superintendent for Cultural and Environmental Heritage. In these roles, the castle fosters a dialogue between the past and the present, connecting generations of Calabrians with their heritage.

Visiting the castle is a journey through time, offering a chance to stand where Greek, Byzantine, Norman, and Aragonese footsteps once echoed. From the panoramic views atop its battlements, you can watch as the sun paints the sky in a thousand shades of gold, casting a warm glow on the city below.

As you leave the castle's shadow and head back into the bustling streets of Reggio Calabria, you carry with you tales of courage, conquest, and endurance. The Aragonese Castle is more than a historical monument; it's a living tapestry of history, as intriguing and captivating as the city it watches over.

So why visit the Aragonese Castle? Because within its stone walls lie the whispers of centuries, the echoes of battles fought and won, the hush of ancient mysteries. It's an invitation to step back in time, to walk the corridors of history, and to lose yourself in the enigma of a past etched in stone. The Aragonese Castle is not just a destination; it's an experience - a plunge into the very heart of Calabria.

The Unmissable Museums and Art Galleries of Calabria

Art lovers, history buffs, and cultural explorers are in for a treat in Calabria. The region is adorned with a multitude of museums and art galleries that enrich its cultural panorama, each offering a unique peek into the region's past and its artistic mastery. Here's a collection of must-visit destinations that will undoubtedly add a vibrant stroke to your Calabrian escapade.

National Archaeological Museum of Locri

In the city of Locri, prepare to be astounded by the wealth of ancient artifacts that have been unearthed from the ruins of the Greek colony of Lokroi Epizephyrioi. The National Archaeological Museum houses a vast collection of archaeological finds that vividly depict the colony's life, culture, and religion. The museum's star attraction is the "Pinax of Persephone," an ancient terracotta tablet intricately painted with scenes from the myth of Persephone.

The Diocesan Museum of Tropea

Situated in the heart of Tropea, this museum serves as a custodian of religious art that spans several centuries. Housed within the Bishop's Palace, the Diocesan Museum hosts a collection of sacred art, including statues, altarpieces, and vestments, each intricately designed and woven with religious and historical significance.

Eco-Museum of the Sea in Borgia

The Eco-Museum of the Sea in Borgia is not your typical museum. It is a dynamic cultural space that aims to conserve and promote Calabria's maritime heritage. Here, you'll find a rich collection of marine artifacts, old seafaring equipment, and installations that shed light on the region's intimate relationship with the sea.

Museum of Byzantine and Medieval Art in Stilo

Delve into the region's Byzantine and medieval past at this museum in Stilo. The exhibit comprises a comprehensive collection of objects, including ceramics, textiles, and metalwork, reflecting the Byzantine aesthetic influence on the region during the Middle Ages.

Each of these destinations offers a unique piece of Calabria's cultural puzzle, inviting you to unravel the region's rich history and artistic flair. So, grab a ticket, soak in the stories, and let the journey to the past begin!

MACA (Museum of Contemporary Art of Acri)

Nestled within the historical center of Acri, the MACA is a gem for contemporary art enthusiasts. The museum is divided into several sections, each dedicated to different art forms like painting, sculpture, and graphics. Not only does it house works by established artists, but it also encourages emerging talents, often serving as a launchpad for new artistic careers.

The National Museum of Magna Graecia in Reggio Calabria

This museum is home to one of Italy's most prestigious collections of Magna Graecia artifacts, featuring a wealth of Greek and Roman statues, terracotta, bronze items, and jewelry. The crowning jewels of the collection are the Riace Bronzes (as we have said before), two exceptional full-size Greek bronzes of naked bearded warriors, considered among the most famous icons of Italian cultural heritage.

The Aragonese Castle of Le Castella's Aquarium

Located in the Aragonese Castle of Le Castella, this aquatic museum takes you on a journey beneath the waves. The aquarium houses several species of marine creatures native to the Ionian Sea and offers visitors a rare opportunity to learn about the region's diverse marine ecosystems within the historic walls of a castle.

The Folklore Museum of Belmonte Calabro

Get a glimpse into the everyday life, traditions, and customs of Calabria's past at this folklore museum. Located in the hilltop village of Belmonte Calabro, the museum displays an array of household items, traditional costumes, and tools used in agriculture and craftsmanship, all collected from local inhabitants.

Each of these sites offers a unique perspective on Calabria's cultural, artistic, and historical identity. These cultural hubs surely enhance the understanding and appreciation of this diverse and vibrant region.

Unearthing the Past: Calabria's Remarkable Archaeological Sites

Delving into Calabria's past is akin to turning the pages of a captivating history book, where every chapter unravels a tale rich with historical narratives, ancient civilizations, and enduring legacies. The region is not only known for its mesmerizing natural beauty or its delectable cuisine, but also for the wealth of archaeological sites that offer windows into its diverse historical epochs. From the fascinating remains of Magna Graecia cities to the vestiges of Roman grandeur and the traces of Byzantine and Norman influences, each site provides a unique lens to understand Calabria's vibrant past. The aura of mystery that surrounds these archaeological wonders further enhances their allure, beckoning history buffs, curious travelers, and culture enthusiasts alike. So grab your adventurer's hat and join us as we embark on this intriguing journey through time, exploring the remarkable archaeological sites that have etched their mark in Calabria's rich historical tapestry.

These are some of the archaeological sites and parks you cannot miss:

Scolacium Archaeological Park

Venture just outside of Catanzaro and you'll discover the breathtaking Scolacium Archaeological Park. This was once the site of the ancient city of Scolacium, one of the most important urban centers of Magna Graecia. Today, it is a treasure trove of archaeological discoveries, where one can wander among the remains of a Roman theater, a Byzantine basilica, and an imposing Norman castle, all while surrounded by a beautiful olive grove overlooking the Ionian Sea. The site offers a rich glimpse into the various civilizations that have graced this land over the centuries.

Sybaris Archaeological Park

Sybaris, located near the Crati river, was one of the most famous cities of the ancient Magna Graecia, celebrated for its significant wealth and luxury. Today, the Sybaris Archaeological Park and National Museum offer a tangible look into the lives of this city's former inhabitants. Although what remains is just a fraction of the grandeur that once was, the foundations of the ancient houses, streets, and public buildings still manage to inspire awe.

Locri Epizephyrii Archaeological Park

Another gem in Calabria's archaeological crown, the ancient city of Locri Epizephyrii, was once a prominent center of Magna Graecia. The site is home to extensive remains of a Greek theater, a necropolis, and numerous temples dedicated to various gods. Particularly intriguing is the Epizephyrian sanctuary of Persephone, a rare example of a mystery cult location from ancient Greek times. Visiting Locri Epizephyrii is like taking a walk back in time, amidst the ruins echoing the grandeur of the past.

Taurianova - Archeological Site of Medma

The archaeological site of Medma, in the modern-day Taurianova, preserves traces of a past stretching back over millennia. Established by the Locrians in the 7th century BC, the site still showcases the fragments of walls, residential structures, and an impressive necropolis. The terracotta artifacts retrieved here, including intriguing figurines and vases, are now exhibited in the National Museum of Reggio Calabria.

Each of these sites is a testament to Calabria's deep and rich history, spanning numerous cultures and eras. By visiting these places, one does not merely observe the remains of ancient civilizations but actively steps into the narrative of humanity's shared heritage.

Celebrating Life: Calabria's Rich Culture and Traditions

When the topic turns to Calabria, it's impossible to avoid the region's robust tapestry of cultural customs, age-old traditions, and vibrant festivals. These elements are deeply woven into the local identity, mirroring the Calabrian spirit and its way of life. From pulsating street parades to tranquil religious ceremonies, and from lively culinary feasts to rich folkloric events, each celebration holds a mirror to the region's history, its joys, and its sorrows.

Yet, the essence of these festivities goes beyond mere spectacle. They symbolize the collective memory of the people, binding them together, and fostering a sense of community that is palpable across the towns and villages. These traditions are the threads that connect the past with the present, offering a tangible link to their ancestry and creating a path that guides their future.

So, prepare to immerse yourself in the living culture of Calabria as we journey through a calendar filled with festivals and events, each promising to offer an unforgettable taste of Calabrian life. From the vibrant dance of the tarantella to the sacred processions of Holy Week, we'll uncover the significance of these traditions and understand why they continue to be celebrated with unabated enthusiasm. Come along, and let the spirit of Calabria sweep you off your feet!

Calabria's Festive Heartbeat: Embracing Tradition and Togetherness

Calabria is not only a feast for the eyes but a jubilant procession of festivities that resonate with the rhythm of its rich culture. From coastal towns to mountain villages, each locale has its unique set of traditions, a shared experience that brings families, friends, and communities together. The celebrations you'll witness across this region are deeply steeped in heritage, an echo of their vibrant past, and a dance with their dynamic present.

Our journey through Calabria's calendar begins with Easter, the cornerstone of Calabrian festivities. The most enchanting spectacle unfolds in Tropea, where the 'Processione dei Misteri' (Procession of the Mysteries) takes place on Good Friday. Locals carry beautiful handmade statues representing scenes from the Passion of Christ through the winding, narrow streets. The procession, bathed in the glow of countless candles, is a sight to behold.

In the sultry summers, Calabria comes alive with the 'Festa della Madonna della Consolazione' in Reggio Calabria. This September celebration is one of the region's most significant religious events, marked by processions, music, and fireworks. It is a tradition passed down through generations, a symbol of devotion and spiritual strength.

Speaking of music, the 'Tarantella Festival' held in August in Caulonia, resonates with the hypnotic rhythm of this traditional folk dance. The Tarantella, an emblematic expression of Calabrian culture, is a captivating performance where dancers, dressed in traditional costumes, move to the rhythm of tambourines, accordions, and the 'chitarra battente' (a traditional Italian folk guitar).

Food, of course, plays a starring role in any Calabrian festivity. Every November, the town of Sant'Onofrio becomes the epicenter for mushroom enthusiasts with the 'Sagra del Fungo.' This delightful festival celebrates the region's wild mushroom varieties, from the fragrant porcini to the elusive black truffle. Food stalls offer an assortment of mushroom-based dishes, allowing visitors to sample this local delicacy in its many delicious forms.

As we journey into the heart of winter, the 'Carnevale di Montalto Uffugo' offers a warm embrace. Known as one of the oldest carnivals in Calabria, the town bursts into color and music, featuring elaborate floats, theatrical performances, and a festive atmosphere that dispels the winter chill.

Each of these celebrations reveals an aspect of the Calabrian soul - a testament to their enduring spirit, respect for their roots, and a love for life's simple pleasures. By immersing yourself in these festivities, you're not just observing a tradition - you're becoming a part of Calabria's living heritage, an experience that is as rewarding as it is unforgettable.

Vibrant Calabria: A Calendar of Cultural Highlights

alabria's event calendar is a vibrant tapestry of celebrations, each weaving together strands of culture, heritage, and the zest for life that is quintessentially Calabrian. These diverse events, ranging from music and cinema to gastronomy and sports, paint a colorful picture of the region's dynamic spirit.

Begin the summer with the 'Paleariza Festival', which takes place in the Bova area during July and August. This unique event showcases the region's Greek roots, featuring traditional music, dance, and theatre performances, creating a moving testament to Calabria's rich cultural heritage.

f the sounds of jazz serenading the summer air intrigue you, don't miss the 'Roccella Jazz Festival' in Roccella Jonica. An annual celebration that attracts renowned musicians from around the world, this festival fuses rhythm, sun, and sea to create an unforgettable melange of experiences.

The allure of Calabria's pristine waters transcends the enjoyment of the sunbathers and fishermen. The 'Tropea Sail Cup' is a spectacular annual regatta held in the sparkling waters of Tropea's bay in September. This thrilling display of sailing prowess is a treat for participants and spectators alike.

Film enthusiasts should not miss the 'Magnà Graecia Film Festival', an international event held annually in Catanzaro. The festival showcases cinematic gems from emerging filmmakers, complemented by engaging workshops and forums—a must-attend for all cinephiles.

For those who find delight in the fiery flavors of Calabrian cuisine, the 'Peperoncino Festival' in Diamante offers a sensory extravaganza. This annual celebra-

tion of Calabria's famed chili pepper features tasting sessions, culinary demonstrations, and a lively chili-eating contest, all set to the soundtrack of live music and merriment.

In December, the region hosts the 'Borgo Incantato', or the 'Enchanted Village' in Santa Severina. This magical event transforms the town into a living nativity scene, complete with crafts, gastronomy, and local traditions—an unforgettable celebration of the Christmas season.

Calabria's events offer visitors a chance to immerse themselves in the region's rhythm and soul. They are more than dates on a calendar—they are an open invitation to step into the local life, experience shared passions, and partake in collective celebrations. So, when you visit Calabria, remember, you are not just a tourist; you become part of a vibrant and welcoming community.

Calabria's Culinary Symphony: A Journey through Flavours and Traditions"

As you step into the sun-drenched landscapes of Calabria, the southernmost region of Italy's boot, you are greeted not only by the azure Mediterranean Sea and towering mountains but also by the mouthwatering aroma of its culinary delights. Calabrian cuisine is a beautiful paradox, as simple as it is complex, a perfect embodiment of the land and the sea, narrating tales of the region's rich history and vibrant culture.

From robust 'nduja, a fiery spreadable sausage, to the delicate flavour of red Tropea onions; from the tangy bite of local pecorino cheese to the sweet notes of bergamot citrus used in teas and sweets, Calabrian cuisine is a veritable feast for the senses. In this chapter, we'll embark on a gastronomic journey, meandering through bustling markets, family-run vineyards, fragrant citrus orchards, and rustic farmhouses, revealing the secrets of Calabria's culinary symphony, one bite at a time. Ready your taste buds, for they're in for a treat!

Typical Calabrian dishes

Calabria, the "toe" of Italy's boot-shaped peninsula, is a land rich in flavour, its gastronomy as passionate as the region's blazing sun, as soulful as its folk music, and as multifaceted as its history. Let's embark on a delightful journey to discover the gastronomic jewels of this rich land, whose dishes are a tribute to simplicity, authenticity, and above all, a deep love for the land and sea.

Start with the famous 'nduja, a unique Calabrian delicacy that sings of the region's fondness for all things fiery. This spicy, spreadable sausage made from pork and Calabrian chili peppers is a cornerstone of local gastronomy. Smear it on crusty bread, mix it into pasta, or melt it onto pizza, the 'nduja imparts a spicy kick and a delectable smoky flavour. Its vibrant red colour is as bold as its taste, indicative of the warmth and vivacity of Calabria's culture.

Start with the famous 'nduja, a unique Calabrian delicacy that sings of the region's fondness for all things fiery. This spicy, spreadable sausage made from pork and Calabrian chili peppers is a cornerstone of local gastronomy. Smear it on crusty bread, mix it into pasta, or melt it onto pizza, the 'nduja imparts a spicy kick and a delectable smoky flavour. Its vibrant red colour is as bold as its taste, indicative of the warmth and vivacity of Calabria's culture.

Then there's the iconic Caciocavallo Silano, a pear-shaped cheese reminiscent of the region's pastoral tradition. This semi-hard cheese, aged to perfection, brings a balance of salty and sweet flavours. It's often pan-seared and served with honey or homemade jams, proving that in Calabrian cuisine, as in life, contrasts harmonize beautifully.

When it comes to comfort food, Calabria serves up the heart-warming melanzane alla parmigiana (eggplant Parmesan). Layers of thinly sliced eggplant, tomato sauce, basil, mozzarella, and Parmesan cheese are baked together until the flavours meld into a luscious, bubbling masterpiece. Each bite is a testament to the Italian way of life, where food is an expression of love, a celebration of togetherness.

Seafood lovers will be enthralled by the swordfish dishes of the Costa degli Dei, the 'Coast of the Gods.' One cannot help but be mesmerized by the skill and bravery of the local fishermen, who use traditional methods to catch this noble fish. Once caught, the swordfish is often simply grilled or prepared in a light sauce, highlighting the fish's delicate flavour.

Pasta is an Italian staple, and Calabria has its unique rendition, the fileja. These hand-rolled spirals of pasta, often served with a hearty ragù or a simple tomato and basil sauce, showcase the region's agricultural wealth. Pair this with a glass of local wine, and you have a meal that embodies the joyous spirit of Calabria.

No gastronomic journey through Calabria would be complete without exploring its delectable pastries. The most famous of them all is likely the tartufo di Pizzo, a delicious ice-cream truffle originating from the town of Pizzo. Encased within a shell of chocolate or hazelnut gelato is a heart of fior di latte ice-cream, enriched with a surprise touch of molten chocolate or fruit syrup.

When we speak of Calabrian cuisine, we speak of more than just the combination of ingredients. We speak of the grandmothers' wisdom passed down generations, the fishermen's tales carried by the wind, the farmers' respect for the land and the seasons, and the inherent warmth of the Calabrian people. As we navigate through each dish, we taste the narratives of this region, vibrant and robust, as flavourful as the dishes themselves. The true beauty of Calabrian cuisine lies not only in its taste but in the stories, it tells and the traditions it preserves. It is a culinary heritage that deserves to be celebrated, savoured, and passed on. It is, after all, love made edible.

Markets and Local Products: A Taste of Authentic Calabria

When it comes to truly immersing oneself in the heart of a place's culinary heritage, nothing beats the vibrancy and authenticity of local markets. It is here, amidst the chatter of vendors and the enticing aromas of freshly cooked food, that the real Calabria can be discovered.

A walk through a Calabrian market is like a vivid sensory journey. From the rich fragrance of cured meats, to the sight of colorful fruits and vegetables piled high, every sense is piqued. These markets, filled with the buzz of locals haggling and engaging in good-natured conversation, offer a glimpse into the age-old customs and traditions of the region.

One product you're likely to come across is the famous 'nduja sausage, a gastronomic symbol of Calabria. Whether spread on a slice of bread or used to enhance a pasta sauce, it's a culinary delight not to be missed. Another essential to taste is the caciocavallo cheese, typically aged and full of flavor, perfect for an appetizing break or to enrich a dish.

The beauty of these markets extends beyond food. You'll also find stalls selling local crafts, with Calabrian ceramics being a popular souvenir. The pottery, often brightly colored and decorated with intricate patterns, tells a story of its own, reflecting the creativity and passion of the local artisans.

And then there's the wine. From robust reds to delicate whites, each bottle promises a taste of the region's sun-soaked vineyards. A stroll around a wine market, or even a local wine shop, is an excellent way to discover and sample the array of local wines.

Calabria's markets are an integral part of the region's social and cultural fabric. They encapsulate the region's culinary soul and provide a vital link between past and present, tradition and innovation. Spending time in these bustling, vibrant spaces allows you to experience the true taste of Calabria, making them an essential stop on any food lover's itinerary.

Calabrian Wine Odyssey: A Stroll through Vineyards and Vintages

Calabria, the toe of Italy's boot, steeped in sunlight and surrounded by seas, beckons you on a wondrous journey through its charming vineyards. The region, with its sublime landscapes and coastal breeze, has been passionately producing vintages for centuries. Imagine walking down lush vine rows, each bend in the road revealing a unique world of aroma and flavor. This isn't just about wine; it's about stepping into a tale as old as time.

In the north, nestled in the Pollino Mountains, you'll encounter the warm, rich tones of Terre di Cosenza DOC wines. The vineyards here bask in the sun during the day, and cool in the mountain air at night, creating a unique thermal variance that gives birth to a sophisticated palette of flavors.

ontinuing towards the coast, where the Ionian Sea laps against the land, Cirò reigns supreme. Arguably the most celebrated Calabrian wine, it has a history that stretches back to ancient Greece. Made predominantly from the Gaglioppo grape, Cirò's robust reds are renowned for their vibrant ruby color, and complex, fruity flavor profile. Be sure to relish a glass alongside local cheese or pasta for a sublime experience.

As we wander deeper into the heart of Calabria, we meet Greco di Bianco, a sweet wine made from late-harvest grapes left to dry in the sun. This enchanting golden elixir is named after the tiny coastal town of Bianco, a place where wine-making is a testament to the harmony between nature and man.

Venturing west, the journey takes you to Bivongi DOC region. The vineyards here, terraced along the slopes, benefit from the cooling maritime influence. Enjoy a glass of Bivongi's white, rosé, or red wines, each delivering a unique melody of taste and aroma, while looking out over the stunningly beautiful Ionian coast.

Our stroll concludes in the hills of Savuto, tucked away in the region's western front. Savuto DOC is a blend of several grapes, creating a harmonious medley of taste that sings a song of Calabria's vibrant viticulture. These wines are earthy, yet light, the perfect companion for the hearty fare of the region.

This journey through Calabrian vineyards is more than an exploration of the region's wines - it's an intimate experience of its soul. Each glass tells a story of the land, of its people's perseverance, and of the enduring love affair between Calabrians and their vines. When you sip on Calabrian wine, you're not just tasting fermented grapes; you're drinking in the sun, the sea, and the spirit of a place that's as beautiful as it is flavorful. So, here's to you, traveler. May your journey through the wines of Calabria be as enriching as it is delightful.

UNIQUE EXPERIENCES IN CALABRIA

Step into the Wild: A Closer Look at Calabria's Hiking Trails

In Calabria, every trail tells a tale, each path beckoning with the promise of new discoveries. Let's delve deeper into the details of some of these fantastic hiking routes, the gems of this southern Italian region.

Tracing History in Pollino National Park

Pollino's diversity shines through in its hiking trails. The 'Horace's Journey' trail isn't just a hike, it's a walk through history. As you trace the footsteps of the Roman poet Horace, you'll pass by the Devil's Bridge on the Lao river, ancient caves that

were once hermit dwellings, and more. Along the way, watch for the Bosnian pine trees, an endangered species that the park protects.

Sila National Park: A Haven of Natural Wonders

The Sila plateau is home to the 'Giant Trees Trail,' where hikers can marvel at some of Europe's oldest and tallest trees. The scenic paths around Lake Cecita, however, remain the highlight. As you amble along the "Sentiero Umberto," listen to the murmurs of the forest, observe the unique bird species, and enjoy the lake's serene beauty that changes with the sunlight.

Serre Calabresi: Where Spirituality Meets Adventure

Serre Calabresi mountains, offer more than physical exertion. It's a spiritual journey that invites hikers to explore their inner selves while appreciating the beauty of nature. Passing through several sanctuaries, this trail serves as a pilgrimage route, adding a divine touch to your adventure.

Breathtaking Beauty of the Coastal Trails

On the 'Footpath of the Gods,' you'll walk high above the Tyrrhenian Sea, where the sweeping views of the coast meet turquoise waters. Make sure to stop at the Belvedere in Capo Vaticano, a panoramic terrace offering a fantastic view of the Aeolian Islands, and if you're lucky, the active volcano Stromboli puffing in the distance.

Aspromonte's Peaks and Valleys

Finally, the Aspromonte National Park, with its towering peaks and deep valleys, provides a rigorous but rewarding experience. The 'Trail of the Gods' leads to Montalto, the highest peak of the park. Here, you can gaze upon the surrounding landscapes and even spot the Sicilian coast on clear days.

For a more interactive experience, consider joining one of the many local guided trekking tours. Not only will you have expert advice on hand, but it's also a wonderful way to learn about the region's rich flora, fauna, and geology in depth.

Let's not forget that hiking in Calabria is more than just walking. It's about pausing

to appreciate a wildflower's bloom, tasting the freshness of mountain spring water, enjoying a friendly chat with locals along the path, or listening to the symphony of birdsong. In essence, it's a way to connect with the land, its history, and its people on a deeper level. As you explore the trails, let your senses guide you, and let each footfall unlock the region's natural and cultural wonders.

Smooth Sailing: Exploring Calabria by Boat

The coastal vistas of Calabria, a land almost surrounded by water, are a spectacle best enjoyed from the sea itself. Let's hoist the sails and embark on a journey where the azure waves meet the pristine beaches and majestic cliffs. But the adventure doesn't stop at the coastline. Calabria's rivers offer a different kind of voyage, one that takes you through the heart of the region's stunning landscapes.

Coasting Along the Tyrrhenian and Ionian Seas

Cruising along Calabria's extensive coastline is a seafarer's delight. Boat tours departing from the charming towns of Tropea and Scilla on the Tyrrhenian Sea or Le Castella on the Ionian side offer a fantastic opportunity to discover hidden coves, secluded beaches, and towering sea cliffs. The 'Costa degli Dei' (Coast of the Gods) from Pizzo to Tropea is a favorite among sailors for its crystalline waters and picturesque landscapes.

Off Tropea, you can anchor near the captivating 'Roccia di Papa' (Pope's Rock) or the sandy strip of 'Grotticelle.' Dive into the transparent waters, explore the sea caves, or simply enjoy the sun-kissed beaches. Over on the Ionian side, the tour from Le Castella takes you along the 'Squillace Gulf,' known for its serene bays and ancient ruins visible even from the water.

Venturing Out to the Aeolian Islands

Located off Calabria's northern coast, the Aeolian Islands, a UNESCO World Heritage site, are a must-visit for boat enthusiasts. Embark on a day trip from the ports of Tropea or Vibo Marina to the island of Stromboli, one of the most active volcanoes in the world. As the sun sets, witness the 'Sciara del Fuoco,' a dramatic fiery spectacle that sends glowing lava into the sea. The islands of Lipari and Vulcano, known for their thermal springs and mud baths, offer yet another unique maritime experience.

Riding the Waves on Lao River

But Calabria's water adventures aren't restricted to the sea. Thrill-seekers can take a raft or kayak down the rapids of the Lao River in Pollino National Park. Meandering through one of the deepest canyons in Italy, this trip offers a unique perspective on the region's natural beauty. Marvel at the towering rock faces, discover hidden waterfalls, and dip in the clear pools along the way. Remember to keep an eye out for otters and kingfishers that often frequent the riverbanks!

Cruising the Crati River

For a more tranquil journey, the Crati River cruise offers a peaceful retreat. This slow-paced tour weaves through the diverse landscapes of the Sila Plateau, from marshes to dense forests. Bird watchers will be delighted by the variety of species found along the river, including herons and cormorants.

Whether you're navigating the high seas, exploring the coastal waters, or cruising the river currents, each journey offers a unique way to experience Calabria's diverse landscapes. These boat trips are not merely modes of travel but doorways to discovery, opening up new and exciting views of the region. Feel the sea spray on your face, listen to the wind singing through the river valleys, and watch the sun paint colors on the water. These are the moments that will make your Calabrian journey truly unforgettable.

A Touch of the Divine: The Codex Purpureus Rossanensis Experience

The history of mankind is recorded and transmitted through various means. Some write on stone, some on paper, but few use the medium of parchment dyed in majestic purple, embossed with text of silver and gold. Among these few treasures is the Codex Purpureus Rossanensis, a regal testament to the creative spirit of ancient times, which continues to captivate contemporary visitors.

Situated in the Diocesan Museum of Rossano in Calabria, the Codex Purpureus Rossanensis or the Purple Codex of Rossano isn't merely a relic; it is a living history that silently narrates an engaging tale of craftsmanship and devotion. To step into the museum is to traverse time, an adventure back to the 6th century, where sacred words were woven into works of art.

The Purple Codex (UNESCO heritage), stands apart from the numerous illuminated manuscripts of the New Testament. Its pages emanate a royal purple hue, once considered the color of emperors and kings. But what truly sets it apart is the ethereal words of the New Testament that dance across the page, penned in silver ink with touches of gold. It is an impressive union of religious reverence and artistic mastery.

Equally fascinating are the surviving full-page miniatures, 14 in number. Each painting invites you into a Biblical story, their characters vibrant, emotions vivid, and messages powerful. As you observe the ancient figures in the frescoes, you're likely to experience a blend of awe and contemplation.

One might wonder how this remarkable artifact survived over a millennium and a half. The Codex's journey has been a miraculous one, seeing it through the Byzantine era to the present day, enduring the rise and fall of empires, witnessing the evolution of societies, and surviving the ravages of time. Each passing century has added another layer of intrigue to its existence, turning it into a symbol of endurance and resilience.

Immersing yourself in this journey through the Codex Purpureus Rossanensis is more than just a sightseeing venture. It's a transformative experience, a unique opportunity to see, touch, and understand history. It's a lesson in the perseverance of beauty, the endurance of faith, and the enduring resonance of human creativity. It's not just a visit; it's a voyage into the past, a voyage you will carry with you long after you've returned to the present.

Savor the Flavor: Calabrian Cooking Classes

Traveling is not just about capturing breathtaking views or visiting historical sites; it's also about immersing oneself in the local culture. And what better way to do that than learning to cook local dishes in the heart of Calabria? The region, known for its robust and fiery flavors, offers a variety of cooking classes to tourists, helping them to bring a piece of Calabrian soul back home in the form of recipes.

In the coastal city of Tropea, numerous cooking schools thrive. The courses usually include trips to local markets to learn about the fresh, local ingredients that make Calabrian cuisine so delightful. It's an incredible experience - bustling markets, fresh produce, and the infectious enthusiasm of the local vendors. Schools such as the Italian Culinary Institute combine traditional cooking classes with additional wine, olive oil, and cheese tasting sessions.

Nestled in the scenic town of Belmonte Calabro, Belmonte Vacanze Cooking School offers a culinary journey of the Italian south. They provide a rich, week-

long cooking course that lets you delve into the region's most beloved dishes. Apart from the culinary lessons, they organize visits to local wine producers and nearby farms, emphasizing the farm-to-table connection.

Another great place to consider is Cucina Calabrese in Reggio Calabria. These classes are less structured, encouraging creativity and adaptation - you won't just be following a recipe, but making it your own. They emphasize local, seasonal produce and traditional techniques, allowing a genuine connection with the cuisine.

For those looking for a more immersive experience, the Awaiting Table Cookery School in Lecce offers week-long courses exploring the food and wine of Calabria. Students stay in the school's historic castle, where they learn traditional cooking techniques and explore local wine and olive oil production.

Each of these classes focuses not only on the preparation of food but also on the cultural context that surrounds it. The courses are filled with anecdotes and historical tidbits that help deepen the understanding of the regional cuisine. They end, typically, with a shared meal – dishes that you cooked, served with local wines, in a setting that is all about togetherness and camaraderie.

Remember, cooking classes are about more than just the food; they're about the people you meet, the stories you hear, and the traditions you become a part of. So, prepare to roll up your sleeves and make memories while making pasta. The scent of simmering tomato sauce, the kick of Calabrian chili, and the tang of local olive oil will forever bring you back to the joyful days spent in the Calabrian kitchen.

Links and useful information

Transportation

Car Rentals

- entalcars.com: **www.rentalcars.com** (Compares car rental deals from various providers)
- Europcar: **www.europcar.com**
- Hertz: **www.hertz.com**

Rome's Fiumicino Airport and Naples' Capodichino Airport are the nearest major airports to Calabria. Several budget airlines offer flights to Lamezia Terme Airport, the region's main airport.

The Italian railway network, Trenitalia, connects most of Calabria's towns. Visit **www.trenitalia.com** for schedules and ticket bookings.

Several bus companies, such as Romano or Federico, offer services throughout Calabria. Their schedules can be found on their respective websites.

Accommodation

In Italy, one of the best ways to stay is to book a room from Booking or Airbnb.

In particular, if you contact the homeowners from Booking, it is very likely that you will find their cell phone number, being able to agree on a cheaper price off Booking.

The same can be done on Airbnb, but not before making a reservation.

Once made, you will have access to the host's phone number, and contact them to arrange to cancel the reservation so that you can pay a lower price in cash once you arrive on site.

Local Tours

TheCalabria Greeters network offers free local tours led by volunteers passionate about their region.

- Visit **www.globalgreeternetwork.com** for more details.
- For guided tours, visit **www.viator.com**, where you can book anything from food and wine tours to boat excursions.

Cooking Classes

- Italian Culinary Institute, Tropea: **www.italianculinary.it**
- Belmonte Vacanze Cooking School, Belmonte Calabro: **www.belmontevacanze.com**
- Cucina Calabrese, Reggio Calabria: **www.cucinacalabrese.com**

Local Events and Festivals

- Eventbrite: **www.eventbrite.it** (For finding local events, meetups, and festivals)
- InCalabriaTour: **www.incalabriatour.it** (Information on Calabrian culture, festivals, and tours)
- Museums and Cultural Sites
- Musei Calabria: **www.museicalabria.it** (Guide to the museums in Calabria)
- Official Tourism Site of Calabria: **www.turiscalabria.it** (Comprehensive information on places to visit, cultural heritage, and more).

A FREE BONUS GUIDE
FOR YOU!

- ✓ The Best High-Level Restaurants
- ✓ 7 Itineraries selected by a true Apulian
- ✓ The Most beautiful experiences
- ✓ The 20 must have items you must pack!
- ✓ The Tastiest Wines

SCAN ME

Scan this QR and download
now your FREE BONUS!

SICILY

TRAVEL GUIDE

Ready to Unearth Italy's Mediterranean Gem?

Discover the Best of Sicily from Distinguished Landmarks to Hidden
Charms, Complete with an Insider's Guide to the Rich Sicilian Cuisine

3 IN 1 FREE BOOK FOR YOU!

✓ BOOK 1 – EVERYDAY ITALIAN PHRASES
✓ BOOK 2 – ITALIAN SLANG
✓ BOOK 3 – ITALIAN TRADITIONS, ETIQUETTE, AND CURIOSITIES

SCAN ME

SCAN THIS QR AND DOWNLOAD NOW YOUR FREE BONUS!

INTRODUCTION TO SICILY

Welcome to Sicily

An island that is not just a geographic entity in the heart of the Mediterranean Sea, but an experiential kaleidoscope, an unfolding story, and a celebration of life that combines the grandeur of history, the allure of nature, and the warmth of its people into an intoxicating blend.

Bathed in the golden Mediterranean sun, Sicily is a melting pot of cultures and eras. From its shores, you can almost reach out and touch the footprints of the ancient Greeks, the whispers of Arabic tales, and the echoes of Norman chivalry. It is a land where each cobblestone has a story to tell, a narrative that stretches back over three millennia.

Imagine, if you will, a patchwork quilt. Each patch carrying its own color, its own design, its own story. But when sewn together, it forms an intricate and coherent tapestry. That's Sicily - a mosaic of experiences and influences.

To the north, the soul-stirring landscapes of Palermo unfold like a well-thumbed book, each page revealing an unexpected surprise. From Byzantine mosaics to bustling markets, from grandiose cathedrals to hushed monasteries, Palermo is a symphony of experiences playing in perfect harmony.

The eastern skyline is dominated by the grandeur of Mount Etna, Europe's largest active volcano. Around its foothills, the city of Catania thrives, its baroque heart pulsing to the rhythm of daily Sicilian life. Beyond, Taormina seduces with its ancient Greek theatre and heart-stopping views of the Ionian Sea.

Venture south, and you'll find Syracuse, once the largest city of the ancient world, its archaeological treasures whispering tales of a glorious past. As you move inland, the landscapes transform into a rolling canvas of hills adorned with vineyards and dotted with timeless villages.

Food and wine aren't mere sustenance here, they're an integral part of Sicily's identity. Sicilian cuisine is a narra-

tive in flavors, a testament to the island's historical intersections and agricultural bounty. From the vineyards that produce globally acclaimed wines to the humble street stalls selling Arancini and Cannoli, gastronomy in Sicily is a joyous celebration of life.

But beyond the tangible - the landmarks, the food, the landscapes - it's the intangible that makes Sicily truly enchanting. It's the chorus of church bells echoing through the narrow streets of a sleepy town. It's the lingering aroma of fresh bread wafting through the morning air. It's the seamless blend of the old with the new, tradition with modernity, that provides the island with a rhythm like no other.

So come, embark on this Sicilian odyssey. Explore its lands, sail its azure waters, savor its culinary delights, live its traditions, and allow the magic of this incredible island to sweep you off your feet. Welcome to Sicily, the Mediterranean's timeless jewel.

A few historical notes

Nestled at the heart of the Mediterranean, the enchanting island of Sicily is a historical treasure trove, each layer revealing a bygone civilization that once graced its land. This is a place where time has wisely chosen to tread gently, leaving remnants of the past beautifully etched into the present.

Long before Sicily welcomed its first foreign settlers, it was home to three ancient tribes – the Sicani, Elymians, and Siculi. Their lives were touched by the first tides of foreign influence when Greek colonists arrived around 750 BC. The Greeks, with their golden era of philosophy, democracy, and arts, breathed life into Sicilian cities, with Syracuse rising as one of the great cities of the Greek world. The island became a canvas painted with the finest strokes of Greek civilization, as can be seen in the Valley of the Temples in Agrigento, and the stunning Greek theatre in Taormina.

Yet, Greek hegemony was not left unchallenged. The island's strategic location and fertile lands drew the attention of the mighty Carthaginians, leading to the Punic Wars with Rome. This turmoil eventually led to Roman rule after their victory in 241 BC. Sicily then served as Rome's granary, its fertile plains supplying Rome with grain, while Roman culture started to mingle and fuse with Greek and native traditions.

Sicily's unique position made it a prime target for invasions, leading to a period of turbulence with the fall of the Roman Empire. Vandals, Ostrogoths, and Byzantines took turns at the helm. However, it was the Arab conquest in the 9th century that left an indelible mark. The island thrived under Arab rule, experiencing advances in agriculture, irrigation, and cuisine that continue to shape the Sicilian identity today.

The island changed hands once more in the 11th century with the arrival of the Normans, who, despite their Northern roots, embraced and augmented the multicultural heritage of Sicily. They were followed by a brief period of German Hohenstaufen rule and then by Spanish dominance. All these rulers left behind a piece of their culture, a layer to the intricate Sicilian tapestry.

The unification of Italy in 1861 brought Sicily under the Italian flag. The 20th century saw the island grappling with poverty, emigration, and the rise of the infamous Sicilian Mafia. Despite these challenges, Sicily emerged resilient, its people fiercely proud of their land and heritage.

The story of Sicily is a saga that spans millennia, a historical mosaic of diverse cultures, each leaving its unique imprint. It's a story that lives in the island's architecture, its cuisine, its language, and most importantly, in the spirit of its people. A visit to Sicily is not just a journey through picturesque landscapes, but a walk through the corridors of time, an exploration of a living museum where history continues to breathe.

Region's geography and climate

Let's journey into the heart of the Mediterranean, to the sun-drenched island of Sicily, where geographical wonders intersect with climatic extravagance. Sicily, the largest island in the Mediterranean, is an enticing patchwork of rolling hills, stark mountains, and turquoise seas that charm every adventurer who steps onto its soil.

The geography of Sicily is remarkably diverse. Its most dramatic feature, without a doubt, is Mount Etna, one of the world's most active volcanoes. Rising to more than 10,000 feet, Etna looms over the landscape, blanketing the surroundings with rich volcanic soil that fuels the growth of vineyards and orchards. Away from Etna's shadow, the Nebrodi and Madonie mountain ranges stretch across the northern coast, providing a haven for hikers, bird watchers, and nature enthusiasts.

But Sicily is not all mountains and rugged landscapes. It also cradles extensive agricultural plains, including the fertile Conca d'Oro outside Palermo, known for its lush citrus groves and artichokes. A notable part of Sicily's geography is its coastline, stretching over a thousand kilometers, shaped by scenic bays, rocky cliffs, and golden sandy beaches that dip into crystal clear waters.

Now, let's talk about the climate. Sicily benefits from a Mediterranean climate, which means warm, dry summers and mild, wet winters. The island is one of the sunniest places in Europe, boasting an average of 2,500 to 3,000 hours of sunshine per year. These sunny spells, combined with the cooling sea breezes, create the perfect climate for the cultivation of grapes, olives, and a plethora of other fruits and vegetables that make Sicilian cuisine so delightful.

However, Sicily's weather is not entirely uniform. Higher altitudes around Mount Etna and the other mountain ranges see cooler temperatures and heavier precipitation. In the winter months, it's not uncommon to see snow caps adorning the peaks of Etna, offering skiing opportunities that juxtapose splendidly with the balmy coast.

It's this extraordinary blend of geography and climate that makes Sicily such a captivating place. From the snowy peaks of Mount Etna to the sun-soaked beaches of the south, from the verdant hillsides teeming with olive groves to the bustling, vibrant cities, Sicily's landscapes and weather patterns invite exploration, promising adventures that are as varied and thrilling as the island's terrain itself.

MAIN CITIES TO VISIT

Palermo: the beating heart of Sicily

Alive with an eclectic mix of architectural marvels, the city is an open-air museum showcasing epochs of rich history. Byzantine mosaics and Arab arches, baroque churches and gothic palaces, all are a testament to the manifold civilizations that left their indelible prints on Palermo's urban fabric. A casual stroll around the city is an immersive lesson in history, as if the stones themselves were whispering tales from the past.

Teatro Massimo stands imperiously as one of the premier opera houses in Europe. Echoing with the tunes of Verdi and Rossini, its awe-inspiring neoclassical facade and lush interiors provide a heavenly setting for evenings of cultural delight. Nearby, the Palermo Cathedral dazzles with its array of architectural styles, each layer telling a story of the city's illustrious past, while the breath-taking mosaics of the Cappella Palatina bring Byzantine art to life.

Yet Palermo isn't merely a city of grand monuments and elegant boulevards. Its soul resides in its bustling markets, where the real lifeblood of the city pumps. The Mercato Ballarò, for instance, is a sensory overload - colourful displays of fresh produce, the calls of vendors echoing around the narrow lanes, and the intoxicating scent of traditional street food permeate the air. Here, the city's Norman-Arab heritage thrives in every corner and every mouthful of food.

Adding to the charm, the locals are warm, engaging, and always up for a chat. Their spirited discussions, quick to laughter or heated debates, are as much part of the city's soundscape as the rustling palm trees or the distant hum of the Mediterranean Sea.

One must not miss the iconic Quattro Canti, the four corners formally known as Piazza Vigliena. This unique intersection of two principal streets in the historic city center is adorned with baroque buildings featuring statues of the four seasons, Spanish kings and the patronesses of Palermo. It's an enchanting architectural testament to Palermo's history, radiating grandeur and intricate beauty.

Just a stone's throw away lies the historic Kalsa district. This former Arabic quarter, named after the Arabic al-Khalisa, meaning "the chosen," is a treasure trove of winding streets, baroque churches, and eclectic eateries. The district is also home to the Regional Archaeological Museum, which harbors a vast collection of artifacts illuminating the history of Sicily from prehistoric times to the late Roman era.

Continuing with our exploration of Palermo's rich past, the Palazzo dei Normanni is a must-visit site. This palace is a striking symbol of the city's Norman past, boasting incredible architecture and home to the mesmerizing Cappella Palatina, with its dazzling Byzantine mosaics. The palace is not just a monument, it is a thriving testament to history, serving as the seat of the Sicilian Regional Assembly.

Palermo's food culture is a universe unto itself. Piazza Marina on a Sunday morning offers a fantastic flea market where one can snack on local treats like the arancini, a deep-fried risotto ball filled with a variety of stuffings. For the more adventurous, Palermo offers a unique street food experience like the "pani ca meusa," a sandwich filled with sautéed spleen, a local delicacy!

Natural beauty also abounds in Palermo. The picturesque promenade at Foro Italico provides a perfect place for an evening stroll, with expansive views of the azure Mediterranean Sea. For the botany enthusiasts, the verdant splendor of the Orto Botanico, the city's botanical gardens, offers a peaceful sanctuary away from the urban hustle.

When night falls, Palermo is a city that knows how to enjoy itself. From chic rooftop bars with stunning views of the city, like the one at Hotel Ambasciatori, to clubs that offer a chance to dance the night away, the city's nightlife buzzes with energy and excitement.

Through all this, what remains with you about Palermo is not just its historical treasures or the tantalizing cuisine, but the indomitable spirit of its people. The 'Palermitani' are a passionate, resilient lot who have weathered many storms yet have retained their warmth, hospitality, and zest for life. Their resilience is as much a part of Palermo's DNA as its centuries-old architecture or its lively markets.

There is a rhythm to Palermo, an almost tangible pulse. Whether in the dance of sunlight and shadow on the cobblestone streets or the orchestrated chaos of its historic markets, the city hums with an energy that is intoxicating and wholly authentic. This, dear friends, is Palermo - a symphony of history, culture, and life's simplest, most beautiful pleasures.

This intricate tapestry of life in Palermo, blending the past with the present, is what makes this city more than just a tourist destination. It's an experience, a heady mix of sights, sounds, and flavors that make you feel like you're not just visiting Palermo, but truly living it.

Catania: a city on lava

Catania, the city built on lava, is the pulsating heart of Sicily's eastern coast. Under the gaze of Mount Etna, Europe's highest and most active volcano, Catania's fertile soil, nourished by numerous eruptions, has fostered a city bursting with life and charm.

Entering Catania is akin to stepping onto the pages of a living history book. An intriguing blend of Baroque architecture, ancient ruins, and vibrant city life offers a feast for the senses. The city was reborn from the ashes of a catastrophic earthquake and a series of volcanic eruptions during the 17th century, which shaped its unique architectural landscape.

Walking through Catania's city center, you can't help but admire the opulence of the Palazzo Biscari. This extravagant 18th-century palace, with its ornate ballrooms and mythological frescoes, embodies the spirit of Sicilian Baroque. The palace's balcony offers a breathtaking panorama of the city, with the volcano's ominous presence in the distance.

A few steps away, you'll find the Catania Cathedral, dedicated to Saint Agatha, the city's patron saint. The cathedral, with its magnificent façade, stands as a testament to the resilience of the people of Catania, having been rebuilt several times due to natural disasters.

Nestled among these historic sites is the Piazza del Duomo, Catania's main square. At its center, the iconic "Liotru," or the Elephant Fountain, stands tall. This black lava stone elephant carrying an obelisk is more than just a city symbol; it's a perfect representation of Catania itself—strong, unique, and inherently tied to the power of Mount Etna.

Just a short walk from the piazza, Catania's Fish Market, or "la pescheria," comes alive every morning. The market is a sensory experience filled with the briny scent of the sea, the cacophony of vendors hawking their fresh catches, and a kaleidoscope of seafood, from crimson prawns to octopuses and sea urchins. Here, the city's intimate relationship with the sea is on full display.

The city, of course, wouldn't be complete without its culinary scene. Catania's gastronomy is a fusion of flavors, with a variety of dishes that reflect its rich cultural history. From Pasta alla Norma, a delicious concoction of tomatoes, fried aubergines, basil, and ricotta, named in honor of Catania's famous composer Vincenzo Bellini's opera, to the city's famous cannoli, a sweet treat of crisp pastry tube filled with creamy ricotta—Catania is a food lover's paradise.

Yet, for all its architectural marvels and tantalizing cuisine, it is the grandeur of nature that steals the show in Catania. A trip to Mount Etna is an unforgettable journey. Its moon-like landscape, the scent of sulfur in the air, and the thrill of being on an active volcano—it's a reminder of nature's indomitable spirit and humbling power.

In the outskirts of the city, the "Riviera dei Ciclopi," or the Cyclops Riviera, offers beautiful beach areas, like the picturesque fishing village of Acitrezza, home to the legendary giant rocks thrown by Polyphemus in Homer's Odyssey.

Catania is a celebration of life in all its vibrancy. It is a city where the old and the new, the earthly and the divine, the fiery temperament of a volcano, and the cool tranquility of the sea coexist. It is a testament to resilience, rebirth, and the eternal dance between civilization and nature. With every cobblestone etched with history and every corner echoing with stories, Catania invites you to live its tale.

Siracusa: the echo of magna Graecia

In the southeastern corner of Sicily, a city has held firm to its roots, an emblem of the island's Greek past and an enduring testament to its rich heritage. Welcome to Siracusa, or Syracuse as it's known in English, the city where echoes of Magna Graecia, or Greater Greece, still reverberate.

The city's history began in 734 BC when Corinthians, led by the aristocrat Archias, founded it. It quickly flourished and grew into one of the ancient world's most influential cities, rivaling even Athens in size and prestige. Its former grandeur may not be immediately apparent in the hustle and bustle of the modern city, but venture into the archaeological park of neapolis, and you'll soon encounter Siracusa's magnificent past.

The Greek Theater, one of the largest and best-preserved in the world, is a testament to the city's cultural eminence. Carved out of the hillside, the theatre's massive stone steps form an imposing semicircle, a venue that once held 15,000 spectators. Here, the works of famed playwrights such as Aeschylus and Euripides came alive, and even today, the annual Greek Theatre Festival revives the ancient tradition of theatrical performances.

Just a stone's throw away from the theater, the Ear of Dionysius, a massive, cave with incredible acoustics, unfolds its peculiar history. Legend has it that the tyrant Dionysius used the cave's acoustics to eavesdrop on his prisoners, a chilling reminder of the city's tumultuous past.

Descending from the neapolis park, the island of Ortygia awaits, the historic heart of Siracusa. This tiny island connected to the mainland by three bridges, is a treasure trove of architectural wonders. Wander through its narrow, winding streets, and you'll be greeted by a labyrinth of enchanting lanes filled with baroque palaces and piazzas, while the salty scent of the Ionian Sea wafts through the air.

In the island's center, the magnificent Piazza Duomo unveils a sublime blend of architectural styles. The Cathedral of Siracusa, a remarkable example of Sicilian Baroque, was built incorporating the ancient Temple of Athena, whose Doric columns are still visible in its structure, creating a remarkable blend of ancient and baroque architecture.

But Ortygia isn't just about historical monuments. It's a living, breathing entity where locals go about their daily lives amid timeless surroundings. The bustling market, alive with the aroma of fresh produce, the chatter of local vendors, and the taste of the best street food in Sicily, infuses the city's Greek and Roman past with its vibrant present.

Siracusa's appeal extends beyond its historical core. The surrounding region, with its picturesque fishing villages, stunning beaches, and the pristine Vendicari Nature Reserve, offers a different kind of beauty, as vibrant and compelling as the city itself.

Siracusa is a place where time has melded the past with the present, creating a city of timeless appeal. With the echoing voices of Greek philosophers, the whispers of Baroque nobility, and the lively hum of local life, Siracusa invites visitors to journey through the pages of history while savoring the vivacious spirit of Sicilian life. Every corner holds a story, every stone a memory of times past, and every wave that laps against Ortygia's shores sings the melody of Magna Grecia.

but the wonder doesn't end there, there's much more to see in Siracusa that a traveler wouldn't want to miss:

The Fountain of Arethusa

According to Greek myth, Arethusa was a nymph who was transformed into a freshwater spring by the goddess Artemis to escape the river god Alpheus. Today, the spring can be found in Ortygia, where it still bubbles up next to the sea, creating a unique freshwater pond inhabited by papyrus plants and ducks.

Archaeological Museum of Paolo Orsi

Named after the prominent archaeologist, the Museo Archeologico Regionale Paolo Orsi is one of the most significant archaeological museums in Europe. It boasts a vast collection of artifacts from prehistoric times to the late antiquity, revealing the profound layers of history that have shaped Siracusa and Sicily as a whole.

The Catacombs of San Giovanni

While not as well-known as Rome's, Siracusa's catacombs provide a fascinating glimpse into early Christianity. The catacombs were initially a burial site during the Greek and Roman eras before becoming a place of worship for early Christians. The extensive underground tunnels serve as a solemn testament to the city's long and diverse history.

The Byzantine Catacombs

Beyond San Giovanni, there are many lesser known but equally fascinating catacombs scattered throughout Siracusa, many dating back to the Byzantine era. These catacombs provide another layer to Siracusa's storied past.

Castello Maniace

At the southern tip of Ortygia, this imposing fortress juts out into the sea. Constructed under the reign of Frederick II in the 13th century, Castello Maniace offers stunning views of the sea and city. While the interior is usually closed to the public, the exterior alone is worth the visit.

Bellomo Palace Museum

Housed in a magnificent 13th-century palace, the Museo del Palazzo Bellomo holds a collection of Sicilian art ranging from the Middle Ages to the 18th century, including Antonello da Messina's iconic "Annunciation."

Taormina: A Balcony on the Sea

h, Taormina! Poised on the eastern coast of Sicily, it's a destination that combines the charm of antiquity with the vibrant warmth of Mediterranean hospitality. With every step you take in this town, history whispers stories of civilizations that have come and gone, each leaving their indelible marks on the land and its people.

The journey to Taormina itself is an introduction to its beauty. As your path winds up the hillside, each twist and turn reveals breathtaking views of the Ionian Sea, kissed by the Mediterranean sun. As the vista expands, you'll spot the silhouette of Mount Etna in the distance, an eternal sentinel that has played a crucial role in shaping Sicily's landscape and psyche.

Taormina's allure starts from its historical heart. Piazza IX Aprile, the town's main square, is framed by the artistic splendor of the Church of Saint Augustine, the Torre dell'Orologio and the classic Baroque stylings of the Church of Saint Joseph. This square, which overlooks the sea, is the social hub of the town and a perfect spot for people watching or catching the extraordinary Sicilian sunsets.

Speaking of antiquity, you can't ignore the Greek Theatre, a jewel of ancient architecture, perched high on the cliffs of Taormina. Built in the third century BC, it is the second largest of its kind in Sicily. Even today, this ancient auditorium echoes with performances during the summer season. The acoustics of the theatre, combined with the panoramic backdrop of Mount Etna and the sea, make every performance there a memorable one.

Nearby is the Public Garden of Taormina, a verdant space adorned with diverse vegetation and peculiar architectural follies. You can enjoy a leisurely stroll through these gardens, and perhaps find a quiet spot for a picnic or simply soak in the stunning view of the coastline.

A few steps away from the park is the charming quarter of Castelmola. It's a quaint little hamlet, perfect for a tranquil afternoon away from the hustle and bustle. Here, you can walk the cobbled streets, explore the Norman ruins, or take in a panoramic view of the coast from the town's highest vantage point.

The Corso Umberto, Taormina's main street, is an adventure in itself. A walk down this bustling thoroughfare takes you through a variety of shops and boutiques, selling everything from high fashion to local Sicilian produce. The street is lined with buildings that showcase architectural styles spanning many centuries, adding to the eclectic feel of the town.

Food lovers will rejoice in Taormina's culinary scene. The town is ripe with cafes and restaurants, each offering their spin on Sicilian cuisine. The local seafood, sourced fresh from the surrounding waters, is a must-try. Pair it with a glass of local Etna wine, and you have a gastronomic experience that caters to all your senses.

Taormina is not just about history and food. For those craving a day at the beach, the town is a gateway to the beautiful bays of Mazzarò, Isola Bella, and Giardini Naxos. Each offers crystal clear waters, sandy beaches, and a plethora of water activities for the adventurous.

In the end, what makes Taormina truly enchanting is its soul. It's the way the golden light drapes over the ancient architecture during sunset, the echo of the church bells through the valleys, the delicate aroma of orange blossoms in the air, and the ever-present symphony of the sea. It's in these moments that you realize Taormina isn't just a place to visit; it's an experience to be lived, an emotion to be felt, a memory to be treasured.

UNKNOWN SICILY: OFF THE BEATEN PATH

While the charming piazzas and cobblestone streets of Palermo, the intriguing lava fields of Catania, the mesmerizing echoes of Magna Grecia in Siracusa, and the breathtaking vistas of Taormina are indeed enchanting, there's a different Sicily awaiting those who dare to tread off the well-worn tourist path. This is a Sicily of raw, unspoiled beauty, where the air is perfumed with wild herbs, where the sunsets over the Mediterranean Sea are an artist's dream, and where ancient traditions persist, untouched by the trappings of modernity. Let's journey together into the heart of this less-known but deeply enchanting Sicily, a place where every turn in the road reveals another stunning vista, another taste of authentic Sicilian life.

Monti Nebrodi: Unspoiled Nature

The allure of the Nebrodi Mountains is magnetic. At nearly 2,000 square kilometers, this protected area is a tapestry of diverse landscapes that transition seamlessly from luscious woodland to rugged mountain terrain, and onto rolling green pastures, each scene as captivating as the last.

For the true adventurer, Nebrodi's hiking trails are a treat. Routes such as the "Dorsale dei Nebrodi," a multi-day trek that traces the park's mountainous spine, presents an immersive journey into the region's wild heart. A walk here is filled with moments of awe as you navigate through dense woods, crossing babbling streams, and clambering over moss-covered rocks.

One of the defining features of Nebrodi is its numerous natural lakes, each possessing a distinct character. Besides the peaceful Lake Maulazzo, there is Lake Biviere, a high-altitude wetland that serves as a migratory stop for a variety of bird species, making it a dream destination for bird-watchers. Nearby, the ethereal beauty of Lake Trearie with its shimmering water mirroring the surrounding beech trees is sure to enchant visitors.

In the heart of the park, scattered amidst the verdant scenery, are scores of pastoral communities. While their architecture and layout are appealing, it's their

inhabitants and their way of life that truly bring these places to life. The traditional practices of cheese-making and bread baking, among others, are very much alive here. A visit to a local cheese farm, for example, offers a unique insight into the production of the famous 'Provola dei Nebrodi', a regional cheese recognized for its exceptional quality and taste.

Archaeological sites dot the landscape of Nebrodi, each providing a unique glimpse into the region's historical and cultural roots. The Argimusco plateau, often dubbed as Sicily's Stonehenge, is an intriguing megalithic site where the shapes of the stones are said to align with astrological phenomena.

Then, there's the Rocche del Crasto, an imposing mountain area known for its large golden eagles. Perched high among the peaks are what remains of old Sicilian settlements, their ruins keeping vigil over the valleys below.

Monti Nebrodi's strength resides not just in its natural beauty but also in its rich culture and traditions, the history etched into its landscapes, and the enduring spirit of its people. Every curve and contour of this untouched region beckons the intrepid explorer to delve deeper and experience Sicily's raw, rugged beauty at its most compelling.

The Most Beautiful Villages: Hidden Sicily

Cradled in the heart of the Mediterranean, Sicily's towns and villages are repositories of culture, history, and tradition, offering unexpected treasures for those willing to stray off the well-trodden path. Amidst emerald mountains, rolling vineyards, and azure waters, you'll discover the real Sicily in its smaller communities, where time seems to stand still.

Gangi

Begin your journey in the unassuming village of Gangi. Tucked away in the Madonie Mountains, this medieval hilltop town was named the 'Most Beautiful Village in Italy' in 2014. Its cobblestone streets wind up the hill, leading you past rustic stone houses and inviting you into quiet squares, where locals gather to exchange pleasantries and share stories. A step into Gangi is a step back in time, where ancient traditions are lovingly preserved.

Montalbano Elicona

Next, make your way to Montalbano Elicona, named one of the most beautiful villages in Italy. With its tangle of winding medieval streets, grand castle, and stunning views over the Nebrodi Mountains, it's a place that thrives on its historical charm. While you're there, make sure to try the local 'provola' cheese, a delicacy produced from the milk of the cows that graze freely in the surrounding countryside.

Erice

On Sicily's west coast, Erice is a village that sits high above the sea, encircled by ancient defensive walls. Its hilltop position affords stunning panoramic views of the region, from the rugged coastline to the sweeping plains inland. Its labyrinthine streets, twelfth-century castle, and venerable pastry shops make Erice a must-visit destination for those seeking the authentic Sicilian experience.

Sambuca di Sicilia

Journey inland to Sambuca di Sicilia, a quaint village that possesses an Arab soul, witnessed in its winding streets, its saracenic layout, and the remnants of an ancient Muslim castle. Here, amidst the golden hues of the landscape and the warm glow of the sun, life is savored, and every moment holds the potential for beauty.

Savoca

On the eastern coast, Savoca charms visitors with its untouched authenticity. Known as the location for several scenes in Francis Ford Coppola's 'The Godfather,' this village offers more than just cinematic connections. Venture into the catacombs of the Capuchin Monastery, where the mummified bodies of local notables provide an intriguing, if somewhat eerie, look into the past. And don't forget to sit and enjoy a lemon granita in the iconic Bar Vitelli, just as Michael Corleone did.

Noto

Venture to the southern edge of Sicily to the Baroque beauty that is Noto. Although not as obscure as the other villages, it's nonetheless a hidden gem that deserves mention. Rebuilt after a devastating earthquake in 1693, the town is a masterpiece of Sicilian Baroque architecture. Wander down the Corso Vittorio Emanuele, marvel at the intricate façades of the honey-colored stone buildings and take a moment to savor the quiet charm of this unassuming town.

Ragusa Ibla

If you travel to the southeast corner of the island, you will come across the town of Ragusa Ibla, the old part of the city of Ragusa, largely rebuilt in the Baroque style after a destructive earthquake in 1693. Ragusa Ibla's beauty is so compelling that it served as the backdrop for the popular Italian TV series "Inspector Montalbano." As you wander through its labyrinthine streets and over its stone bridges, you can't help but feel like you've stepped onto a film set, where every corner promises intrigue and drama.

Scopello

Moving westward, you'll find the picturesque village of Scopello, not far from the city of Trapani. A former tuna fishing village, Scopello charms visitors with its unspoiled landscape and crystal-clear waters. Film aficionados may recognize Scopello from scenes in the Hollywood blockbuster "Ocean's Twelve." Be sure to visit the tonnara (tuna fishery) and the nearby Zingaro Nature Reserve, one of Sicily's natural gems, with its seven kilometers of unspoiled coastline.

Castelmola

Lastly, Castelmola, perched high above the well-known town of Taormina, is a place of stunning vistas and quiet charm. Its strategic location and panoramic terraces made it an ideal setting for scenes in the film "The Big Blue." Explore the village's quaint streets, visit the remains of its Norman castle, and be sure to stop at Bar Turrisi for a taste of their famous almond wine.

These lesser-known villages of Sicily not only provide a welcome escape from the bustling tourist hotspots but also offer a journey into the very soul of Sicily – its traditions, its history, and, most importantly, its people. There's something quite magical about venturing into these off-the-beaten-path locales, where centuries-old traditions still thrive, and every stone, every street, and every smile tells a story. So, ready your spirit for adventure, and embrace the allure of hidden Sicily, where every turn leads you closer to the heart of this Mediterranean jewel.

SICILIAN ISLANDS – JEWELS OF THE MEDITERRANEAN

In the warm embrace of the Mediterranean lie the Sicilian Islands, each possessing a distinct character that embodies the diversity of Sicily as a whole. Lush vineyards, imposing volcanoes, crystal clear waters and rich histories punctuate these islands, presenting a plethora of adventures waiting to be discovered.

Sicily's Volcanic Trio: The Aeolian Islands

In the cobalt expanse of the Tyrrhenian Sea, north of Sicily, the Aeolian Islands rise dramatically from the waters. Composed of seven islands and various volcanic formations, the Aeolian archipelago encapsulates the mesmerizing power of nature and the alluring charm of Mediterranean culture.

Stromboli: The Lighthouse of the Mediterranean

Imagine a skyline perforated by a smoking silhouette and a night sky flickering with nature's fireworks. That's Stromboli, the ever-active volcano island known as the "Lighthouse of the Mediterranean." Its constant volcanic activity makes for a hypnotic spectacle, especially at night when the glowing lava lights up the darkness. The Sciara del Fuoco, a large scar in the island's side, is where the lava

flows freely into the sea, a sight that leaves visitors in awe. For the adventurous, guided hikes allow you to witness this primordial showcase up close.

Aside from the volcano, Stromboli offers delightful black sand beaches, crystal-clear waters, and quaint settlements. The island's whitewashed houses, blue sea, and fiery mountain make a picture-postcard view, while the small village of Ginostra, only reachable by boat, offers tranquility in an old-world setting.

Vulcano: A Geologist's Dream

South of Stromboli, Vulcano, as its name suggests, is known for its volcanic phenomena. It's a living geology lesson, where you can walk on a crater's edge, bathe in thermal mud baths famed for their therapeutic properties, and swim in warm, bubbling sea waters heated by volcanic fumaroles.

The island is dominated by the large Fossa crater, a walkable volcano where you can witness the power of Mother Nature as sulfuric gases escape from the Earth's crust. From the top, the vista across the Aeolian Islands is unparalleled. Beyond its geology, Vulcano has some lovely beaches. Porto di Levante, with its shallow, warm waters and black sands, offers an ideal spot to relax after a day of exploring.

Lipari: The Aeolian Queen

The largest and most populated of the Aeolian Islands, Lipari serves as the archipelago's vibrant heart. Rich in history, the island's past is recorded at the Aeolian Archaeological Museum, where remnants from prehistoric times to the Greek period are displayed.

A stroll around Lipari Town reveals charming streets, a historic castle, and bustling piazzas filled with local cafes serving fresh seafood and the island's renowned Malvasia wine. Outside the town, you'll find a rugged coastline adorned with beautiful coves and beaches, such as Spiaggia Bianca, known for its pumice-white sand.

The Aeolian Islands, each with its unique character and appeal, offer an enchanting blend of awe-inspiring nature, inviting Mediterranean culture, and fascinating history. Their volcanic origins have given birth to breathtaking landscapes and formed a backdrop to a distinctive way of life. To visit these islands is to embark on a memorable journey that straddles the elemental forces of the earth and the tranquil allure of the sea.

Pantelleria: The Black Pearl of the Mediterranean

Venture south of Sicily, almost halfway to Tunisia, and you'll find the solitary

island of Pantelleria - the Black Pearl of the Mediterranean. The island is a testament to the remarkable symbiosis between the wild, primeval forces of nature and the resilient human spirit. This unique harmony is evident in the island's architecture, culture, and gastronomy, all shaped by the powerful volcanic forces.

Elemental Landscape

Pantelleria is primarily known for its strikingly rugged landscape formed by past volcanic activity. The coastline is a dramatic spectacle of jagged black cliffs and capricious lava formations plunging into the deep blue sea. At the heart of the island lies the Montagna Grande, a dormant volcano covered in a thick Mediterranean macchia, a testament to nature's tenacity.

A Storied Past

Pantelleria's history is rich and captivating, with traces of its past still visible. Discover prehistoric archaeological sites like the Sesi, tombs built by the island's earliest settlers. Visit the remains of the Roman acropolis at San Marco and Santa Teresa, where thermal baths hint at a luxurious Roman lifestyle.

Architectural Harmony

Pantelleria is famed for its unique vernacular architecture - the dammuso. Traditional Pantescan homes, dammusi are built from local black lava stone with characteristic domed roofs designed to capture precious rainwater. Their thick walls keep interiors pleasantly cool during scorching summer months, demonstrating the ingenuity of traditional architectural solutions.

Taste of the Island

Pantelleria boasts a distinctive cuisine, reflecting the island's fusion of Italian and North African influences. Zibibbo grapes thrive in the volcanic soil, producing Passito di Pantelleria, an exquisite dessert wine appreciated worldwide. The island's capers, with their intense flavor, have received protected designation of origin status and are a must-try delicacy.

Natural Wonders

For nature lovers, Pantelleria offers extraordinary experiences. Hike the scenic trails of the Montagna Grande and soak in the panoramic views from its peak. Immerse yourself in the rejuvenating thermal waters of Lago di Venere or the steamy sauna caves of Scauri. For the ultimate Pantescan experience, visit the Specchio di Venere, a lake in a volcanic crater where you can swim in warm, therapeutic mud.

Pantelleria offers an authentic and compelling experience far from the conventional tourist routes. The profound bond between the people and the land, shaped by volcanic forces and historical shifts, has created an island of distinctive character and untamed beauty. It's a place where you can truly experience the transformative power of nature.

Lampedusa & Linosa: Europe's Southern Frontier

Beyond the southern tip of Sicily and closer to the coasts of Tunisia than Italy, you'll find the Pelagie Islands – the last frontier of Europe. These are Lampedusa and Linosa, two lesser-known pearls, each with its unique character, brimming with untamed beauty and charm.

Lampedusa: The Sea Turtle Sanctuary

Known for its crystal-clear turquoise waters and fine sandy beaches, Lampedusa is the largest of the Pelagie archipelago. However, it's not just sun-seeking vacationers that flock to its shores. Lampedusa's most famous beach, the iconic Spiaggia dei Conigli or 'Rabbit Beach', serves as a crucial nesting ground for loggerhead sea turtles. These majestic creatures return every year to lay their eggs, an awe-inspiring spectacle that visitors can witness if timed right.

Lampedusa's character extends beyond the beach. Inhabited for over two millennia, the island has a rich history visible in the archaeological ruins of Roman and Phoenician settlements. A stroll through the lively town center reveals a blend of cultures – Italian, African, and Mediterranean – a true melting pot shaped by geography and history.

Linosa: Volcanic Splendor

In contrast to Lampedusa's sandy shores, Linosa, the archipelago's second-largest island, is an explosion of color. Here, the volcanic origins are immediately apparent: three extinct craters rise above a landscape of black volcanic sand and fields painted with a kaleidoscope of wildflowers. The island's coast is adorned with steep cliffs, interrupted occasionally by small beaches and charming coves.

The vibrant landscapes continue beneath the waterline. Snorkeling or diving in the waters off Linosa is like stepping into a living aquarium, teeming with a myriad of marine life – a paradise for underwater enthusiasts.

Linosa's tiny village exudes an atmosphere of simplicity and tranquility, reflective of its island life. Colorful cubic houses line the narrow streets, where time seems to have paused, and the rest of the world feels a million miles away.

A Journey Worth Making

Both Lampedusa and Linosa provide the opportunity to disconnect from the outside world and immerse oneself in the simple beauty of island life. From the enchanting sea turtle spectacle of Lampedusa to the radiant blooms against the volcanic backdrop of Linosa, the islands present a humble yet rich experience of nature's grandeur.

Visiting these islands is not just about the exquisite natural environment; it's about the welcoming locals, the slow pace of life, and the cultures shaped by the surrounding sea. These are places of refuge and escape, a glimpse into a way of life dictated by the rhythms of nature, where every moment feels like a stolen piece of paradise. Together, Lampedusa and Linosa serve as a unique and refreshing reminder of the diverse treasures hidden within Europe's Southern Frontier.

Egadi Islands: Unspoiled Mediterranean Beauty

When we think of untouched Mediterranean beauty, the Egadi Islands instantly come to mind. This archipelago, nestled off the western coast of Sicily, consists of three principal islands: Favignana, Levanzo, and Marettimo. Each island, while sharing the azure backdrop of the Tyrrhenian Sea, offers a distinctive charm and allure.

Favignana: The Butterfly Island

Shaped like a butterfly, Favignana is the largest and most accessible of the Egadi Islands. Her shores alternate between dramatic cliffs and enchanting coves, the

most notable of which is the famous Cala Rossa. This beach, a mesmerizing fusion of turquoise waters and an ancient tufa quarry, embodies the juxtaposition of nature and history that defines Favignana.

The island is known for its historical significance in tuna fishing. The ancient 'Tonnara' or tuna fishery is a testament to this past, hosting the 'mattanza,' a traditional and choreographed capture of tuna, until the early 21st century. Today, it stands as a museum, providing insights into the island's cultural heritage.

Levanzo: A Dive into Prehistory

The smallest and perhaps the most charming of the Egadi, Levanzo, is like a glimpse into a bygone era. Its main attraction is the Grotta del Genovese, a prehistoric cave adorned with Neolithic cave paintings and Paleolithic petroglyphs - a silent narrative of human history etched on stone.

Levanzo is also home to an array of serene, pebble-lined beaches and azure bays. Its coastal paths lead to hidden bathing spots, accessible only by foot or boat, providing an intimate encounter with the island's stunning maritime landscape.

Marettimo: The Wild Island

Marettimo, the furthest from the mainland, is the wildest and most untouched of the trio. It's a hiker's paradise with a network of trails that traverse through its lush vegetation, leading up to panoramic peaks, and down to secret sea caves. The island is also a haven for scuba divers, who are drawn to its thriving underwater ecosystem, full of caves and archaeological treasures.

Its sparse population and remote location have preserved Marettimo's traditional character. The white houses of its single village, fringed with vibrant bougainvillea, stand as a beacon against the backdrop of the Mediterranean, seemingly lost in time.

Discovering the Egadi

The Egadi Islands capture the essence of the Mediterranean, a harmony of brilliant landscapes, rich history, and warm hospitality. A voyage here feels less like a trip and more like a slow dance with nature. Whether it's the allure of Favignana's past, the captivating simplicity of Levanzo, or the untamed wilds of Marettimo, the Egadi Islands offer a detour from the usual path, transporting visitors to a world that feels both ancient and new. Each island promises a unique exploration, a journey that unravels the heart and soul of the Mediterranean, in all its unspoiled beauty.

SICILIAN CUISINE: A CULINARY JOURNEY

If you're looking for a culinary adventure that's as thrilling and diverse as the landscape itself, prepare to be dazzled by Sicily. Sicilian cuisine, a delightful concoction of Greek, Arabic, Spanish, and French influences, is renowned for its bold and vibrant flavors, varied textures, and a marvelous range of both sweet and savory offerings. This is a cuisine shaped by the island's history, geography, and climate - a gastronomic tale of invasions, trade, and an abundance of locally-sourced ingredients.

Every aspect of Sicilian food is a testament to the island's richness, from the dazzling array of seafood caught off its coast, to the luscious fruits, almonds, olives and wheat cultivated in its fertile soils, and the herds of sheep that produce high-quality dairy products.

Seafood is a staple, particularly tuna, swordfish, sardines, and cuttlefish, which are typically grilled, baked, or made into hearty stews. It graces the tables of both humble homes and sophisticated restaurants, offering an authentic taste of the island's maritime heritage. The coastline also provides a variety of crustaceans and mollusks, adding a unique touch to pastas and risottos.

Sicilian pastas are diverse, with shapes and sauces that differ from region to region. Pasta alla Norma, from Catania, is an iconic dish, featuring fried eggplant, tomatoes, basil and a generous sprinkling of salty ricotta salata. Pasta con le Sarde, on the other hand, is a delightful mix of fresh sardines, wild fennel, saffron, pine nuts, and raisins.

The Sicilian palate isn't solely dedicated to the savory. Sicilian desserts are among Italy's most iconic, inspired by centuries of Convent baking and Arabic sweet making. The famed Cannoli are tubular shells of fried pastry dough filled with a sweet, creamy ricotta. Then there's the divine Cassata, a colorful sponge  cake layered with ricotta, covered with a green almond paste and elegantly decorated with candied fruits.

Street food, a world in its own right, is at the very heart of Sicilian cuisine. Arancini, deep-fried balls of saffron risotto with a heart of ragu and peas, are a popular pick. Panelle, chickpea fritters, are typically served in a sesame-seeded bun at street stalls, while Pani ca Meusa offers a taste of the exotic with its filling of veal spleen and lung.

Of course, no culinary journey in Sicily would be complete without a taste of the island's famed cheeses. From the strong and spicy Pecorino Siciliano, to the delicate and creamy Caciocavallo, Sicilian cheeses alone could command a gastronomic tour.

From the breakfast granita and brioche in the bustling bars of Palermo, to the seafood feast in the Trattorias of Catania, every meal in Sicily is a journey of discovery. It's a cuisine that surprises and satisfies, inviting you to explore the island's rich history, culture, and indomitable spirit, one delicious bite at a time.

In the end, Sicilian food is more than a mere list of dishes and ingredients. It is, instead, a reflection of the island's unique character, echoing the rhythm of the seasons, the diversity of its landscape, and the spirit of its people. Exploring this gastronomic paradise is like unearthing hidden treasures, an experience that transcends the sense of taste, and reveals the soul of Sicily itself.

Food Walk in Sicily:
A Step-by-Step Culinary Adventure

Embarking on a food walk in Sicily is like exploring an open-air museum dedicated to the art of gastronomy, an immersive journey punctuated by delightful encounters with local vendors, bustling markets, and centuries-old family-run establishments. Picture strolling down sun-drenched lanes, savoring the scents of simmering sauces and frying fish, exchanging smiles with passionate food artisans, and of course, tasting the fruits of their labor.

Begin your food walk in the heart of Palermo, a city renowned for its street food

culture. The vibrant Ballarò Market is a feast for the senses, teeming with stalls piled high with fresh fruits, vegetables, and an array of locally-caught seafood. The chatter of vendors, the vibrant colors of the produce, the sizzle of frying panelle, and the aroma of grilling meats create an atmosphere that's as intoxicating as it is inspiring.

Don't miss a chance to taste the iconic Arancini, golden orbs of crispy, saffron-infused rice with a molten core of ragu, peas, and melting mozzarella. Stop by a stall selling Pani ca Meusa, a soft bun filled with tender veal spleen and lung, a dish that dates back to the Middle Ages and exemplifies the 'nose-to-tail' approach of Sicilian cooking. Finish your street food adventure with a Sfincione, Palermo's take on pizza, a soft, thick, dough topped with tomatoes, onions, anchovies, and a sprinkling of caciocavallo cheese.

Next, venture east to the Baroque city of Catania. At the Pescheria, the city's ancient fish market, watch as chefs and locals haggle over the day's catch. Take a moment to appreciate the mountains of prawns, mussels, clams, octopus, and a myriad of fish species laid out in all their fresh, briny glory.

In Catania, seafood is the star of the show. Sample Pasta alla Norma, a delightful concoction of fresh tomatoes, fried eggplant, salty ricotta salata, and basil, or Pasta con le Sarde, a traditional pasta dish featuring fresh sardines, wild fennel, pine nuts, and raisins.

As you journey through Sicily's southeast, the town of Modica awaits with its unique contribution to the world of sweets: the famous Cioccolato Modicano. This chocolate, made according to ancient Aztec methods brought to Sicily by the Spanish, is grainy, aromatic, and comes in an array of flavors like cinnamon, vanilla, and even chili.

Your food walk wouldn't be complete without a pilgrimage to Ragusa to taste its famous Caciocavallo Ragusano. This stretched-curd cheese, made from the milk of Modicana cows and aged for a minimum of six months, is a must-try for any cheese enthusiast.

Finally, let the tantalizing aroma of lemon groves guide you to the hills surrounding Syracuse. It's here where the world-renowned Siracusa lemons grow, their juice a coveted ingredient in Sicilian cooking and the star of refreshing granita, a semi-frozen dessert that's as Sicilian as the summer sun.

A food walk in Sicily is more than an exercise in indulgence; it's an insight into the island's identity, seen through the prism of its cuisine. It's a testament to the Sicilian spirit, resilient and passionate, creative, and above all, welcoming. So, come hungry, bring your curiosity, and prepare for a gastronomic journey that is as rich, vibrant, and irresistible as Sicily itself.

Sicilian Wines: A Toast to the Sun-Kissed Vineyards

The essence of Sicily, a sun-drenched jewel of the Mediterranean, is beautifully encapsulated in the island's eclectic spectrum of wines. The story of Sicilian wine is a fascinating chronicle, rooted in a rich tapestry of cultures, climates, and landscapes that have each left their unique imprint on the island's viniculture.

To begin, one cannot overlook the importance of the varied terroir. Sicily's diverse landscape, ranging from the volcanic soils of Mount Etna to the sun-baked plains of the south, offers a nurturing cradle for a plethora of indigenous and imported grape varieties. This diverse terrain is the cornerstone behind the distinctive character of Sicilian wines - a fascinating blend of boldness, complexity, and charm that speaks volumes of their place of origin.

The Nero d'Avola, Sicily's signature red grape, has steadily grown in popularity for its wines that are both robust and versatile. Wines produced from this grape are redolent with the fragrances of ripe cherry, plum, and peppery spice, their ruby-colored depths echoing the warm Sicilian sunshine. Grown throughout the island, this grape variety is a testament to Sicily's ability to produce full-bodied reds that pair beautifully with the hearty local cuisine.

Contrasting this is the Nerello Mascalese, a grape largely grown on the northern slopes of Mount Etna. The wines produced from this grape reflect the mineral-rich volcanic soil, boasting elegant flavors that are reminiscent of the revered wines of Burgundy. Their refined structure, along with their notes of ripe berries and spices, make them ideal companions for more sophisticated dishes.

In terms of white grapes, the Grillo is a star. Thriving in the intense Sicilian heat, this grape produces wines that are remarkably refreshing, characterized by a vivacious acidity and notes of citrus and tropical fruits. Grillo wines are the embodiment of a Sicilian summer - light, breezy, and undeniably charismatic.

The fortified Marsala, a legacy of Sicily's winemaking tradition, cannot go unmentioned. Created from a blend of white grapes, including Grillo, Inzolia, and

Catarratto, Marsala wines are a sensory delight, their complex flavors ranging from sweet to dry, with notes of caramel, vanilla, and apricot.

Winemaking in Sicily is more than a centuries-old tradition. It's a testament to the island's resilience, its ability to merge the old with the new. Modern winemaking techniques are being utilized alongside traditional methods, giving rise to wines that not only respect their heritage but also appeal to the evolving tastes of contemporary wine enthusiasts.

Sicilian wines, in essence, are a liquid narrative of the island's vibrant history, its varied landscapes, and its warm, passionate people. A toast to Sicilian wines is more than a mere celebration of their exquisite taste - it's a tribute to the enduring spirit of Sicily itself.

The Wine Routes of Sicily: A Journey through Taste and Tradition

The wine routes of Sicily are a tantalizing invitation to explore the island's winemaking heritage, blending scenic landscapes, historical intrigue, and, of course, the allure of Sicilian wines. This exploration is not merely a journey across vine-laden hills and sun-kissed coasts; it is an intimate encounter with Sicily's soul, its people, its traditions, and its love for la buona vita.

Start your wine journey in the heartland of the Etna Wine Route. Here, the power of nature is evident in every vine that battles the mineral-rich volcanic soils. Wineries like the Benanti Winery and the Barone di Villagrande offer guided tours, where visitors can explore the vineyards, discover the intricacies of the winemaking process, and partake in tastings. Each sip of their signature Nerello Mascalese-based wines is a testament to the enduring spirit of the island, echoing the smoky nuances of the volcanic terrain.

In the southwestern part of the island, the Menfi Wine Route boasts picturesque vineyards that are caressed by the Mediterranean breezes. Planeta, one of the most renowned wineries of the region, offers the opportunity to discover the charm of their wines, alongside a feast of local Sicilian cuisine. The bold flavors of their Nero d'Avola and the crisp freshness of their white wines offer a fascinating counterpoint, their diversity mirroring the multifaceted character of Sicily itself.

The Marsala Wine Route, a trail immortalized by the English merchant John Woodhouse, offers a taste of Sicily's vinous history. The historic wineries of Florio and Pellegrino offer guided tours of their cellars, where time-honored traditions meet modern techniques. The tasting of Marsala, an iconic Sicilian fortified wine, is a sensory journey through notes of caramel, dried fruits, and vanilla - a taste of Sicily in every drop.

The Wine Route of the Sicani Mountains meanders through a region that's an amalgamation of ancient traditions and spectacular landscapes. Here, indigenous grapes such as Inzolia and Catarratto flourish alongside the likes of Chardonnay and Merlot. The Regaleali Estate, a piece of paradise tucked away in the Sicilian hinterland, offers a holistic wine experience - one that encompasses vineyard tours, wine tastings, and a celebration of the Sicilian farm-to-table concept.

Every wine route in Sicily is dotted with charming agriturismi, where visitors can immerse themselves in the rural Sicilian lifestyle. Amidst the tranquil vineyards, the promise of a home-cooked Sicilian meal, accompanied by a glass of the estate's wine, is the epitome of simple pleasures.

Each wine route in Sicily has its unique narrative, its dedicated grape varieties, and its distinct wines. Yet, they are all bound by a common thread - an unwavering respect for the land, a passion for their craft, and a warm Sicilian welcome that instantly makes you feel at home.

So, come and lose yourself in the wine routes of Sicily. Let the whispering vines tell their stories, let the wines introduce you to the soul of the island, and let the people of Sicily show you what it means to truly celebrate life. It's more than a journey - it's an experience that stays with you, long after the last drops of wine have been savored.

AGRIGENTO:
ECHOES OF ANCIENT GREECE IN SICILY

As our Sicilian journey continues, we find ourselves heading towards the southern coast, where history, culture, and natural beauty coalesce in the remarkable city of Agrigento. This new chapter, promises a mesmerizing blend of ancient grandeur and idyllic Mediterranean charm that makes this city a must-visit for any traveler.

Tucked into Sicily's sun-drenched southern coast, Agrigento was once one of the leading cities of Magna Graecia during the golden age of Ancient Greece. The city, originally called Akragas, has an incredibly rich history that has left an indelible imprint in the form of spectacular ruins, grand temples, and evocative archaeological sites.

Our journey to Agrigento will unveil a unique perspective on ancient Greek civilization, far from the mainland Greece, offering an intriguing fusion of Greek, Roman, and Norman influences that have shaped its culture, architecture, and the very fabric of life in this captivating city.

But Agrigento is not just about ancient ruins. Its medieval old town, with its winding alleys, beautiful squares, and charming local eateries, promises a delightful exploration of Sicilian life in all its vibrancy. The stunning natural landscape, particularly the striking coastal formation known as Scala dei Turchi, adds to Agrigento's multifaceted allure.

So, get ready to delve into Agrigento, a place that elegantly straddles the line between the past and the present, offering an unforgettable travel experience. From the shadowy outlines of ancient temples to the warm, inviting Mediterranean seascape, Agrigento is a testament to Sicily's timeless charm.

Valley of the Temples: A Walk with the Gods

Unveiling Agrigento's crown jewel, we take a winding path towards the magnificent Valley of the Temples, a UNESCO World Heritage Site that encapsulates the city's ancient grandeur. We are destined to traverse time, to the age of Greek dominance, where philosophy, democracy, and art thrived.

Walking in the Valley of the Temples is an immersive experience, where one can't help but feel the powerful echoes of history. Laid out along a sacred way, this elongated ridge hosts a series of well-preserved Doric temples, dedicated to various deities, serving as magnificent testimony to the city's Hellenistic past.

Among these architectural wonders, the most captivating is the Temple of Concordia, one of the world's best-preserved Greek temples. Its harmonious proportions and its remarkably intact structure create an awe-inspiring spectacle. Close your eyes for a moment and imagine the priests who once roamed these sacred grounds, the chants, the prayers and the smoke from the offerings curling up towards the azure Sicilian sky.

Not far from the Temple of Concordia, one can explore the ruins of the Temple of Hera, dedicated to the Greek goddess of women and marriage. Despite the ravages of time and human intervention, the surviving columns still hold an aura of sacredness and mystery.

As we stroll further, we encounter the remains of the Temple of Heracles, the oldest in the valley, and the once grand Temple of Olympian Zeus, whose original plans aimed to make it the largest Doric temple ever built. The enormity of its ambitious scale can still be perceived in the colossal ruins.

Every stone, every column in the Valley of the Temples holds a story, a narrative of a thriving civilization that shaped the Western world. The power of this place lies not just in its remarkable preservation but in its ability to transport visitors back in time, offering them a chance to tread the same paths as the ancients, to breathe in the same air and to witness the undying legacy of a once-mighty civilization.

As the sun dips below the horizon, bathing the ancient stone in a golden glow, the Valley of the Temples takes on a magical aura, the shadows of the past becoming almost tangible. It is, without doubt, a journey that stirs the soul and sparks the imagination, and a reminder of how Agrigento, and indeed Sicily itself, has been a crossroads of cultures and civilizations for millennia.

Museo Archeologico Regionale: A Dive into the Past

Lost in the heartland of the Mediterranean, steeped in the echoes of ancient civilizations, the city of Agrigento emerges as an ode to the grandeur of bygone times. Amongst its most precious treasures lies the Museo Archeologico Regionale. This museum, tucked away within Agrigento's picturesque setting, serves as an exceptional gate to the past.

Once you cross the threshold of this cultural sanctuary, it's as if time stands still. You're no longer a visitor, but a time-traveller voyaging through an enchanting world of ancient relics, statues, and artifacts that breathe life into the illustrious history of Sicily. The museum houses an extensive collection of archaeological findings from Agrigento and its environs, offering an unmatched depth of insights into the life, culture, and society of ancient Sicily.

An unmissable sight is the Telamon - a colossal statue, once a supporting figure of the Temple of Zeus, which never fails to stun visitors with its towering presence. It serves as a mute testament to the engineering marvels and artistic splendor of a civilization that has long vanished into the annals of history.

The Ephebe of Agrigento, a bronze statue of exceptional beauty, strikes a balance between a youthful charm and a divine aura. This celebrated Greek sculpture, exuding an aura of timelessness, stands as the museum's crown jewel, subtly captivating anyone who lays their eyes upon it.

But the museum isn't just about statues. From terracotta vases to intricate frescoes, from delicate jewellery to ancient weapons, every piece has a story to narrate. The coin collections, for instance, provide unique insights into the economic systems of antiquity.

However, the charm of the Museo Archeologico Regionale doesn't solely reside within its walls. Its location atop a hill offers sweeping panoramic views of the Valley of the Temples below. Imagine the vista of sun setting over these ancient ruins, painting the sky in shades of crimson and gold - a scene that truly marks an indelible memory.

A visit to the Museo Archeologico Regionale is more than a detour; it's an immersive historical adventure that accentuates the experience of Agrigento. So, if you are keen on uncovering layers of time and catching a glimpse of the rich tapestry of human civilization, make sure to allocate a day for this treasure trove of history.

Scala dei Turchi: Nature's Marvel

In the unspoiled wilds of Sicily, where the azure sea meets the firmament, nature reveals a masterpiece carved with meticulous precision - the Scala dei Turchi. Evoking visions of a stairway to heaven, this natural marvel in Agrigento is a spectacle of arresting beauty, rightfully earning its reputation as one of the island's most awe-inspiring landmarks.

The Scala dei Turchi, or the 'Stair of the Turks,' is a dazzling white marl cliff that gently descends into the Mediterranean. Formed over millions of years by wind

and wave erosion, the cliff takes its intriguing name from the invading Turkish pirates who allegedly used it as a convenient hideout. Today, it's far from a hideout, becoming instead a much sought-after destination for nature-lovers and wanderlust-chasers alike.

Approaching the Scala, one is first struck by the stark contrast of colors. The chalky white marl and clay cliffs, made luminous by the southern sun, set against the vivid blues of the sea and the sky, create an enchanting spectacle. Climbing this natural staircase is a surreal experience, and with every step, the breathtaking panorama of the Mediterranean unfolds further.

If you manage to peel your gaze away from the stunning vistas, do spare a moment to appreciate the cliff itself. Weathered over ages, the rock formations morph into various shapes and textures, telling tales of the relentless passage of time. Here, the ground beneath your feet turns into an open book, recounting the geological history of Sicily.

Once at the top, take a moment to marvel at the sun as it dips below the horizon, painting the sky with vibrant strokes of orange and pink. It's in this moment that you truly appreciate the natural splendor of the Scala dei Turchi, as the soft glow of the setting sun accentuates the cliff's ethereal beauty.

Beyond the mere viewing pleasure, Scala dei Turchi also offers an inviting beach where visitors can relax, soak up the Sicilian sun, and take a dip in the crystal-clear water. The azure waves gently lapping against the bright white cliffs add a soothing rhythm to this idyllic setting, making it a perfect spot for unwinding.

Moreover, the area surrounding the Scala dei Turchi is abundant with flora and fauna. From seagulls circling the sky to the fragrant Mediterranean shrubs that dot the landscape, nature thrives in its unspoiled glory.

However, the Scala dei Turchi is m more than just a picturesque spot; it's a symbol of Sicily's enduring charm. It's where the rhythm of the waves, the whisper of the wind, and the beauty of the terrain come together in a harmonious symphony. Every step taken on this natural staircase is a step taken in the lap of mesmerizing beauty, a beauty that reverberates with the timelessness of nature itself.

Embarking on a journey to the Scala dei Turchi is a pilgrimage to the heart of nature's artistry. This stunning monument of natural architecture, sculpted by time and weather, stands today as a testament to the eternal allure of Sicily. It's a place where one can't help but stand in awe, humbled by the sheer beauty of our planet. As you leave, you carry with you a piece of its charm, a memory of the white cliff gleaming under the Mediterranean sun, etched in your heart forever.

Agrigento: Timeless Echoes of the Greek Past

Agrigento, once a leading city of Ancient Greece, now a spellbinding amalgamation of ancient tales and modern life, invites travelers on a timeless journey. Traces of its Greek heritage are woven seamlessly into the city's tapestry, casting an intriguing blend of old-world charm and contemporary vibrancy.

A stroll through the city's historic center is like stepping into a living museum. Encased within the labyrinth of narrow, winding streets are treasures waiting to be discovered. Each turn, each cobblestone, echoes with tales of its glorious past, stories waiting to be told to those who listen. Here, in the heart of Agrigento, you find yourself stepping back in time, walking the same paths as the Greeks did centuries ago.

Agrigento, once a leading city of Ancient Greece, now a spellbinding amalgamation of ancient tales and modern life, invites travelers on a timeless journey. Traces of its Greek heritage are woven seamlessly into the city's tapestry, casting an intriguing blend of old-world charm and contemporary vibrancy.

A stroll through the city's historic center is like stepping into a living museum. Encased within the labyrinth of narrow, winding streets are treasures waiting to be discovered. Each turn, each cobblestone, echoes with tales of its glorious past, stories waiting to be told to those who listen. Here, in the heart of Agrigento, you find yourself stepping back in time, walking the same paths as the Greeks did centuries ago.

The city's old quarter, known as 'Girgenti,' is a testament to its Greek roots. As you meander through its arteries, you are greeted with a wealth of stunning baroque architecture. Facades of sun-bleached limestone houses stand tall, preserving the character and charm of the city. Don't miss the opportunity to explore the splendid Palazzo Municipale and the intricate Chiesa di Santa Maria dei Greci, built directly over the remains of a Greek temple, merging ancient history and baroque splendor.

Venture into the heart of Agrigento, and you are welcomed by the grandeur of Piazza Pirandello, the city's main square. Named after the famed playwright Luigi Pirandello, a native son of Agrigento, the square stands as a vibrant center of modern life amid the historical landscape. Cafés, shops, and locals going about their daily lives create a lively ambiance, reminiscent of an age-old Italian painting.

Just a stone's throw from the bustling square, the Museo Diocesano reveals a collection of ecclesiastical artifacts, while the Agrigento Cathedral offers panoramic vistas of the cityscape. Climb to the top, and let your gaze sweep across the rooftops, down to the glittering Mediterranean Sea.

Beyond the city's limits, the landscape is a vision of rustic Sicily, untouched and serene. Olive groves and vineyards stretch as far as the eye can see, providing a striking contrast to the historic urban landscape.

Agrigento is not merely a city; it's an experience. A place where time is told not by the ticking clock but by the age-old tales whispered in the wind. A city that wears its Greek heritage with pride, welcoming visitors to uncover its treasures and make them their own. Come, journey into the past, and let Agrigento write a chapter in your travel story, one you will cherish forever.

EVENTS AND FESTIVALS IN SICILY

An overture of distant music, the scent of citrus and roasted nuts wafting through the air, a kaleidoscope of colors whirling in the streets—there's no experience quite like stepping into the heart of a Sicilian festival. These vibrant events, rooted in history yet pulsating with life, offer an intoxicating dive into the soul of Sicily.

In the "Sicilian Events and Festivals" chapter, we'll walk the cobblestones of time-honored celebrations, taste tradition in the street food, and dance along to the heartbeat of Sicilian culture. As each town has its unique rhythm, so does it have a unique festival, setting the stage for a fascinating exploration of this island's rich tapestry of customs.

Prepare to feast your senses on a journey through Sicily's calendar of events, from raucous carnivals to solemn religious processions, effervescent music festivals to lively food fairs. Each event is a vibrant thread in the cultural fabric of Sicily, echoing the island's multifaceted history, the resilience of its people, and their passion for celebrating life. Here's to the magic that unfolds when the streets of Sicily come alive!

Traditional festivals

There are numerous other events and festivals that color the cultural fabric of Sicily, each celebrating a unique aspect of this fascinating land.

Every year in Palermo, in July, the Festival of Saint Rosalia, the city's patron saint, comes alive with grand processions, music, and fireworks. Rosalia's effigy is paraded through the city, accompanied by the faithful and curious, celebrating a tradition that harks back to the 17th century when the saint supposedly saved Palermo from a devastating plague.

Head over to Catania in February for the Feast of Saint Agatha. This event is one of the most important religious festivals in Italy and the world. Devotees carry candles and wear traditional white garb as they follow the jewelled casket of the martyr Saint Agatha through the city streets, a spectacle of faith and devotion unlike any other.

In Siracusa, every May, the ancient Greek dramas come to life in the Teatro Greco, a tradition dating back to 1914. This incredible mix of culture, history, and entertainment known as the "Ciclo di Rappresentazioni Classiche", attracts spectators from around the world who marvel at timeless tales under the stars in the ancient theatre.

But it's not just the cities that hold these vibrant celebrations. The smaller towns have their share of captivating festivals too.

Take, for instance, the Festa dei Giudei in San Fratello. This centuries-old Easter tradition sees locals dressing as "Giudei," wearing red costumes, and making a raucous with music and laughter. This unique celebration, whose origins are shrouded in mystery, presents an intriguing blend of solemn religious observance and boisterous merriment.

Further inland, in the town of Buscemi, the Festa di San Sebastiano is observed in August. A long-standing tradition, it culminates in a grand procession where the saint's statue is carried by the faithful. Not to be missed is the "u fistinu" (the feast), a grand banquet of local dishes, uniting the community in festive feasting.

Or venture to Scicli for the Uomo Vivo (Living Man) Easter procession. This event, deeply rooted in the town's history, sees a wooden statue of the Risen Christ paraded through the town to the rhythm of local music, a sight both emotional and mesmerizing.

In the realm of religious tradition, one cannot miss the striking Misteri Procession in Trapani, taking place during Holy Week. This 24-hour long procession is one of the oldest continuously running religious events in Europe, dating back to the Middle Ages. It features groups of sculpted wooden statues, or 'mysteries,' depicting scenes from the Passion of Christ, carried by the faithful through the streets from Good Friday into Holy Saturday. It is a deeply moving spectacle, reflecting the potent spirituality interwoven with the Sicilian identity.

Piazza Armerina, a town located in the heart of Sicily, hosts the Palio dei Normanni every August, a three-day event commemorating the Norman conquest of Sicily in the 11th century. Participants don traditional medieval costumes, and the highlight is an intense horse race, a vibrant, chivalric spectacle harking back to the island's medieval past.

And if you're looking for something a little different, why not immerse yourself

in the Carnival of Acireale? Held in February, it is one of the most beautiful and oldest carnivals in Italy, with its roots in the 16th century. The town bursts with vibrant floats, stunning flower displays, traditional Sicilian music, and tantalizing food stalls. It is a joyous, convivial event that truly exemplifies the spirit of Sicilian hospitality and festivity.

In the small hilltop town of Sutera, the Presepe Vivente (Living Nativity) is held every Christmas. Here, the town's narrow medieval streets and ancient buildings serve as the perfect backdrop for a living re-enactment of the Nativity story. It's a magical experience that seamlessly blends religious tradition with community spirit, creating an enchanting journey back in time.

And lastly, we must not forget the Sagra del Mandorlo in Fiore (Almond Blossom Festival) in Agrigento, taking place in February. This event celebrates the arrival of spring, marked by the blooming of almond trees. It includes traditional music, dance performances, and an international folk festival, where participants from around the world share their cultural traditions. It's a splendid showcase of diversity and unity, set against a backdrop of blooming almond trees – a sight and experience truly unique to Sicily.

These are just a few of the countless traditional celebrations that grace the Sicilian calendar, each with its rhythms and rituals, each a heartfelt expression of Sicily's diverse and deeply rooted cultural heritage. They paint a vivid picture of Sicily not just as a place, but as a living, breathing tapestry of history and human spirit. Engaging in these celebrations offers more than just a glimpse into the soul of Sicily—it's an invitation to become a part of it.

Celebrating Diversity: Sicily's International Festivals and Cultural Events

Sicily doesn't just shine with religious and traditional festivals but also hosts a wide array of international and cultural events. Let's embark on a journey to uncover these unique celebrations.

Taormina Film Fest and Taormina Arte

Every June, the ancient Greek theater of Taormina transforms into an impressive open-air cinema. With the glittering Ionian Sea as a backdrop, the festival has attracted A-list actors, directors, and film enthusiasts for over six decades, cementing its position as one of Italy's foremost film events.

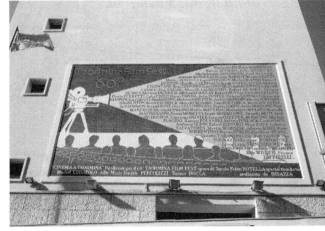

Besides the famous film fest, Taormina Arte is an annual summer-long arts bonanza held in the same magical Greek Theater of Taormina, featuring theater, dance, and music performances from renowned international artists.

Cous Cous Fest in San Vito Lo Capo

Celebrated in late September, this international gastronomic event is a delightful sensory journey embracing the Mediterranean's cultures. Amidst beach settings, this week-long festival involves professional chefs from different countries competing in making the best couscous, accompanied by music concerts and wine tasting events.

The International Kite Festival on the Beach of San Vito Lo Capo

Every May, the sky of San Vito Lo Capo is painted with colors. Kite-makers from around the world converge on this Sicilian town to participate in this international event that combines creativity, art, and entertainment.

Ortigia Film Festival

This annual film festival, usually held in July in Syracuse, attracts filmmakers from across the globe. The event showcases international feature films, shorts, and documentaries, with a special emphasis on first and second works and the promotion of young Italian and European authors.

Sherbeth Festival in Cefalù

An international ice-cream festival that takes place in the picturesque town of Cefalù every September. Ice cream makers from all around the globe gather to showcase their unique flavors, and visitors can indulge in a vast array of ice creams.

Sicilian Jazz Festival

This musical event, spread across various locations in Sicily during July, has been celebrating the best of local and international jazz since 1983. Over the years, it has grown in size and stature, attracting an impressive lineup of jazz musicians and enthusiasts alike.

Eurochocolate in Modica

Modica is renowned for its unique and delectable chocolate, a tradition dating back to the Spanish rule in the 16th century. In December, the town becomes a chocoholic's paradise during Eurochocolate, where attendees can sample exquisite Modican chocolates, watch demonstrations, and even take part in chocolate-making workshops.

The Mediterranean Offshore Sailing Championship

Held in Syracuse in March, this prestigious sailing event attracts sailors from around the world. The clear, azure waters of the Mediterranean provide a perfect setting for this thrilling competition, while spectators can enjoy the spectacle from the city's beautiful coastline.

Palermo's International Teatro di Verdura Music Festival

Every summer, this open-air theater in the capital of Sicily hosts a series of concerts spanning across genres from classical to jazz to pop. The historical setting, under the stars, offers a magical atmosphere for enjoying music.

The International Puppet Theatre Festival in Palermo

Sicily's traditional puppet theater, known as Opera dei Pupi, is celebrated every year at this event in November. Puppeteers from around the world come to perform their shows, preserving and promoting this unique form of storytelling art.

Artistic Ceramic Exhibition in Santo Stefano di Camastra

This town, located between Palermo and Messina, is one of the principal ceramic production centers in Sicily. Each year, in September, the town holds an exhibition showcasing the rich tradition of Sicilian ceramic artistry.

These international and cultural events represent another vibrant side of Sicily's social and cultural life, further enriching the island's diverse character.

NAVIGATING SICILY –
A PRACTICAL GUIDE FOR THE TRAVELER

Arriving in Sicily: Gateway to the Mediterranean

There are various routes you can take to get to Sicily, depending on your starting point. If you're traveling from mainland Italy, you could take the train or drive across the iconic Strait of Messina. This strait, dotted with ferries, connects the toe of Italy's boot with the island of Sicily. For those who prefer a more panoramic approach, a ferry ride can offer breathtaking views of the sparkling Mediterranean Sea.

If you're coming from farther afield, Sicily is home to several international airports. The largest is Catania-Fontanarossa, located on the eastern side of the island. Palermo Falcone-Borsellino airport, located in the island's capital, and Trapani Vincenzo Florio airport, situated on the western coast, also offer a wide array of international and domestic flights.

Traveling Around Sicily: A Journey through Tim and Terrain

Once you've arrived in Sicily, getting around is part of the fun. The island has a variety of transport options tailored to different travel styles. Renting a car is the most flexible option, as it allows you to explore at your own pace and venture into more remote areas. However, keep in mind that Sicily's winding roads and free-spirited driving style can be challenging for some.

Alternatively, Sicily's trains and buses can take you to most cities and towns. The island's railway system, operated by Trenitalia, provides a leisurely and scenic way to travel, especially along the coastal routes. Buses, on the other hand, are the go-to option for reaching smaller villages and archaeological sites.

If you're planning on staying within city limits, both Palermo and Catania have efficient public transportation systems, including buses and trams. And of course, don't miss out on the chance to take a slow-paced stroll through the city streets, as walking is often the best way to soak up the local atmosphere and discover hidden gems.

Remember, traveling in Sicily isn't just about getting from point A to point B – it's a chance to savor the journey, taking in the stunning landscapes, vibrant culture, and warm hospitality that define this incredible island. Whether you choose to traverse the bustling city streets or venture into the serene countryside, each path offers a unique glimpse into Sicily's enduring charm.

Finding Your Sicilian Home: A Guide to Accommodations

Whether you're yearning for a room with a sea-view, a quiet cottage nestled in an olive grove, or an apartment in the heart of a bustling city, Sicily offers a wealth of accommodations tailored to a range of budgets and tastes.

For those seeking an authentic experience steeped in history and culture, consider staying in a renovated palazzo or a charming bed and breakfast in one of Sicily's historic centers. These lodgings are often family-run and offer a personal touch. They're the perfect choice if you want to wake up to the aroma of freshly baked cannoli or the sound of church bells echoing through the narrow, winding streets. Cities like Palermo, Catania, and Syracuse are renowned for their architectural gems, many of which have been transformed into unique places to stay.

If you prefer to wake up to the sound of waves, Sicily's stunning coastline is dotted with a variety of beachfront hotels, resorts, and villas. Taormina, Cefalù, and the Aeolian Islands are among the most sought-after coastal destinations, providing luxury accommodations with access to private beaches, exquisite local seafood, and unrivaled Mediterranean views.

Alternatively, the Sicilian countryside offers tranquil agriturismo stays – working farms that also function as B&Bs. This is a delightful way to experience rural Sicily's laid-back lifestyle while supporting local businesses. Most of these farmhouses, scattered across regions like Ragusa and Agrigento, provide home-cooked meals prepared with produce grown on the premises. Some even offer cooking classes, horseback riding, and wine tasting experiences.

For independent travelers, or families, renting a self-catered apartment or a villa can provide the freedom to explore Sicily at your own pace. These options, popular in places like the baroque towns of the Val di Noto or the picturesque village of Castellammare del Golfo, often come with kitchen facilities, giving you the opportunity to try your hand at Sicilian cuisine with local ingredients from the market.

Sicily is also welcoming to the backpacker community with its hostels. While not as widespread as in other parts of Europe, you'll find some excellent options in Palermo and Catania. These are sociable spaces where you can swap stories with fellow travelers, usually with the bonus of a communal kitchen and organized group activities.

One last tip: wherever you choose to stay, it's recommended to book in advance, especially during the summer months and holiday seasons when accommodations can fill up quickly. Above all, keep in mind that the best place to stay in Sicily is the one that makes you feel most connected to the island's vibrant character, welcoming warmth, and enduring history. After all, isn't that what travel is all about?

Navigating Your Sicilian Adventure: Essential Resources and Links

Planning a trip can feel like piecing together a puzzle, especially when you're traveling to a place as diverse and rich as Sicily. To assist you in assembling your Sicilian adventure, here are a few online resources and links that can prove invaluable:

Visit Sicily Official Website - **www.visitsicily.info** - As the official tourism website of Sicily, it provides comprehensive information on places to visit, cultural events, and traditional cuisine. A true encyclopedia for anyone wishing to explore the island.

Trenitalia - **www.trenitalia.com** - For up-to-date information about train services, schedules, and ticket prices in Sicily, this is the official site of the Italian State Railways.

Interbus - **www.interbus.it** - If you plan on navigating the island by bus, check out Interbus for timetables, routes, and fares.

Parco Archeologico della Valle dei Templi - **www.valleyofthetemples.com** - Official site for the Valley of the Temples in Agrigento. You can find information about opening hours, ticket prices, and available guided tours.

Aeroporto di Catania - **www.aeroporto.catania.it** - Catania's airport official site with flight information, car rental options, and more.

Aeroporto di Palermo - **www.aeroportodipalermo.it** - Official website of Palermo's airport with flight information and more.

Booking.com - **www.booking.com** - For accommodation options ranging from luxury hotels to charming bed and breakfasts, this site allows you to filter your search based on your needs and preferences.

Airbnb - **www.airbnb.com** - If you prefer a more homely feel or are traveling with a larger group, Airbnb can provide options for entire homes or apartments.

Trapani Welcome - **www.trapaniwelcome.it** - A useful resource for anyone planning to visit Trapani and its surroundings, from cultural sites to nature trails.

Etna3340 - **www.etna3340.com** - For guided tours of Mount Etna, including hikes, wine tours, and more.

Sicily on Food and Wine Travel - **www.foodandwinetravel.com.au** - For those gastronomically inclined, this website provides information on food and wine tours in Sicily.

TripAdvisor Sicily - **www.tripadvisor.com** - Here you can read reviews, tips and Q&As from fellow travellers about attractions, restaurants, and hotels in Sicily.

Discover Sicily - **www.discoversicily.com** - This website provides detailed itineraries for those looking to self-guide their tours of Sicily.

Eco Sicily Travel - **www.ecosicilytravel.com** - For eco-conscious travelers, this website offers sustainable and nature-based tourism options in Sicily.

ANAS (National Roads Agency) - **www.stradeanas.it** - Provides up-to-date information on road conditions, closures and traffic across Italy, including Sicily.

Palermo for 91 Days Travel Guide - **www.amazon.com** - A comprehensive travel guide to Palermo, available for purchase on Amazon.

Culture Trip Sicily - **www.theculturetrip.com** - Offers curated local insights and tips about cultural attractions in Sicily.

TREKKING AND NATURE: FROM THE MOUNTAINS TO THE SEA

There's an old saying, "In every walk with nature, one receives far more than he seeks." And indeed, nothing quite matches the exhilarating thrill of stepping into the wild, of treading paths untrodden, of discovering sights unseen. In this chapter, we dive headfirst into the diverse and awe-inspiring natural landscapes of Sicily, where adventure seekers can experience the island from a completely unique and invigorating perspective.

From the sun-drenched coastlines to the grand peaks of Mount Etna, Sicily, with its diverse landscapes and unique microclimates, offers a breadth of trekking and outdoor opportunities like no other.

Let us guide you through a selection of Sicily's most breathtaking hiking trails, mountain biking routes, and outdoor activities. We will also delve into the various flora and fauna you can expect to encounter, the best seasons to plan your nature-filled excursions, and essential tips to ensure a safe and memorable adventure.

Are you ready to lace up your hiking boots and embark on an unforgettable journey through Sicily's picturesque and rugged landscapes? Keep your eyes open and your senses sharp, for we're not merely passing through these paths - we are immersing ourselves into a world that brims with life, beauty, and surprises at every turn.

Journeying Through Nature: Sicily's Spectacular Trekking Trails

Mount Etna

Rising to a height of more than 3300 meters, Etna is not only the highest active volcano in Europe but also one of the most active in the world. Trekkers visiting Etna have the opportunity to explore an intriguing mix of environments, from lush vineyards and orchards at lower altitudes to the almost lunar landscapes of the summit area. If you're up for a more challenging trek, consider the route from Sapienza Refuge to the Central Crater. It's a steep and demanding journey but offers unparalleled views over the island.

The Madonie Mountains

Located within the Madonie Regional Natural Park, this mountain range holds some of the highest peaks in Sicily. The Piano Battaglia route, which weaves through dense forests of oak and beech trees and offers stunning views from the mountain's summit, is a favorite among trekkers. During the winter, this trail is also a popular destination for skiing.

Riserva Naturale dello Zingaro

The Zingaro Reserve, stretching along about 7km of unspoilt coastline, offers seven main trails that cater to various levels of trekking proficiency. Each trail will reward you with panoramic views of the Mediterranean and access to secluded beaches where you can relax and take a swim.

Monte Cofano Nature Reserve

Here, you can explore trails that range from easy strolls to challenging treks, making Monte Cofano suitable for all fitness levels. For history enthusiasts, the paths leading to prehistoric caves are a must. The rocky coastline, teeming with diverse marine life, also makes it a popular spot for snorkeling and diving.

Pantalica Nature Reserve

Pantalica offers a combination of history and natural beauty, with its ancient rock-cut tombs and stunning landscapes. The most popular route is the 'Royal Path', which takes you across the Anapo Valley, offering the chance to appreciate the reserve's rich biodiversity.

Nebrodi National Park

As the largest protected area in Sicily, Nebrodi offers a host of trekking trails that meander through dense forests, across rolling hills, and around sparkling lakes. The trails in this area are well-marked and varied, making it an excellent destination for family-friendly treks and picnics.

Mount Soro

This peak in the Nebrodi Mountains is a challenge but offers unparalleled panoramic views that stretch over the Tyrrhenian Sea and Mount Etna. The flora and fauna here are unique, including the Nebrodi black pig and the San Fratello horse, both endemic species.

Vendicari Nature Reserve

This reserve offers trekkers the chance to explore coastal landscapes, bird-watch in the lagoons, and relax on untouched sandy beaches. Walking along the trails, you will stumble upon the historical remnants of the tuna fishery, an activity that has marked the history of this area.

When embarking on any of these treks, remember to bring plenty of water, wear appropriate clothing, and leave no trace behind. Happy trekking!

Embracing Adventure: Sicily's Call of the Wild

Bird Watching in Vendicari Nature Reserve

Imagine being hushed into silence by the symphony of the avian world in Vendicari Nature Reserve. As you stroll along the marshy landscapes, eyes peeled to your binoculars, the sight of flamingos against a crimson sunset would leave an imprint on your heart.

Horse Riding in the Madonie Mountains

Picture galloping through vast meadows, underneath the cooling shadows of the Madonie Mountains. As your steed leads you on undulating trails, every curve reveals a new panorama, each more breathtaking than the last.

Diving and Snorkeling in Ustica

Imagine plunging into the aquamarine depths of the Ustica sea, where underwater vistas teem with vibrant corals, mystic caves, and a spectacular array of marine life. Each dive is a unique voyage into a hidden world.

Mountain Biking on Mount Etna

Feel your pulse race as you pedal furiously on the rocky trails of Mount Etna. The volcanic landscape offers a thrilling backdrop to your adventure, while the prospect of cycling on an active volcano adds to the adrenaline rush.

Canyoning in the Alcantara Gorges

Picture yourself navigating through the Alcantara Gorges, as the river water challenges your every step. The sight of waterfalls cascading down basaltic walls is a reward worth the thrilling climb.

Caving in the Monte Conca Cave

Step into the Monte Conca cave, an underground realm where stalactites meet stalagmites. The echo of dripping water and the chill of the dark create an eerie yet mesmerizing atmosphere.

Sea Kayaking along the Aeolian Islands

Picture paddling through the azure waters of the Aeolian Islands, with the wind in your hair and sun on your back. Every stroke brings you closer to secluded beaches and secret coves waiting to be discovered.

Sailing around the Egadi Islands

Imagine gliding on the Mediterranean waves, with the wind filling your sail as you maneuver around the Egadi Islands. The sunsets seen from your deck are postcards come alive.

Botanical Tours in the Ficuzza Wood

Envision wandering through Ficuzza Wood, a living library of flora and fauna. With every step, you'll learn more about the biodiversity of this magical forest, guided by experts who know every leaf and tree.

Paragliding in Pollina

Close your eyes and imagine soaring like a bird over the Sicilian coast in Pollina. The panoramic view from the sky is a sight to behold, with the azure sea meeting the green coastline under the golden sunlight.

These activities invite travelers to step out of the ordinary and embrace the adventurous spirit of Sicily. They offer a chance to not just observe the island's beauty, but to immerse oneself in it, to become a part of Sicily's spectacular and diverse natural tapestry.